PROFITABLE MANAGEMENT FOR THE SUBCONTRACTOR

PROFITABLE MANAGEMENT FOR THE SUBCONTRACTOR

ROBERT L. TEETS

McGraw-Hill Book Company

New York St. Louis San Francisco Auckland Düsseldorf Johannesburg
Kuala Lumpur London Mexico Montreal New Delhi Panama Paris
São Paulo Singapore Sydney Tokyo Toronto

Library of Congress Cataloging in Publication Data
Teets, Robert L
  Profitable management for the subcontractor.

  Includes index.
  1. Construction industry—Subcontracting—Management.   I. Title.
HD9715.A2T43   658'.92'4   75-34237
ISBN 0-07-063387-8

  2 3 4 5 6 7 8 9 0   K P K P   7 8 4 3 2 1 0 9 8 7

The editors for this book were Jeremy Robinson and
Carolyn Nagy, the designer was Elliot Epstein, and the
production supervisor was Teresa F. Leaden. It was set
in Baskerville by University Graphics, Inc.

Printed and bound by The Kingsport Press.

DEDICATION

I have been abundantly blessed with the most valuable thing that one can acquire—friends. The experiences that I have realized, that made this book possible, are the results of associations with truly dedicated friends, people who have repeatedly indicated their friendship by lending a helping hand when needed. These friends include people from all walks of our industry:

Union officials
Fellow union members
Electrical inspectors
Trade association officials, NECA
General contractors
Electrical contractors
Contractors of other trades
Business associates
Those who have worked under my direction

Those who directly participated, contributed, or motivated me are:

Helen Teets, my wife
Florence Reynolds, my personal secretary
Nathan Rosenmutter, President of General Iron Industries

My wife, Helen, supported and encouraged my ambitions during 25 years of pursuing knowledge and experience.

My secretary, Miss Reynolds, was the impetus that made finalization of the book possible.

Nathan Rosenmutter provided the vehicle that allowed me to apply and develop my engineering skills and continually encouraged and supported me in all of my undertakings during my entire business career.

I thank God for all these people, and it is to them that this book is dedicated.

CONTENTS

PREFACE

This book is directed to those who have mastered the mechanical know-how of the construction industry and want to know more about its management and administration. It will give those who are already in construction management a greater appreciation of the depth and detail of the responsibility involved in managing a construction subcontracting firm. It is written to serve as a textbook for those who aspire to become subcontractors.

Although all references to gender are directed to the male, it is intended to apply to both men and women. Use of the male gender is to satisfy ease of communication only.

All businesses are the same, no matter how large or how small. Whether they are construction, manufacturing, retail, or a service organization, none is more difficult or easier than the others. The concepts, techniques, procedures, and forms outlined here are not new to the industrial world. In one form or another, they have all been utilized for over 100 years.

The material presented in this book is, however, applicable specifically to construction subcontracting and is based on 30 years of successful application.

Robert L. Teets

PROFITABLE MANAGEMENT FOR THE SUBCONTRACTOR

1 INTRODUCTION

All businesses have two basic common ingredients: people and the need for profit. Profit is the objective. All other desired results are by-products of profit. The by-products of no profit are all undesirable.

A company is an odd thing. It is alive. It has feelings. It has emotions. It is either growing or dying. It becomes older each day, but yet it is not really any of these things. You can't feel it. It really isn't a living being, yet if you treat it as if it isn't a living being, it will surely fail. For practical purposes, let's say the company is alive, and that it has feelings and emotions. Then the life blood, or that which keeps a company alive and growing, is profit. Every endeavor of everyone in the company, at all times, must be a contribution toward generating a profit. When anyone's efforts cease to contribute toward generating a profit, or when the activities he is performing do not contribute to profits, then changes must be made.

The difference between a successful business and a mediocre or failing one is that a mediocre or failing business has problems and a successful business has events. The synonym for the word "problem" is "mystery." The definition for "problem" is "a question proposed for solution." Many people say that the construction industry is more difficult than other industries because of its problems. This is not true. For the "pro," the so-called problems are events. For the beginner the events are problems. All of the endeavors required to build a building, run a sewer, lay a road, build a bridge, etc., are repetitive events. These include all activities within the business, including estimating, accounting, purchasing, and doing the work.

The American civilization is based on materialistic achievements. To the layman there is nothing more phenomenal or complicated than a television set. We can sit in our living room and watch and hear something that is just happening on the other side of the world. Television people could claim their industry is the most difficult, with the most problems, because their product is so complicated. However, the human hands that build this fantastic thing are unskilled hands. The minds guiding those unskilled hands don't have to know what makes a television set work. The reason that these unskilled hands can produce such a thing is that all of their working operations are recognized as being repetitive. The entire production process is broken down into repetitive tasks that do not require overall knowledge by the workman.

The same thing can be done in the construction industry, because the work required to build a bridge, road, building, or sewer is repetitive. Construction industry people are mechanically skilled; therefore, the job should be much easier to set up than a television set.

1

If events in a company are looked upon as problems, then either the company's management or its personnel are inexperienced. If this situation reaches higher into management than apprentices and trainees, the company will generate failure.

The construction industry is not unique, difficult, or full of problems. In fact, it is a rather simple, but intriguing, industry.

Whether a company consists of 1 person or 100 people, it *must* have organization. The work must be organized. The main ingredient in an organized effort is discipline (orderliness). To achieve discipline one must have a method, a system, or a way of doing things; more so when there is more than one person involved. Because discipline is so necessary, systems, methods, procedures, customs and practices, etc., have been developed and/or have grown in the business world.

The construction industry is just waking up to the fact that these business principles cannot be violated. People used to think that the construction industry could operate differently from the rest of the business world. They thought they didn't have to worry about such things as objectives, capital, collections, systems, procedures, orderliness, etc. Many have attempted, and are *still* attempting, to operate without a profit!

Just knowing how to install wiring or plumbing or how to build a building, etc., will not allow a person to satisfy today's business requirements. A construction firm manager must know accounting, cash flow, payables, receivables, sales, liens, purchasing, insurance, etc., as well as how to motivate, direct, and control people. Just being the boss will not get the job done.

A typical business consists of many people, hopefully working toward a common goal. Based on the need to utilize people in a disciplined manner and to utilize these concepts as an asset, one can organize a construction company properly by following the sound, tried, and proven business principles being utilized in all other industries.

Construction subcontracting is the business of selling and executing the installation, repair, or maintenance of an on-site constructed facility. It comprises many types of work, including:

1. New residential construction

2. Service (jobbing) and repair—domestic

3. Service (jobbing) and repair—commercial, industrial, and institutional

4. Highway, street, and bridge construction

5. Maintenance

6. Miscellaneous small construction

7. Institutional construction

8. Steel mill construction

9. Light manufacturing construction

10. Heavy manufacturing construction

11. Commercial construction

12. High-rise building construction

13. Power plant and substation construction

14. Electrical transmission and distribution construction

15. Pipeline construction

16. Commercial and institutional remodeling

17. Manufacturing and industrial revamping

Every company must have objectives: What size company is desired? What types of work are to be pursued? What geographical areas are to be worked? What type of return do the owners, or owner-operators, expect?

Regardless of the objectives of the owners or owner-operators, there are eight specific basic requirements that must be satisfied to realize the objectives.

1. Adequate financing

2. Sales

    a. Representation in the marketplace (personal contact)

    b. Realistic and accurate estimating capability

3. Effective materials and tool management

4. Effective flow of information to the workmen

5. Proper planning, scheduling, and directing the work

6. Payment for all work performed

7. Cost control—measure, record, analyze

8. Aggressive and effective management

No single one of these basic requirements is the "key" requirement or the most important. Without completely satisfying each, the organization will fail. Note that the conventional cocktail-hour-conversation type of requirements are not included. Many will say, even after reading this book, "All we need is some people who will work instead of loafing," or "The problem in our industry is productivity."

There is no question that productivity is a major factor. If we were to analyze many contractors, we would find in varying degrees the following (stressed) philosophy being employed. "Joe, you are one hell of a good mechanic, you know your trade, and you are a good worker; so take these blueprints and make me money. If you need anything, just call the office."

A year and a half later the job is finished. Joe has used all the tricks and techniques within his experience. The few times he called the office he was disappointed, and so he worked the situations out himself by scrounging for what he needed. He applied himself diligently and worked hard. The customer, well satisfied, congratulates and thanks Joe for a job well done and tells the contractor, "What a fine man Joe is!" The contractor looks at the job costs, and lo and behold, the labor and material are appreciably over the estimate. Joe is called to the office. On the way to the office Joe thinks the boss is now going to congratulate him with a bonus and a pat on the back. The contractor informs Joe of the loss and states he is very disappointed in him. He tells Joe that he let him down and that Joe had better look for another job. Who let whom down? The contractor certainly let Joe down. He did not support him properly.

The eight basic requirements include support to the man in the field. If all eight requirements are satisfied by the contractor, there isn't any room for poor productivity and other inefficiencies by the workman. With poor support, the most capable field personnel will fail to produce a profit. With capable and effective support, less capable field personnel will produce a profit. If the contractor had told Joe, "Here are the prints, the material, the tools, the installation information; this is what I have contracted for, and this is what I have not contracted for, and I will be here each day to determine what else I can get for you," the job would have produced a profit. The difference is that the contractor must provide the management while Joe installs the work. Not, "Joe, you install the work and be your own manager too."

If management will support the workman, the workman will support management. The workmen cannot support management without management's supporting them first. Supporting the workman with effective management includes satisfying the eight basic requirements. The subcontractor must know the details of each requirement thoroughly.

BASIC REQUIREMENT NO. 1. ADEQUATE FINANCING

Every company, whether it is new, old, small, or large, has a limited amount of liquid assets (cash) plus credit. The total of these two equals the financial capability of the company. Every job requires a specific amount of money to be invested. This amount will vary during the life of the job.

The amount of cash and credit available determines the company's financial ability to support work in progress. Credit includes both short- and long-term borrowing, plus the amount of credit extended by suppliers. The company's debtors are a source of cash. This source is the most overlooked and neglected of all. To utilize it, payment of all invoices should be immediately collected when due.

For every sales dollar committed there must be enough financing available to support the sale. This is called "pipeline money." Financial capability to support work in progress is not totally determined by the dollar value of working capital (difference between current assets and current liabilities). With poorly organized cash flow management, working capital will not support the volume of sales that organized cash flow management will; that is, with prudent cash management you can get more mileage from existing dollars. To do this, a company not only must have the money, but also must know how to use it the best way. Adequate financing includes having the required cash, credit, and cash management know-how.

BASIC REQUIREMENT NO. 2. SALES

Sales prime the pump of any company. Without them, nothing happens. Construction industry sales include two major activities: (1) being known in the marketplace and (2) giving realistic and accurate estimates.

There are only three ways for subcontractors to become known in the marketplace: (1) personal contact, (2) word of mouth (being recommended by someone else), and (3) indirect communication, including advertising and direct mail. So far, the only workable way to produce sales has been by personal contact. Unfortunately, this is the most expensive way of selling. The only time it is not necessary is when a subcontractor is bidding competitively on public work.

Once the subcontractor has reached the marketplace, he must give realistic and accurate estimates which are put together in an orderly and standard manner. The sales effort will be of no value unless the estimate is realistic and accurate. Sales aren't often made unless the subcontractor comes in with a low bid. Unfortunately, the estimate, which establishes the job cost and the selling price, is 90 percent of the total cost of getting sales. Yet its only contribution is to provide numbers necessary to make the sale. The more accurate an estimate, the more valuable it is in making the sale. When it is put together in an orderly and standard manner, it will be accurate. Then it becomes useful for more than just providing numbers for the sale. After the subcontractor gets a job, he can use the orderly estimate as a guide to installing the work. It also becomes the base for purchasing, cost control, and breakdown for payout. A disorderly estimate would not be accurate and would be of no value for other uses because it could not be understood by others. Have you ever tried to read and understand an estimate prepared by someone else in a haphazard method on scratch paper?

The selling portion of the total sales activity is the responsibility that is mostly dependent on the subcontractor personally. As previously stated, the only effective selling method available to construction firms is personal contact. This personal contact requires something of the subcontractor as a person. With the exception of large firms, the customer often feels he or she is doing business with the subcontractor as a person as opposed to a company. The subcontractor, therefore, must be a personable salesman and knowledgeable in his trade, in addition to being an owner and a manager.

BASIC REQUIREMENT NO. 3. EFFECTIVE MATERIALS AND TOOL MANAGEMENT

Material from the manufacturer is hardly ever changed on the job. Most of the time, it is merely assembled into a building, sewer, bridge, or road. To do this, the subcontractor needs manpower and tools at the right time and in the right place. Once a piece of material is assembled into the job, it is no longer available. Therefore, to keep his men assembling, the subcontractor must keep the right material coming, steadily. As the man moves on, his tools must move with him. The minute that either material or tools are not where the work is to be installed, then the work cannot continue.

Material flow has to be timely. Materials cannot arrive too late at the point where they are to be assembled and installed. Yet they can't be too early. If materials are sent to the job or point of assembly before they are needed, chances are that they will become lost, disarranged, or weathered, and as a result they won't be totally available in the required quantity and form when the work force is ready to assemble and install them.

To assure that materials and tools are at the place where the work is to be performed, management and control of their flow is required. This flow is similar to the flow of guns and ammunition to the soldiers on the front lines of a war.

Picture the tools as guns and the material as ammunition. As the soldier uses up the ammunition, so too the construction worker uses up material by installing it. As the soldier needs the guns to fire the ammunition, so too the construction worker needs the tools to install the material.

As the soldier fights the war, his position changes (hopefully forward), thereby changing the location where the ammunition and guns are required next. As a construction worker installs the material, his position changes (hopefully forward), thereby changing the location where the material and tools are needed next. In the military, the science of the flow (movement) of ammunition and guns is called logistics. In construction, the flow (movement) of materials and tools is called materials management or material handling. As with the soldier, the construction worker cannot install materials without the materials being at the place where they are to be installed. As the soldier cannot fire the ammunition without the guns, the construction worker cannot install the materials without tools.

In most trades, materials represent an appreciable portion of the total cost of a job. The degree of efficiency of labor is appreciably affected by the efficiency of the materials movement to the point where the work is to be performed. There is no better excuse for poor productivity than no material, not enough material, or the wrong material. Poor materials management and flow of materials to and within a construction site is synonymous with poor control of labor. Materials management includes procurement (purchasing), delivery to job, on-job storage, and distribution within the job site.

The manufacturing industry has long recognized the importance of effective materials flow to its machines to produce its products. The construction industry has only recently recognized the importance of materials flow, handling, and control within the construction site.

Workers should never be assigned to the job unless the required material and tools are there, and the material should never be delivered until the workers are assigned.

BASIC REQUIREMENT NO. 4. EFFECTIVE FLOW OF INFORMATION TO THE WORKMEN

Details of where, how, what, and how much material is to be installed are never fully developed at the start of a project. This is caused by a constant flow of additions, deletions, changes in locations, and additional information which come as the project moves along.

These changes come in from the architects, owners, engineers, suppliers and manufacturers of materials, general contractors, subcontractors, the Good Lord, changes in union contracts, etc. As this information comes in from all these sources it must be evaluated, combined, and reduced to instructions as to where, how, what, and how much material is to be installed.

This information must flow to the man assembling and installing the work. He must have it just before he needs it; otherwise he will either install the work wrong, or not at all. However, it cannot be given to him too early. He should be concerned only with the information needed at the time. He should not have to remember that which he was directed to do prior to the time he is to do it. The information must be given at the time of need, not too early and not too late.

Here is an example of poor timing. A plumbing contractor informs his plumber, "Joe, the fifth house down the block gets a pink sink instead of the usual blue one. You will find the pink one in the warehouse. Now, don't forget."

The chances of a pink sink being installed in the fifth house down the block are very remote. The chances of a pink sink being installed in any house are remote. Whose fault will it be? The contractor's, of course. The plumber is paid to install the sinks, not to be a memory bank. The contractor should give Joe, the plumber, a schedule for each house, with each house identified by address or lot number. The schedule should list all changes, etc.

If the plumbing contractor wanted to use a face-to-face verbal information system, he should have waited until Joe got to the fifth house down the block and then given him the information about the pink sink, with the pink sink under his arm.

To assure that the required information is established and forwarded through managers, superintendents, general foremen, and foremen to the person performing the work requires an orderly system even when the flow involves only two people. The biggest deterrent to an effective flow of information through an organization is the inability of people to communicate accurately.

The flow of information through a construction firm is via blueprints, work orders, change orders, copies of purchase orders, copies of material requisitions, manufacturers' catalog cuts, memos, sketches, copies of contracts, copies of proposals, etc., *and verbal exchange.* Each of these, without being part of an organized, recognized system for the flow of information, will contribute to poor and wrong communication.

All information in the construction business is subject to change at any moment. The person receiving the information must have a means to know whether the information is the latest, if it supersedes previous information, and if it has been committed to by the contractor. A work order or change order which conflicts with a previously issued order will create confusion unless the last work order states, "This order supersedes the previous order, number so and so."

Issuance of revised blueprints always has been dangerous without a system. How does the contractor know if the workmen are using the latest drawings, or those which he has contracted for, and how does the workman know if the contractor has accepted the latest drawings?

The practice of forwarding copies of purchase orders, material requisitions, etc., to the man in the field many times is confusing. The man in the field ends up with so much paper he gives up on all of it. The information given should be specific and confined to the particular need.

Many contractors send as a work order a copy of the proposal that was sent to the customer, with the amount of the contract blocked out, to the man who is to perform the work. A proposal or contract does not state how the work is to be performed, it merely states what the finished product will be. A separate work order should be given to the man, directing him to install so many widgets in a particular location, in thus and so manner, using such and such material.

If there are blueprints involved, the work order should authorize the man to install the work in accordance with particular dated plans to which the contractor has committed himself. Revised drawings to which the contractor has committed himself should be authorized for use by a change order directing the man to use the revised drawings in lieu of previous drawings.

Ineffective methods of not making sure that the men are installing only that which the contractor has agreed to are the greatest source of costs that will not be paid for. Information regarding structural changes which do not involve additional charges or credits to the contract that does not flow to the man performing the work is another appreciable source of additional costs. Information that does not involve additional charges or credits can appreciably affect the cost of the installation. The flow of this information also is very vital.

The flow of information is vital to every aspect of an installation, both in getting the job done and in getting paid for it. In the military, information is called "intelligence." The flow of intelligence is recognized as having equal importance to all other major functions. As the soldier needs guns, ammunition, and intelligence, so too the construction worker needs material, tools, and information. Don't be like the plumbing contractor with the pink sink!

BASIC REQUIREMENT NO. 5. PROPER PLANNING, SCHEDULING, AND DIRECTING THE WORK

In addition to the tools, materials, and information, the work must be scheduled and directed. It must be broken up into work tasks involving specific numbers of men for specific periods of time at specific locations. After these tasks are developed, they must be scheduled into a sequential work plan.

Frequently there is more than one method to physically accomplish the work task. The most applicable and economical method must be determined. The man assigned to the work task must be told what method to use and given the required information concerning that method.

On large projects, planning, scheduling, and directing the work is performed on the job site by engineers, superintendents, general foremen, and foremen. On a smaller-sized job, the contractor does the planning, scheduling, and directing himself or delegates it to his superintendent, estimator, or some other key person. Planning involves layout of the work, which denotes materials, tools, and the number of men required to perform the job. Scheduling involves determining when the work can or must be performed, delivering the material and tools, and assigning the men. Directing involves physically explaining to the man or men who are to perform the work exactly how it is to be done. Here is an example. An electrical conduit running from a wall switch, across the room to a wall outlet, can be installed in several ways. It can be run down from the switch over to the other wall and up to the outlet, or it can be run from the wall switch up to the ceiling and over to the other wall and down to the outlet. Down, over, and up; or up, over, and down. In almost every case one way is better and easier than the other.

The man who is to install the work must be directed as to how to install it. The alternative is to allow the man to decide himself. But what happens if he decides the opposite way than that for which the material to be used was supplied? What happens when he finds out (too late) that the conduit is in the way of the heating duct?

To allow the workman to direct himself is employing the trial-and-error method throughout the installation. Remember what the workmen are being paid for. Are they being paid for managing and/or being administrators, or supervising, or are they being paid to install the work?

The environment and conditions that the contractor sets up surely are inviting and conducive to loafing. Did you ever visit a construction site and marvel at how the building ever got built? Rarely do you see workmen working. You can see many workmen walking, carrying ladders, carrying tools, carrying blueprints, standing, pointing, and talking about the work. You see them carrying material, going for this, going for that, and there is always the human endeavor of loafing. The adverse behavior of the construction workmen is in most instances a result of the contractors' on-the-job management deficiencies.

Material handling should be done by material handlers, supervision by supervisors, and the work installed by workmen. These activities are separate, and should be assigned and controlled separately.

Did you ever try to pick out a bad apple from a bushel of mixed fruit—red apples, oranges, grapes, lemons, yellow apples, plums, etc? Wouldn't a bad apple be more apparent if there were just red apples, or just yellow apples in the basket? If the contractor does his part—that is, manage and provide the proper support—the workmen have no other alternative than to work. If they don't, they will stand out like a bad apple.

There is nothing wrong with the same man (on small jobs) performing the material and tool handling, layout supervising, etc. He must, however, do each as a separate activity, not all of them at once. The sequence for a one-man installation is:

1. Decide how to install the work.

2. Make a list of material required to install the work in that manner.

3. Decide what tools are required to install that material.

4. Assemble the material and tools.

5. Install the work.

This sequence is treating each activity separately in its logical sequence. If the activities were thrown in all together, the man would obtain the first obvious bit of material, install it, then decide what is needed next, get it, install it, decide on the next item, get it, install it, and so on and so on. Which is the effective way? It is the contractor's responsibility that the work is *planned, scheduled, and directed* effectively.

BASIC REQUIREMENT NO. 6. PAYMENT FOR ALL WORK PERFORMED

Payment for all work performed includes three basic activities:

1. Recognizing, recording, and invoicing all additions to the contract

2. Billing (invoicing) all contracted work

3. Collecting the money

Most systems and organizations are fairly effective in billing contracted work and in collecting the money for the invoices rendered. Most of them, however, neglect to recognize, and get authorization for, additions to the contract effectively. The effective way is to keep adequate records and report the additions so that an invoice that cannot be challenged can be developed and documented and can subsequently be paid.

Unfortunately, in the construction industry, more often than not the dollar amount of changes (additions) to the original contract exceeds the gross profit. If the additions are not identified, recorded, and subsequently paid, the job will surely produce a loss.

If, by failure of the organization or the system, payment is not realized for all invoices, and a write-off as "bad debts" occurs, the job has subsequently produced a loss. If the organization and system fails to render invoices for the basic contracts, those contracts involved produce a loss.

So often it is left to the man performing the work to decide what is included in the contract and what is not included. This becomes difficult, for in most cases he has never seen the contract, and even if he had he would have been unable to make the determination.

Getting paid for what is installed starts with the contract, which should include a description of what work is to be installed and, more specifically, what work is *not* included in the contract. A work order should be written, converting the language of the contract to installation information language and mentioning what is not included in the contract.

The workman now has been given written instructions as to what he is to install, and what he is not to install. *All that which is not to be installed, plus anything not listed as to be installed, is an addition to the contract (extra).* With this information the workman can readily recognize what constitutes an extra. He can now notify the subcontractor that the customer has requested something to be installed that is not included in his work order. After the subcontractor has reached an agreement of price and terms of payment with the customer for the additional work, he can authorize the workman to proceed with additional work. He does this by issuing a supplemental work order for the additional work to the workman. This supplemental work order frequently is called a "change order."

Now the subcontractor has the basis for billing for the additional work, and also knows from where and when to expect payment, and more importantly, so does the customer. The chance of getting paid for all work performed is much greater under this system than by expecting the workman both to determine by intuition what is an extra and then to make arrangements for the customer to pay for the additional work. Did you ever know a workman who was overly concerned as to how and when the boss was going to get paid? The answer is, "No," and rightly so. It is the subcontractor's responsibility to get paid for the work performed, not the workman's.

BASIC REQUIREMENT NO. 7. COST
CONTROL: MEASURE, RECORD, ANALYZE

Because the life blood and main objective of all business activities is profit, we must control that which controls profit. What controls profit? Cost of materials, labor, and other direct job costs, plus overhead costs. Costs, which are the direct determining factor of profit, must be controlled, and the need for the control must be recognized.

Before something can be controlled, it must be measured. But measurement in itself will not provide the control. The measurement must be recorded and then analyzed. The costs established must be compared with the estimate. Differences between established costs and the estimate are then recognized. Analyzing these differences provides the means for cost control. For negative differences, means must be set up to correct or cope with that which is making them negative. For the favorable differences, means must be set up to perpetuate that which is contributing them. The results of no organized cost control are without exception negative, and will surely lead to the business becoming a fatality. The accounting system must provide job costs accurately and promptly. Accounting in itself is the reporting of economic history (after the fact). In cost control this is not good enough. The ideal would be to record the costs before they occur. This is obviously impossible, and so we have to settle for the next best thing, immediate reporting of cost.

Reported labor cost should be no later than 10 days after the first day of a weekly pay period. That is, the recording of labor expended on Monday (of a Monday-through-Sunday pay period), should be no later than Wednesday of the following week. For labor expended on Tuesday, the delay should be no longer than 9 days, for Wednesday, 8 days, and for the entire week, 3 days. It usually takes 1 to 2 days to run the payroll; on the third day the labor costs are distributed to the job cost ledgers. Material and other costs should be recorded no later than 5 days after shipment. It usually takes 3 days for the supplier to make up the invoice and for it to be received in the mail. Two additional days are ample for recording in the job cost ledger.

The subcontractor should have on his desk each week the total costs for each job through the close of the preceding week. With this he can evaluate the condition of each job and take appropriate control action while there is still time for his action to have effect.

It is impossible to recover costs that were lost as a result of a deficiency. They are gone! They are gone! That's all that can be said. It is possible, fortunately, to reverse the loss and still produce a profit if the deficiency is discovered early enough. The longer the deficiency exists, the more costs are lost forever, and the bigger the loss that will have to be overcome before a profit can be realized.

As in football, the more points the other side gets, the more points it takes to beat them, and for every minute that continues without reversing the trend, the less time there is to get the field goals and touchdowns required to win the game. In football this is called "running out of time." In golf it is called "running out of real estate." In construction it is called "building a monument."

A construction monument is a building, bridge, sewer, or street in which a contractor has invested heavily through losses but does not own any shares. He can walk in or on it, he can feel it, he can talk about it, he can take his family for a ride on Sunday and show it off, but he does not own it, or any part of it. The objective in contracting is to invest in as few monuments as possible.

Construction contracting at its best, with everything ideal and with the best expertise in all functions and activities, is a gamble. Without cost control it is more than a gamble. It is Russian roulette. Without cost control the contractor will be a builder of monuments.

BASIC REQUIREMENT NO. 8. AGGRESSIVE AND EFFECTIVE MANAGEMENT

The resources of a company, which are people and money, must be utilized effectively. This requires planning, coordination, control. and development. Management is the prime mover for these functions. Management is responsible for planning, coordination, control, and development of the resources. The way management acts is the way all things follow.

The personality and effectiveness of a company are directly determined by the attitudes, disposition, behavior, ability, and discipline of management. If management fails to manage, the company will surely fail. If management is efficient and effective, the company will succeed. Management is responsible for all things, including the other seven basic requirements. The following chapters will attempt to further explain the responsibilities and functions of the managing process.

2 ANALYSIS OF THE SUBCONTRACTOR — THE PERSON

M ost of today's contractors are first or second generation. With few exceptions, first-generation contractors came up through the tools; therefore, they have a field background only. Second-generation contractors inherit their status. Their backgrounds include college and on-the-job training with their fathers. Second-generation backgrounds rarely include business or management expertise by either experience or training.

Neither first- nor second-generation contractors are business managers by training or profession. They are just contractors. This leaves a great part of the construction industry without formal professional management.

In every organization there is an owner and a manager. These two positions are separate and distinct. Each has specific responsibilities and authority. An owner has only three responsibilities: (1) to provide the required equity capital, (2) to employ a capable manager, and (3) to set the objectives of the company. A manager has but two responsibilities: (1) to manage the company to meet the owner's objectives and (2) to generate an acceptable return on the owner's investment.

In most contracting firms the owner employs himself as the manager. However, most owners are not management experts, especially in the early stages of the company, or in the early stages of the second generation having taken command. This is highly unfortunate because it occurs during the most critical period of the company's life. Management expertise is an art and a specific profession that calls for learning, experience, known techniques, etc. When the inexperienced owner of a new company, or new owner of an existing company, wears both owner and manager hats, he has failed in one of his three responsibilities, that is, to employ a capable manager. In doing so he not only has failed in 33 percent of his responsibilities as an owner, but he has put himself, as the manager, in a position of compromise and conflicting interest. An owner cannot by nature manage a company without the instinct for self-preservation of his assets. He therefore becomes "self-guarded." This, added to his lack of management know-how, provides the ingredients for a nongrowth company.

When an owner or a board of directors of larger firms employs a manager, they investigate his training, experience, and track record as a manager. If most owner-managers would say, "Self! What experience have you had as a manager?" "Self! What is your track record as a manager?" "Self! What management training have you had?" Their answer would be, "None." "I have no track record." "None."

Managing a company must be completely without emotions. A manager who is not the owner has a much better chance of making the major day-to-day decisions without emotions. The owner who is the manager never requires his manager to report to him nor to be responsible to him as a manager. The management of the company, therefore, does not have to answer for the results of the managing process. This allows this vital function to be neglected.

The owner is compensated on a "return on investment" (commonly called ROI) basis. Return on investment is the result of the total business endeavor after *all* costs have been satisfied, *including the salary of the manager.*

The manager is compensated on salary basis. His salary is part of the routine costs of operating a business. It is not part of the return on investment. When the owner is also the manager, the compensation he receives as salary for being the manager *is not part of the return on his investment.*

The return on the owner's investment and the manager's salary are two separate and distinct compensations. One cannot be substituted for the other. A company that is managed by the owner must still compensate both separately: the owner each year with an acceptable rate of return on the owner's investment, and the manager with a salary worthy of his responsibilities and capabilities. Many times an owner-manager will accept a salary for his total compensation, forgetting that the company also must produce a return on his investment. No one would work for a firm for a salary that depended upon making a hefty investment without any return on it. Unfortunately, many owner-managers do just that. They invest the company's total net worth back into the company each year without expecting a return on that investment, for the privilege of working for the company for a fixed salary plus a few fringes.

The owner part of the owner-manager, however, is usually aware of and concerned about his investment *and* the return or lack of return. Every company has a net worth. Each year the net worth from the previous years is invested. A rate of return is required on this investment from the next year's operations, the same as if the same amount of money were invested in another endeavor.

Rates of returns on investments historically have been based on the risk or exposure to loss of the investment. Construction contracting, even under the most desirable circumstances, is a gamble.

Example

A medium-size construction firm has a net worth of $100,000. This means that the owner is going to invest $100,000 into a high-risk venture the following year. If the owner were asked to invest his $100,000 in an oil well with an expected rate of return (if the well produced) of 10 percent, he would laugh at the proposition. He would say, "You're crazy if you think I'm dumb enough to risk losing an appreciable part of $100,000 for a *potential* return of only 10 percent." He would, however, be more inclined to risk losing part of his $100,000 if the potential rate of return were 50 percent.

Unfortunately, year after year, owners of construction firms invest their company's net worth and accept as a matter of course losses or rates of return as low as passbook savings account returns. It is hard to understand why an owner who would refuse to invest his money in a high-risk oil well with a low rate of return invests his money in *high-risk contracting* and readily *accepts* from it a very low rate of return.

When the results of the owner's investment in his construction firm are not desirable and do not match the risk and, therefore, become unacceptable, the owner-manager doesn't say, "Self! You are not managing this company in a manner that is acceptable to me as the owner. If you cannot correct things in 6 months, I will be forced to replace you."

With this lack of accountability, the mismanagement continues and the cause of the undesirable or unacceptable results continues. The owner, not having a manager that he can hold accountable, blames the operating personnel. The operating personnel, who are operating autonomously (that is, without being managed), think they are doing a good job. When they are blamed by the owner for bad results, they are demotivated.

In the early stages of every contracting firm, the owner must wear both the owner's and manager's hats. This is not only a necessity, but it is also very prudent. The owner *must,* however, realize at all times that he is wearing both hats. When he is making decisions not related to his investment he must remember that he is the manager and not the owner. He also must know when his firm has outgrown the two-hat stage. Then he must wear the owner's hat only and hire a *capable manager.*

At this point, the owner can expand his activities into the many functions that do not interfere with the unemotional managing process. Sales work is a prime example. Sales are vital to any firm. The owners of contracting firms make ideal marketing people. Fortunately, this is the contracting function and is often the function in which the owners *do* have expertise. The owner then truly becomes the *contractor,* rather than the *manager.*

Marketing (sales), providing required equity (capital), and keeping employed a capable manager are more than a full-time job. Managing any appreciable-size contracting firm is also a full-time job. It is rare for a contracting firm to grow past a particular point without a separate owner and a separate manager. There are exceptions where the owners, through experience and study, become very capable managers. When this occurs they still must call upon key assistants as management people, for it is impossible for one man to both own and operate a sizable construction firm successfully.

In that most new and aggressive construction firms are owner managed, the industry as a whole is adversely affected. For example, look at the owner-manager's attitude on estimating. Estimating in the construction industry is an art. The process accurately forecasts the cost of material required to be installed and the labor to install it. The owner-manager adds all additional costs (nonproductive, administrative, etc.) to the labor and material costs that the estimator has forecast. Being an owner-manager, he is influenced by the emotions of desire, greed, fear, revenge, and skepticism about the estimator's costs. The emotion that is the strongest at the time determines the validity of the costs and gross profit (markup) that are added to labor and material costs. This is the way the selling price is determined.

Without fail, the emotion of desire to remain competitive and get the job causes the owner-manager to rationalize that the add-on costs are really not necessary on this job, and he proceeds to reduce them or completely leave them off. This same desire further motivates him to reduce the gross profit (markup) below a feasible point. This drastically reduces his bid (selling price).

On the other hand, the manager who is accountable to an owner for the profits of the company *must* add all required costs, plus a realistic gross profit. If he neglects either, the profit-and-loss statement will reflect his deficiency. This will affect the stability of his position. What owner would keep on a manager who was not producing an acceptable return on investment which matches the risk?

In every construction firm that has had a desirable profitable growth rate, one of the following has occurred:

1. The owner, through experience, study, etc., has become a capable manager and is able to function as a manager *only* and not as an owner-manager.

2. A professional manager has been employed.

3. A manager has emerged from the ranks and has been offi-

cially recognized and given the responsibility and authority as such by the owner.

4. There has been an unofficial, unrecognized employee who assimilated enough know-how to function as the manager.

Because of the owner's emotion of pride, he pictures himself as a capable manager. No. 4 fits most firms which achieve a mediocre success. For the firm this is fortunate, but for the individual involved it is unfortunate. Companies where this situation exists would often experience a greater, more profitable, and better-founded growth if the owner would allow No. 3 to occur. The owner then could hold the manager accountable for the management process which he (the unofficial manager) has been doing unofficially.

NO CONSTRUCTION COMPANY CAN GROW AND REMAIN PROFITABLE BY THE EXCLUSIVE EFFORTS OF ONE MAN. OFFICIALLY OR UNOFFICIALLY, TWO PERSONS ARE REQUIRED.

Let's follow a typical construction company from its inception through its various growth stages to a mature and founded firm. Let's call it Cletsowitz Construction Company. Frank Cletsowitz was a journeyman, having started as an apprentice. He learned his trade well and was an aggressive and efficient mechanic. He also was an extrovert who enjoyed presenting himself to others. His ambitions caused him to not be satisfied either with working 40 hours or with the income of a journeyman. He also needed the additional satisfaction of accomplishment that was not available in physically performing his trade.

To satisfy these needs Frank took advantage of offers to perform work on his own, commonly called "moonlighting." Frank soon realized that this additional activity was exciting and also rewarding in that it provided additional income and the satisfaction from obtaining and performing work on his own.

He continued to accept all offers for moonlighting, and as the word spread that he was available to perform work at less cost than from a contractor, his volume increased. He soon discovered that he was working as many hours moonlighting as he was working on his regular job. His regular job became a drag and was taking valuable hours from his newly found love, that of performing work on his own.

About this time a friend told him about a factory which was going to do some remodeling. He was pretty sure he could get Frank the job. The job, however, was a little too big to perform at night and on weekends. The day of the first big decision was at hand. Should Frank quit his regular job and contract for the job at the factory? Quitting his job was a frightful thought. With a family, could he afford the insecurity of not having a steady job? The responsibilities to his family and the emotional need for security told him to forget all this extra monkey business and settle down to earning a living and raising a family as his father had done, and as his friends were doing. His ambitions and need for self-accomplishment urged him to do what he felt he was capable of. The knowledge of the known future as a journeyman versus the excitement of an unknown future on his own urged him to accept the contract from the factory.

So! The first major decision of his business career had been made. Fortunately for Frank the decision had been based strictly on emotions, for at that point, had Frank realized how ill-equipped he was to become a contractor, he would have remained a journeyman.

Frank's price for the factory job, as for all others at that time, was based on what Frank would have to pay for the material he would use, plus what he wanted for his labor. He had previously borrowed the required tools from his employer. This little fringe, which Frank had overlooked as not being available to him after he quit his job, presented him with his first exposure to the needs of a business: *initial invested capital.*

All his previous jobs had not required any investment. They had required a small amount of working capital to support a short-term cash flow for materials. He would buy the materials for cash and by the end of the same day have the cash back from the cash money paid to him for the job. He had failed to realize that he had provided working capital and had a cash flow for those few hours for each job.

Frank tackled the factory job with vigor and enthusiasm. He bought some of the tools he needed and rented the rest. He bought the material he needed each day with cash. The job would take Frank approximately 1 month to complete.

At the end of the first week his wife asked for the usual paycheck so she could pay the house rent, buy the food, and get the kids new shoes. Frank gave her the needed money from their savings, the same source of the money for the tools and material purchases.

Frank worked through the weekend on his other moonlight jobs and received cash from them. He sure felt good on Monday morning, for he had the cash he had earned over the weekend to buy more material for the factory job. He sure wished the factory job was shorter or smaller, or paid more often. He suddenly realized that he had not given any thought to how or when he would be paid for the factory job, nor had he made any arrangements with the owners for payment.

That night he sat up until four o'clock in the morning projecting how much money he would need for material to finish the factory job and how much he would need for his family until he collected. The amount was more than his savings. What was he to do? He readily recognized he could not continue to pay cash each day for material.

This brought about his second decision as a businessman—to open an account at a supply house. This decision was based on a projected need and was truly a business decision.

He arrived the next morning at the supply house, the same supply house with which he had been doing a cash business for over 2 years. The same supply house where he knew everyone. The same supply house where everyone knew him. He proudly announced that he had selected that particular supply house to open his first account. He was confident that within 15 minutes he would be on his way with the required material for the day, purchased on credit. He also was confident that he would collect from the factory before he would have to pay the supply house. Why shouldn't he feel this way? All the rest of his customers had paid immediately when he finished the job.

His first big disappointment tore his heart out—the supply house didn't jump at the chance of being his prime supplier and now requested of him things he didn't have, such as trade credit references and a financial statement. Also, he was asked questions which he felt were personal and none of their business. What was he worth? Did he have a personal bank account? Did he own his home? Was it paid for? Did he own his automobile? Where did his father work, etc? He went along with all this nonsense only because at that moment he had no choice. He needed material, and he didn't have the money to pay for it. Unknowingly he had recognized the need for credit for his yet unborn company. The supply house finally agreed to extend the credit, with a limit on the total amount and Frank promising to submit a financial statement within a week.

Frank was now requested to take the first step to giving birth to his new company: hiring an accountant to prepare a financial statement. He never did make it to the factory that day. However, he did accomplish a great deal. He had obtained credit at a supply house and had hired an accountant.

Frank thought of what the day had cost him. No material installed, no material cost; no labor expended at the factory, no labor costs. Oh, wait a minute! Although Frank had not worked at the factory that day, the day had passed and his wife would still require money to run the house, even though Frank had not installed any work at the factory. Frank then thought, "But I did work; boy, did I work! Today was harder work than if I had worked with the tools at the factory."

Frank had now experienced his first overhead costs. The cost of his labor for the day and the cost of an accountant to prepare the financial statement. Frank said to himself, "Well I guess it was worth it; at least I won't have to do that again. I can now get to work and make some money."

The next day he arrived at the factory with renewed enthusiasm and started to work when, lo and behold, an inspector arrived and rudely asked Frank for a permit. His pride prevented him from admitting he didn't have a permit and couldn't get one because he didn't have a license, and so he stood there saying, "Aba, aba, aba." His next thought turned to embarrassment should the owner of the factory find out. He would lose the contract, he had already quit his regular job, his savings were now all tied up in tools, material, and money to feed his kids. Boy, what a mess he'd got himself in! Again, Frank was fortunate in not knowing the pitfalls of a contractor, for this kind of fun had just begun.

The inspector, to whom Frank had been indifferent while working for a contractor, was now the demon of all times. The inspector, realizing he had uncovered an unlicensed, naive tradesman posing as a contractor, didn't go out of his way to make it easy for Frank. It appeared to Frank that the inspector was deliberately making it difficult for him. Then fear struck Frank. He couldn't even allow his name to become known for fear he would lose his union card, and with it the last shred of possible recovery from this terrible mess he was in.

Well, Frank finally got his license, permit, and finished the factory job, but 3 months had passed before he collected his money. He got through this period by borrowing from his in-laws and a couple of close friends.

He was no longer the cocky journeyman ready to take the world on. If one were to look closely, a bit of humility could be detected. Frank had now lived through the labor pains and had given birth to his own contracting firm. His enthusiasm had returned, as he was now a contractor. He had obtained a license, established credit, hired an accountant, bought some tools, had a clientele, owed money (short term to his supplier and his wife, and long term to his in-laws and friends), and some money was owed to him. There was even money in the pipeline of jobs in process. He had climbed the hill and was surely on the downhill side now, *he thought!*

Frank's enthusiasm, knowledge of his trade, exuberance, and low prices attracted additional work. It was fortunate for Frank that he did not realize his prices were low, or why. The reason for his low prices was that Frank was not including any overhead in his estimates, mainly because he had none; well, almost none. He didn't realize he would eventually have to pay interest on the money he had borrowed, and he didn't count the gas and wear and tear on his car or the expendable tools he was using.

He was still using his personal checking account; he forgot he paid for the checks. He also forgot the hours and days he was spending on estimating, picking up materials, and looking at jobs for which he was paying himself by continuing to support his family from his contracting endeavors. Of course, the telephone didn't count; it was his home phone.

Well, anyway, Frank felt he was doing well; in fact, work had increased to where he was hiring a moonlighter to assist him on weekends. He had cajoled his wife into writing the checks to pay the bills and the wages of the moonlighter. He had even gone along with the accountant and established earnings records and payroll deductions for himself and his moonlighter assistant. He didn't recognize his wife as an employee, nor did he recognize her time as a contribution to and a further investment in the company; nor did he recognize any need for a return on the investment he had made in his firm with the money he had taken from his savings account and the amount borrowed.

Not counting all these and eliminating necessary business requirements, Frank was doing fine and expanding rapidly and thought he was making money and experiencing success. Again, Frank was fortunate to not be aware of the facts. He had depleted his savings, was up to his neck in debt, and was working 16 hours a day; his wife was working several hours a week; and the money he had been able to take each week was less than half that of a journeyman's pay for 40 hours.

Frank continued on. His volume increased, he hired full-time journeymen, and he began to produce a factual profit. His profit continued to increase along with a steady increase in volume. He was now realizing more profit than he had dreamed possible. Frank was working 16 hours a day, his wife was now a full-time clerk and bookkeeper, and their home and entire life-style were changed to satisfy the demands of the business. Even with these physical and mental demands on himself, his wife, and his family, Frank's enthusiasm was at its peak. Of course, he never stopped to consider that had he been working the same number of hours as a journeyman and his wife had been working the same hours as a waitress, and if he had been earning savings account interest on the money that would have been in the bank, the combined income would have been more than it presently was, without any risk. But that wouldn't have been any fun, would it?

He personally was involved with every detail of every activity, including sales, performance of the work, buying, delivering, paying bills, invoicing, payroll, collection, and customer relations. Productivity was very high because Frank was always there to make sure it was high. He made personally sure that his men had the tools they needed, the material required, and instructions as to what, how, and where to install it. He was in the first stage of a business, that of *direct supervision*. That is the stage during which the contractor supervises every activity directly.

As his volume increased, he was unknowingly approaching the edge of the first plateau of expansion. His wife could no longer keep up with the administrative activities. The vendors' invoices had now become voluminous. Frank knew by experience that each one had to be checked thoroughly before payment.

His wife had fallen behind in getting his invoices out. Frank had delegated the billing to his wife a long time ago because he didn't have time for such unimportant activities. But now she was behind, mainly because Frank wasn't giving her the billing information. In reality he was behind, but he blamed her.

This led to discontent and frequent husband-and-wife arguments. His wife was now fed up with living a business 24 hours a day in her home. Frank knew his business had outgrown his home and the Ma-and-Pa arrangement with his wife.

Well, he would just have to open an office and hire a full-time clerk. His first office was small, modest, and appealing. Frank was very proud. There was no question as to his success. The satisfaction of self-accomplishment was wonderful. It was a joyful week.

The following Sunday Frank made a sudden return to earth. Seated in his new office he started to put some numbers together. Rent, clerk's salary, telephone, utilities—all of a sudden these costs were a reality. Where was the money for these costs to come from? Profits? That was a horrible thought. The only other place would be to add these costs to his estimates. "Say! That's a good idea," he thought. In that way the customer pays for these costs. He now knew what overhead was and he now knew how to recover it. He worked out a formula to put on each estimate its proportionate share of the overhead costs.

Up to now Frank's batting average on obtaining jobs he had estimated was 1.000. Within a month this had dropped to .700. It didn't take him long to find out why he wasn't getting all the jobs. His customers, who previously had been the most wonderful people in the world, all of a sudden weren't so wonderful. Frank thought, "Why, they don't even trust me. They got estimates from others to check on me. All the time I thought they were giving me the work because of their confidence in me and the quality of my work, and the service I was giving them. They really don't care about me. All they care about is my price." Frank felt the same hurt as he felt when the supply house didn't extend open arms to him when he opened his first account.

Another thought entered his hurt mind. Those sneaky contractors who also had bid on the job. The whole world is sneaky, thought Frank. The customer didn't indicate in any way that he was getting other bids. It was now evident to Frank that the customer had led him on. Frank thought of the time and effort he had spent estimating the jobs he lost. Boy, that surely was a waste of time.

Frank wondered. What he was going to do to overcome this newly encountered obstacle: competition. He immediately recognized the cause of the problem, that damned overhead! If he hadn't included that in his estimates he wouldn't have lost the job. The money to pay for that miserable overhead had to come from somewhere. But there were only two places it could come from: either out of his profits or from the customer as part of the costs. Frank felt it wasn't fair for it to come out of the profits. What was he going to do? Those lousy sneaky contractors that he now realized were his competition wouldn't let him add it to his job cost. There was no other alternative than to take it out of his profits.

Frank had unknowingly separated his profit into *gross profit* and *net profit*. And Frank did what he had to do. He stopped putting his overhead costs in his estimates. His batting average immediately increased.

Well, anyway, he was back to normal, his sales were expanding, and business was booming again. A few weeks later Frank's accountant was in to take care of his books. He told Frank he would like to go over his profit and loss statement with him. He pointed out to Frank that up until a few weeks ago Frank's profit was increasing proportionately with the increase in sales. Then all of a sudden, even though Frank's sales had continued to increase, his rate of profit had decreased. Frank told his accountant what had happened when he added overhead to his estimates and that he either had to drop his price by leaving the overhead out of his estimates or lose the jobs. Frank had increased his cost of doing business when he moved into his office and hired a clerk, but had failed in being able to pass this cost onto his customers.

Frank had stepped onto the second plateau of expansion. In so doing he had increased his capacity for more sales and was realizing the cost of this additional capacity, but he didn't have the sales yet to fill that capacity. Frank was feeling the same way as he did when he went from grade school to high school. While in the eighth grade of grade school he was the big shot. He was promoted and, although he was moving forward, he found himself in somewhat of a starting-over position as a freshman in high school. The same thing happened when he went from a senior in high school to a freshman in college.

Frank could see the same thing was going to happen with his company. As he would expand his sales, his profits would expand proportionately until he had reached the total capacity of his company. At that point his rate of profits would be high. Frank knew at that point he would have to increase his capacity by changing his company in some major way, which would immediately reduce his rate of profit again.

Frank discussed this with his accountant, and his accountant indicated that a drop in rate of profit which was caused by deliberately increasing the capacity of a company was healthy, but that a drop in rate of profit for any other reason could be an indication of a serious problem.

Frank and his accountant agreed that several plateaus of expansion lay ahead, and the accountant pointed out that moving from one plateau to another were very critical periods. He stated that each plateau presented a completely different ball game and that at each one Frank would have to decide whether or not to expand to the next one, because there was no turning back. The accountant pointed out that many companies fail during the transition from one plateau to another. He also pointed out that to increase sales beyond the capabilities of a company without expanding to the next plateau also was fatal.

With the added ability derived from his additional administrative capacity he continued to add sales, manpower, tools, etc. Frank was now working the same 16 hours per day, but at twice the speed. He realized that with all his effort, speed, and long hours he was not covering all the bases adequately. The time required for him to take care of meeting customers, estimating, collecting money, seeing inspectors, etc., was causing him to neglect the field. He knew that his men weren't getting the material when and where they needed it. He knew they weren't being instructed as to how, when, and where to install work. He knew the overall performance of the field was slipping. Frank recognized that he had two choices: hire an assistant for sales, estimating, etc., or hire a superintendent to assist in directing the field. He chose to hire a superintendent.

His thoughts turned to his experience with the added costs of his office and clerk. Once again he was adding overhead and once again he had no place to cover the added cost except to take it from profits. Frank immediately calculated the amount of additional sales that he would have to get to pay for the cost of the superintendent. Well, Frank kept his price low and went out and beat the bushes and got the additional sales. Of course, this took several months at the same speed, effort, and 16-hour days that were now commonplace for him.

The result of these additional sales gave birth to another catastrophe. Although his rate of profit had dropped as a result of adding the superintendent, the increase in sales was maintaining a profit. So why all of a sudden wasn't there any money to pay his bills and for payroll? He surely wasn't taking any money from the company. In fact, he was the lowest-paid person in the company.

Frank never realized that for every dollar of sales he added to his volume, an average of 20 cents would be required to pay bills and payroll which that sale would create. All Frank recognized was that he was showing a profit on the books, he had worked hard on collections, and they were in pretty good shape—yet there was no money.

Frank's in-laws were out of money and he was out of friends with money. He had heard of the "friendly banker," and so he decided that he had no other choice than to find out just how friendly a banker could be. Surprisingly, the banker turned out to be very friendly. Frank was able to borrow the money he needed. Again, Frank did not realize that the reason the banker was so friendly was that Frank's financial statement showed that Frank was producing a profit. It really wasn't Frank's good looks. If his statement didn't show a profit, the banker would have been very unfriendly. Frank also did not realize that by borrowing money from the bank he was creating additional overhead costs: *interest.* His involvement with sales, money, and directing the clerk and the superintendent had now moved Frank's company into its second stage, that of *indirect supervision.* That is the stage during which the contractor directs the supervision.

To maintain the additional volume that was required to overcome the additional overhead costs of the superintendent, Frank was required to hire an estimator. Although this increased the overall capacity of the company, it had the same effects and requirements as the two previous significant increases had had in overhead. The first was the office and clerk, and the second was the superintendent. The effects and requirements were the need for additional sales volume to overcome the costs, additional money to support the additional sales (more borrowing and more interest), and a drop in the rate of profit.

Each significant increase in overhead which caused an increase in volume, or vice versa, represented the move from one plateau to another, that is, an increase in sales but a decrease in profit, both by dollars and by percentage. Frank's company continued this treadmill of more overhead requiring more sales volume and the additional sales volume requiring more overhead until the company had grown to the third stage of development, that of *indirect control* by the contractor.

The first stage was direct supervision, the second was indirect supervision, and now Frank found himself at the stage of indirect control. He was now controlling his company indirectly through management systems. Through these systems he was measuring the performance of the people who were controlling the efficiency of the company. Frank was now a large contractor. He had the respect of the union, the business community, and his peers. He was very "well off" financially. Well, at least he was well off financially on paper; that is, his balance sheet showed a healthy net worth.

But what had Frank really accomplished? Well, he wasn't working 16 hours a day any more, just 12 hours a day; he wasn't working 7 days a week any more, just 6½ days a week. He did have a fine home (with a mortgage that would choke a horse). He had an American Express credit card, with no one to question how or to what extent he used it. The amount he was able to take from the company as income somehow was controlled by something that never ceased to haunt him—cash flow. He was still on the treadmill of higher overhead, requiring more sales volume. This still kept him up at night worrying whether he would be the low bidder on the job that was due the next day. He had found a new reason to worry. He would worry about losing a job from not bidding low enough and he would worry about being the low bidder because that usually indicated he was going to lose money on the job.

But with all this Frank was happy. He was happy because he had completely forgotten what it was like to be able to go home at 4:30 and on the way home plan how he would spend the evening with his family, and what would he plan for the weekend—fishing, golf, or just loafing. Yes, he had forgotten that other type of life and, yes, he was indeed happy because *he had done it his way* and was experiencing the complete satisfaction of accomplishment. Yes, he was a contractor in every sense of the word.

We have looked at the characteristics of a contractor's background that caused him to become a contractor. We also have looked at the birth of a contracting firm and the contractor through maturity. Let's now look at what human characteristics a contractor, the person, must have to be successful. He must, above all, be self-disciplined. Discipline, as used here, is defined as "orderliness and compliance." That is, all is done in an orderly manner in compliance with established ways. Self-discipline is causing one's self to perform in an orderly manner and to comply. Self-discipline is no doubt the the most important characteristic necessary for the subcontractor to successfully manage his company. The subcontractor must be an effective manager. To be an effective manager one must be self-disciplined. Self-discipline includes carrying out that which you propose, self-denial, and organizing one's activities.

The difference between an effective and an ineffective manager is that an ineffective manager will come up with the ideas and the know-how to achieve a specific objective, but not with the self-denial and fortitude necessary to work and see his ideas through to conclusion. The effective manager will always carry out that which he proposes. The entire responsibility of management is based on a logical analysis of a need, establishing a course of action, controlling, measuring, correcting, and concluding the course of action. This requires discipline by all concerned and self-denial by the manager.

Self-denial means putting the management responsibility before all else, before personal desires and, in many cases, before responsibilities to one's family. If the logic of the responsibility dictates that the manager perform an activity or be at a specific location which conflicts with a personal need or desire, the personal need or desire must take second place. There is no room in management responsibility for giving in to the superfluities of life.

Seldom do the monetary rewards or the recognition match the effort and time expended by the manager. The only reward is the personal satisfaction of accomplishment within one's self.

The disciplined manager will do that which he knows must be done, at the time it must be done, even though it may be emotionally or physically difficult or awkward. To be self-disciplined, the effective manager must organize all his activities to get the most from his time and effort. Every activity must apply to a specific objective, or must satisfy a specific function. The manager must know at all times what specific function he is satisfying or the specific objective he is pursuing. He cannot perform more than one activity toward more than one objective or more than one function at the same time. Seldom can the manager perform his function or activities without external interruptions. He must, however, be so organized that as soon as the interruption has been established, recorded, and the next course of action developed, he can immediately revert to the job he was doing before the interruption. He will not (if at all possible) follow the course of action caused by the interruption immediately. Instead, he will schedule this to be done after the job he was already doing.

The tasks or activities chosen by the manager are usually ones that cannot be delegated. Therefore, with few exceptions, they are very important. Because of this, they cannot be done on a catch-as-catch-can basis. They must be pursued with as much continuity and diligence as possible.

It is only human for a manager to want to clear up the external interruption immediately before returning to his previous work. It requires considerable self-discipline on his part to record, establish, and develop the next course of action without doing it "right now." If the manager does not use this discipline, the work that cannot be delegated will be done some way, somehow, but it will cause the manager to be grossly inefficient and ineffective. He must organize his work to be as routine as possible. Good self-discipline will help him stay with his routine.

The contractor's profile must be above average in many characteristics. His aptitudes must be high in verbal thinking speed, mechanical insight, sales drive, general information, and logical reasoning.

His personality makeup must be that of an extrovert. He must be self-sufficient (independent) and dominant. He must be firm, frank, and persistent, and a free thinker.

Competition, the need to solve problems, and economics must all motivate the contractor. With his independence, extroversion, dominance, and persistence he also must be cooperative and flexible in his attitude and manner toward others.

One might say the above profile requirements are that of the perfect man. Because of the nature of the construction business, these requirements are there and are necessary. Deficiency in any one of them has a direct effect on the degree of success of the company. Remember, the entire company will take on the personality, attitude, disciplines, and abilities of the contractor.

The way the contractor operates as a person is the way his company will operate as a company. A contractor must know himself, and above all, he must be truthful to himself. If the contractor is weak in any of the above aptitude, personality, or motivation requirements, he must be aware of it and make up for the weakness. He can minimize the effect of such weaknesses by either strengthening himself against the weakness or by delegating the function affected by the weakness to a person who is strong in the particular requirement. For instance, if a contractor is weak in sales drive he should have a good, hard-driving salesman-estimator. If he is weak in mechanical insight and dominance, he should have an experienced, hard-nosed field superintendent. The personality, self-discipline, and motivation requirements cannot be delegated. Weaknesses in these requirements must be improved by the contractor himself. The contractor must be many things at all times.

All of the contractor's responsibilities include working with people. He is constantly working with his customers, his employees, and with his suppliers. He has customers, he is a customer, and he is an employer. His customers include many different types of people. They include highly educated and intelligent people and people who are not educated, and some who are not intelligent. They include architects, engineers, purchasing agents, handymen, plant superintendents, public officials, "pipsqueaks,"* accountants, lawyers, housewives, owners of huge companies, owners of small companies, etc.

His suppliers, to whom he is a customer, are of different levels and professions. They include owners of large and small supply houses, managers of large and small supply houses, supply house salesmen, supply house order takers, delivery men, gas station owners, gas station attendants, one-man operators of businesses that perform services as sub-subcontractors, etc.

His employees include people with professions, people with trades, and

---

*People in insignificant positions who are, however, a link in the chain of control.

the unskilled. Unlike managers in other trades, the contractor is constantly in direct contact with the customers, suppliers, inspectors, union representatives, sub-subcontractors, and employees. Satisfying the people requirements of all these different levels of individuals requires the near-perfect man. The ability to get along with people and the need to cause the other person to do it the contractor's way requires the perfect man. Successfully getting along with people while at the same time causing them to do it your way is called "negotiating."

③ INDUSTRY ASSOCIATES

The subcontractor has many groups of people within the construction industry with whom he must associate on an amiable basis and with whom he must constantly negotiate. These groups are: (1) customers, (2) industry peers, (3) competitors, and (4) employees. It is important to identify each category and to determine which category any given person is in. Customers consist of owners, representatives of owners, architects, engineers, and general contractors. Industry peers consist of union officials, inspectors, architects, engineers, general contractors, sub-subcontractors, suppliers, and manufacturers' representatives. Competitors consist of other contractors. Also included in this category are trade association managers and administrators. Employees consist of the administrative personnel, professional people, and field tradesmen of the industry.

Within the above categories lies the basis of who caters to whom and when. The subcontractor is either catering or being catered to or is on a peer basis with his associates. As it is important in negotiating to know who is the negotiatee and who is the negotiator, it also is important to always know who is supposed to be catering to whom, if at all.

In the American way of life, everyone gets a turn at being catered to and of catering to the other person. Catering to a person in a palatable manner requires skill, and being catered to in a manner that does not cause the person doing the catering to feel awkward is also a skill. In the industry peer category are people who are on even ground with the subcontractor. There is a fine line between associating with people as peers and catering or being catered to.

Construction selling consists of selling, negotiating, and motivating. The subcontractor must sell himself to the customer, then he must motivate him into a position where he can negotiate with him. This obviously does not hold true in public work. Unfortunately, with all the above, one more vital thing must be included—the low bid. Conversely, it is also unfortunate that with the low bid, the job still cannot be obtained without selling, negotiating, and catering.

After the subcontractor is given the job, the relationship turns to negotiating and catering. The subcontractor must constantly negotiate with the customer or his representative during the life of the job. This is primarily generated by changes (extras). To survive, the subcontractor must win as many of the negotiations as possible, while at the same time catering to the customer. This is necessary because of the need for the next job.

All those listed as industry peers are vital and play an important role in the construction industry. Subsequently, the relationship between each and the subcontractor appreciably affects the subcontractor's success. Construction requires a design, labor of various trades, materials, coordination of the subcontractor, installation of the material, and enforcement of the safety of the installation. The people involved in the above are industry peers, all working together to construct a thing. Catering is out of place and is not necessary between industry peers. Cooperation, however, is vital.

The architect and engineers are responsible for the design. Construction industry unions have assumed the responsibility of the discipline of the workmen. They have assumed jointly with the contractors the responsibility for training the workmen. The union also provides other vital functions to the industry, including uniformity of labor costs. The general contractors and/or the architects have assumed responsibility for the coordination of the subcontractors. The municipal inspection bureaus have assumed the responsibility for enforcement of the installation's safety; OSHA has responsibility for the workmen's safety during construction; and the subcontractors assume the responsibility of making the installation. In order to grow and be successful, the subcontractor must have the cooperation of all the people in the above groups.

A person has full control over the degree of his cooperation with others. Cooperation from others, however, is more difficult to come by. The personalities, attitudes, and dispositions of industry peers are all very important to gaining cooperation. Everyone is prone to feel that his position and contribution to the industry is more important and prestigious than others. Architects, engineers, union officials, inspectors, and general contractors all have varying degrees of enforcement responsibility over the subcontractor.

The architect and engineers are commissioned to see that the installation is done in accordance with the plans, the specifications, and the contract. The union officials are elected by the union members and are charged with the enforcement of the union rules involving the contractor, union members, and the union contract. The inspectors are law enforcement officers, responsible for the enforcement of code ordinances designed to provide safe facilities for the public. OSHA officials are representatives of the federal government, responsible for safe working conditions during construction. The general contractor is responsible for the timely coordination of all the subcontractors and compliance with the construction schedule. With this responsibility the general contractor has the authority to direct the subcontractor when and where to work.

The enforcement relationship of the architect, engineer, union official, inspector, and general contractor with the subcontractor places these industry peers in an innuendo position of authority over the subcontractor. This innuendo authority affects people in different ways. Authority to some is a badge of power. Authority to others is merely an aid to helping them meet their responsibility.

Cooperation with those who wear responsibility and innuendo authority as a badge of power is very difficult. Unfortunately, each seems to have an ax to grind with the subcontractor. Some architects and engineers are motivated (to perpetuate their clientele) to impress the owner whom they represent by making it difficult for the subcontractor. They feel the best way to make sure the owner is aware of their expert representation is to force compliance from the subcontractor to the nth degree, past the point of practicality.

Union officials must appear to force the subcontractor to comply with the union contract and applicable union rules without compromise to prevent criticism from the membership. Outward fraternization and cooperation with the subcontractor causes the membership to feel they are being misrepresented. Unions are political bodies consisting of the "ins" and the "outs." The outs are constantly monitoring the ins for misrepresentation in order to support their candidacies.

In that construction union officials come up through the trade, they have experienced the physical hardships and the rough-and-tumble life of the tradesman. Some deal with their membership in a rough-and-tumble manner. Some present themselves to the industry in a rough-and-tumble manner. Many union officials are capable leaders and astute managers who can meet with their membership in kind and can also present themselves to the business world as professional businessmen.

Unfortunately, some union officials are not leaders and managers and wear their responsibility to the construction industry as a badge of power. To make up for their lack of ability as leaders and managers, they thwart their responsibility with power methods of the past. The person most susceptible to this adversity is the subcontractor.

Inspectors have the technical knowledge of a construction craft and are the authority on municipal construction and safety codes and regulations. Most are dedicated and practical. Unfortunately, a few see themselves as police officers with the authority to arrest people and cause them to be punished. The subcontractor is ready prey for this type of inspector. The capable and practical inspector has a responsibility to the public which he is sincerely dedicated to satisfy. The subcontractor is the person to whom this dedication is directed.

Although general contractors are contractors, they differ from subcontractors appreciably. The general contractor's responsibility to a project includes many functions that a subcontractor's does not. These include coordinating other subcontractors, meeting completion schedules for the entire project, payout administration, etc.

It is the rare exception when the subcontractor is not subordinate to the general contractor for some functions. The only time that this isn't true is when the owner or architect does the coordinating, scheduling, and payout administration. For this reason, and because on most projects the general contract includes all the trades, the general contractors look upon the subcontractors as "subs." The term sub means under, down, lower, etc. In that the general contractor looks down on the subcontractor, he feels he is above, better, and more important to the project than the subcontractor.

If the general contract includes all the trades, this discrimination begins with the letting of the subcontracts. Although the general contractor has in his bid the amount of the low bid for each subcontract, he still goes out for rebids. He subsequently is able to buy each subcontract for less than he had in his original bid. (The subcontractors also are guilty of this with quoted costs from their suppliers.) The subcontractors to whom the general contractor sublets contracts are members of the team he has selected to build the project. He establishes an atmosphere detrimental to the teamwork and cooperation between him and his subs by taking advantage of them in the beginning by making money at the subcontractor's expense. It's like Jackie Gleason saying to Alice, "I'm the king and you are nothing."

The general contractor will continually coordinate, schedule, and cause the project to be constructed in a sequence that will benefit his image and financial interest. He does this with complete disregard for the adverse effects generated against the subcontractors. The general contractor backcharges the subcontractors without their authorization. He reduces payout requests without approval of the subcontractor. He even holds back payouts without the subcontractor's concurrence. Because he holds the purse strings, the general contractor is successful in passing to the subcontractors many costs that were in the general contract without including them in the subcontracts. These are costs that the subcontractor did not include in his bid; they therefore represent gains to the general contractor and losses to the subcontractor.

Obviously not all architects, engineers, union officials, inspectors, and general contractors are guilty of the above inequities against the subcontractors. Unfortunately, there are enough to make it appear that the minute a subcontractor gets a job everyone sets out to do him in. The subcontractor feels he is swimming upstream against an already fast current while everyone else is standing on the shore throwing debris in the water to make it even more difficult to swim. What can the subcontractor do to combat this horrible characteristic of the construction industry? Well, he certainly can't fight back. The architect, engineer, and general contractor may be the customer on the next job. If the subcontractor fights back and alienates himself, he certainly won't get a chance at the next job. The union official and inspector are in a position to make life more miserable on the next job.

It should be very obvious that the subcontractor needs cooperation from many friends. There is no way a subcontractor can survive without cooperation. The best people to get cooperation from are friends. Making and keeping friends is vital to the subcontractor. The friendships must be real, based on true feelings, and not on ulterior motives of the subcontractor. To receive cooperation, a person must give cooperation. To receive help, a person must give help.

One of the best ways to set the stage for cooperation by union officials and inspectors is compliance with the codes, the union rules, and the union contract. The subcontractor must learn the code, OSHA safety regulations, and the union rules and contract, and learn how to work within the framework of each. The greatest source of noncooperation is noncompliance as a result of not knowing these. It is the responsibility of the subcontractor to know the codes, regulations, rules, and contract infinitely.

The subcontractor is a member of an industry which he expects will provide him with the good things of life. To be able to take, the subcontractor must give of himself to the industry. The best vehicle for this is the trade association. Membership and active participation in a trade association enables the subcontractor to contribute to the industry and at the same time build up meaningful friendships with industry peers.

Participation in industrywide committees, social functions, and political and training endeavors will maintain recognition. Cooperation from industry peers is a by-product of sincere personal contribution to the industry.

Architects and general contractors provide a combined service to an owner. On many projects, the architects and engineers provide feasibility studies, space requirement studies, budgets, design (plans and specifications), taking of bids, letting of contracts, finance and payout administration, change-order administration, supervision and coordination of the installation, and plans and specification enforcement (punch-list requirements).

On many projects the general contractor provides or assists the architect and engineer in many of the above functions. To satisfy these responsibilities, each must have a team upon which he can depend. The team includes subcontractors. An architect or general contractor has a group of subcontractors from each trade in whom he has confidence and on whom he can depend to perform the work in an efficient, prompt, and cooperative manner. He knows that each is mechanically capable to perform the work, can provide the necessary financing, and has the required administrative capability. These are the subcontractors from whom he takes bids. In that he has equal confidence in each, he is fair and awards the job to the lowest bidder. If one of the bids is extremely low and it is obvious that a mistake has been made, the architect or general contractor will tell the subcontractor to go over his bid. During the progress of the job, the architect, general contractor, and subcontractors cooperate with each other because each will need the other on future jobs. The subcontractor should get on as many of these teams as possible, (They *do* exist.) This is done by personal contact, doing a good job, and cooperation.

Unfortunately, this type of cooperation does not prevail on public work. The architect has very little control over who the bidders are. Many times his team is made up of complete strangers. This contributes to the noncooperative environment explained before.

Other industry peers with whom the subcontractor associates are suppliers, manufacturers' representatives, and sub-subcontractors. Each is a vital link in the construction industry chain. The supplier is not only the coordinator of thousands of items of construction materials, equipment, and tools, but is also the finance buffer between the manufacturer and the subcontractor. The manufacturer, by precedent, requires immediate payment for his products. The subcontractor, by necessity, cannot pay immediately. The supplier pays the manufacturer and extends credit to the subcontractor. The manufacturer's representative is the direct technical link between the manufacturer and the subcontractor. This allows the subcontractor to work directly with the manufacturer on engineering and design requirements. The sub-subcontractor provides services that are included in the subcontract which the subcontractor is not geared to perform. The supplier, manufacturer's representative, and sub-subcontractor provide the subcontractor with his turn to be catered to. He needs their cooperation. It can be obtained by merely returning the courtesies. The third group of people with whom the subcontractor must associate is his competitors. This association is vital in that it is not the customer who controls the prices, it is competitors. The subcontractor must meet or beat his competitor's price, not a price that the customer has set.

Remember Frank Cletsowitz. When he realized that his prices weren't enough to cover his costs plus overhead, he tried to raise them, but his competitors' bids wouldn't permit it. Remember that when Frank first started, he got almost every job he bid. Also remember that he was unaware that the reason he got all the jobs was that his price was extremely low. Not only was he unaware that his price was extremely low, but he was also unaware why. There is an old saying that is very true. "Everyone knows who the low bidder is except the low bidder."

The best competitor is a healthy, well-informed, and astute business-man. A struggling or naive company which is lowering its price in an attempt to survive or which just doesn't know and doesn't include all the costs in its bid is a cancer in the industry. The isolationist theory of "his problems are his" is not applicable in the construction industry. The financial health of a competitor's company, the degree of business know-how, and the all-around contracting ability of a competitor directly in-fluence the success of each subcontractor.

Each subcontractor must help teach his competitor subcontracting. This can be best accomplished through the trade associations. Directly helping a competitor to understand and upgrade his organization is also a good way. Association and cooperation between subcontractors are very vital to the success of all.

Cooperation from customers, industry peers, and competitors can be obtained by associating with each and cooperating with them.

The remaining group of people with whom the subcontractor must associate is his employees. Employees are of three distinct groups: admin-istrative personnel, professional people, and field tradesmen. Coopera-tion from employees must be obtained by motivating them and by earning their respect. In that each group of employees has different backgrounds, different life-styles, and different interests, they must be recognized separately. Associating with employees as "one of the boys" will not motivate, instill respect, or produce the necessary cooperation. The best way to obtain cooperation from employees is to support them in their endeavors. That is, do the job that a subcontractor is required to do. To do the required job the contractor must be organized. His organization must be developed, implemented, and maintained. This holds true for all sizes of companies. All the functions in a large company are also in a small company.

An employee who is part of a recognizable team, and who knows what the rules of the game are, what is expected of him, what he can expect of others, and is provided the wherewithal to do a good job, will cooperate. Being an employee of a disorganized, unstructured company is aggravat-ing and demotivating and will not produce cooperation.

4 DEVELOPING THE ORGANIZATION, SYSTEMS, AND PROCEDURES

Aptitude and capability tests indicate the average person has an acceptable degree of capability for given endeavors; however, he must be in a structured situation to be effective and efficient.

Endeavors involving one or two people with little or no dependence from one to the other, and with very few separate activities, require no designed organizational frame to work within. When people or number of activities are added, though, a structured organization becomes necessary. The subcontractor must cause the collective activities and people performance to be effective and efficient.

Large companies with many employees require a well-structured organization to coordinate the collective efforts and activities of all. The smaller the company, and the fewer the people, the more vital it is that there be a structured organization.

This is especially true with construction contracting. Unfortunately, the small company with few people has the same activities to perform as a large company with many people. The difference between a large company and a small company is that each person in the small company performs many different activities. Each wears several hats. This is why it is more difficult to identify each activity in a small company. Very frequently many overlap. Many activities cannot be readily identified because of their informal characteristics, but nevertheless they are there.

In any size company, whether measured by number of people, by sales volume, or by any other means, all the activities are there and must be performed. In a structured organization they will be performed effectively. In an unstructured situation they will be performed ineffectively.

All construction is mechanically simple and consists of very similar mechanical functions. Activities that support the installation also are simple. The number of activities, however, in itself causes the support functions to become complex. Adverse complexity can be avoided with a well-structured organization.

Following is a representative list of activities that are required to be performed in the average subcontracting firm. Their sheer number should show the damaging complexity that could grow in an unstructured situation. For ease of identification, and to provide the basis on an organizational structure, the activities are divided into the major functions of a company: accounting and administration; purchasing—materials management; production—installation of the work; sales—estimating; and management.

   I. Accounting and Administration

      A. Cash flow (finance)

         1. Payables

            a. Approving vendors' invoices for payment

            b. Paying bills

            c. Establishing and maintaining payable cycles for each vendor

         2. Cash receipts

            a. Collecting

            b. Depositing

            c. Policing customer receivable cycles

         3. Cash needs projection

            a. Estimating what money will be coming in and when

            b. Estimating what bills must be paid and when

         4. Bank borrowing

            a. Determining how much to borrow and for how long

      B. Invoicing (billing)

         1. Work order administration

            a. Initiating commitment to expend labor and/or material

            b. Obtaining authorization for extras and authorizing extra work to be performed

         2. Cost accumulation of basic job and extras

         3. Determining applicable method of payment

         4. Establishing when to invoice

         5. Invoice preparation

      a. Determining type and format

      b. Determining type and preparing documentation required

    6. Forwarding of invoices

C. Insurance

    1. Determining type, coverages, and limits

    2. Keeping in force by paying premiums

    3. Policy—security and control (filing)

    4. Accident reports

    5. Property damage reports

D. Vendor invoice and material from stock requisition administration

    1. Pricing

    2. Approving for payment

E. Accounting and bookkeeping

    1. Maintenance of journals and ledgers

      a. Posting to the journals

        (1) Sales journal

        (2) Purchase journal

        (3) Cash receipts journal

        (4) Cash disbursements journal

        (5) General journal

      b. Posting to the ledgers

        (1) General ledger

        (2) Vendors ledger

        (3) Receivable ledger

        (4) Job cost ledger

        (5) Other subsidiary ledgers

      c. Reconciling bank statements

  d. Timekeeping control

  e. Preparing reports

   (1) Union

   (2) State

   (3) City (if applicable)

   (4) Federal

   (5) OSHA

   (6) Labor costs

  f. Distribution of labor costs to job cost ledgers

  g. Preparation and delivery of payroll checks

  h. Maintenance and administration of payroll bank account

   (1) Transfer of funds from general account to payroll account for:

    (*a*) Net payroll

    (*b*) Withholding funds

    (*c*) Payroll taxes and insurance premiums

   (2) Preparation of checks and payment of:

    (*a*) Federal, state, and city funds withheld

    (*b*) Payroll taxes and insurance premiums

   (3) Rate and salary control

   (4) Wage garnishments

   (5) Severence checks, writing and recording, for:

    (*a*) Layoffs

    (*b*) Discharges

 F. Management reporting

  1. Profit and loss statements

  2. Job costs

3. Aged payables

4. Aged receivables

5. Special

G. Audit preparation

H. Legal aspects

 1. Corporate minutes maintenance

 2. Stock administration

 3. Suits—defense

 4. Liens and waivers—giving notice and perfecting

 5. Purchase and sale of property for office and warehouse

 6. Contracts—compliance

 7. Taxes—administration and payment

   a. Income (company earnings)

   b. Personal property

   c. Real estate

   d. Capital stock

   e. Miscellaneous

 8. Claims against the company—defense and administration

 9. Bank agreements—originating and complying

10. Other agreements—originating and complying

11. Forgery and fidelity—prevention of dishonesty of employees

12. Bodily injury—reports to insurance company, claims, and defense

13. Personal property damage—claims and defense

14. Defense of unemployment insurance claims

I. Cost control

1. Establishing costs
2. Recording costs
3. Reporting costs to control personnel

II. Purchasing—Materials Management

   A. Developing the needs

     1. Items
     2. Quantity
     3. Type
     4. Size

   B. Developing a purchasing schedule

     1. Selecting manufacturers
     2. Selecting distributors
     3. Determining appropriate time of need

   C. Purchasing

     1. Types

       a. Material and equipment to be installed on jobs
       b. Tools (expendable)
       c. Capital expenditures

         (1) Tools (capitalized)
         (2) Vehicles
         (3) Facility improvements

           (*a*) On-the-job facilities
           (*b*) Office equipment

         (4) Office supplies
         (5) Arranging for release for shipment

   D. Selection of type of order

     1. Legal recourse to vendor
     2. Insurance requirements of vendor

E. Submitting equipment and material brochure and catalog

1. Obtaining from manufacturer

2. Submitting and obtaining approval

3. Distributing

F. Overbuying

1. Canceling orders

2. Returning unused items

G. Underbuying

1. Adding to additional purchase

H. Expediting

1. Initial purchases

2. Back orders

I. Executing inventory policies

1. No inventory

2. Inventory

3. Warehouse upkeep

J. Arranging and controlling delivery

1. Company trucks

2. Delivery by vendors

3. Direct shipments

K. Maintaining desired vendor relations

L. Vendor invoice approval administration

1. Authenticating receipt of items (matching shipping ticket with invoice)

2. Checking extensions and totals

3. Checking price of each item

4. Approval for payment

5. Pricing "material used on extras" lists

III. Production—Installation of the Work

    A. Attending job progress meetings

    B. Determining job setup material requirements

    C. Determining job setup tool requirements

    D. Determining and developing installation drawings

    E. Selecting and assigning supervision

    F. Assignment and transfer of field personnel

    G. Meeting union requirements

    H. Execution of all work required by contracts

    I. Timekeeping

    J. Capturing all changes to the contract (additions and deletions)

    K. Requisition of materials, tools, fixtures, specialties, etc., for additions

    L. Hiring and severing field personnel

    M. Administering an apprentice program

    N. Providing estimating section with time studies as required

    O. Curse the world, curse the men

IV. Sales—Estimating

    A. Developing means to determine potential sales leads

    B. Making all customer contacts (initial and repetitive)

    C. Procuring plans for estimating

    D. Estimating

    E. Taking time studies

    F. Planning deposit refund control

    G. Procuring performance bonds and bid bonds

    H. Writing proposals

    I. Submitting proposals

    J. Negotiating sales

    K. Worrying that bid is too high

    L. Attending bid openings

    M. Worrying that bid is too low

    N. Procuring plans required to execute the work

    O. Initiating work orders (with complete information covering all contract requirements)

    P. Providing field personnel with breakdown of estimated hours and purchase requirements

    Q. Providing accounting personnel with payout procedures

    R. Determining required special insurances

    S. Procuring insurance certificates

V. Management

    A. Administering corporate finance

    B. Administering all legal proceedings and requirements

    C. Establishing variances to union wage rates, for union personnel

    D. Establishing wage rates of all personnel not controlled by union rates

    E. Establishing and maintaining all policies

    F. Establishing and maintaining adequate standard operating procedures for all functions

    G. Hiring and severing nonproductive personnel

    H. Coordinating and supervising activities of all groups

    I. Worrying

    J. Controlling all overhead expenditures

    K. Planning and developing short-term and long-term objectives

    L. Trying to ignore unfounded employee complaints

Each of the above activities includes several subactivities.

Before proceeding further, remember the purpose of all this:

PROFIT PROFIT PROFIT PROFIT PROFIT

Subcontracting includes the mechanics of installing the work, layout of the work, superintending, engineering, purchasing (negotiating with suppliers), selling (negotiating with customers), estimating, accounting, administration, training, managing, and much more.

Many subcontractors find that one or two of these major endeavors are exciting and that they enjoy performing them. Some subcontractors become attached to the excitement of one endeavor and neglect the others. When this occurs, the self-satisfaction of accomplishment toward the specific endeavor causes the subcontractor to forget the real purpose of his responsibility as a subcontractor and the manager of a company:

PROFIT PROFIT PROFIT PROFIT PROFIT

The subcontractor cannot afford the luxury of getting carried away and enjoying his job like an employee. With the sole purpose of the company, and therefore the sole responsibility of the subcontractor, having been identified as *profit,* let's proceed with the nitty-gritty of developing an organization—systems, procedures, and disciplines—that will produce that profit. When developing the organizational structure, keep in mind at all times that all activities must contribute to satisfying one of the eight basic requirements discussed in Chapter 1.

The previously established five major functions and groups of activities form the basic organizational structure. No matter how large or small the operation is, all these must be performed. In the smaller operations individuals may perform more than one of these activities. The larger the operation is, the fewer the separate activities that are performed by an individual or group of individuals. In huge organizations, the five groups become departments where several people serve each group separately.

In a small operation there is certainly nothing wrong in having one individual involved in more than one of the groups; in fact, it is desirable. However, each person involved must know what hat he is wearing at the time he is wearing it. When he is involved in sales or estimating, for instance, he shouldn't be wearing the procurement hat. The categories are separate and distinct and must be satisfied completely. An individual who doesn't know he is satisfying a particular activity at the time he is doing it won't be able to perform well or tie up the loose ends.

While these activity groups provide the basis for the organizational structure, there is no law or rule that says they have to be grouped as presented here. However, it is an absolute must for a profitable operation that all the activities be grouped and assigned to ensure that they are performed.

ORGANIZING STEPS

The first thing in organizing is to list all the activities necessary to satisfy the eight basic requirements. Then, group these activities. Finally, assign the activities.

Let's take Cletsowitz Construction Co., which had seven people in the office to perform the support activities. These people consisted of Frank Cletsowitz, the contractor, owner, and manager; Mary, the bookkeeper; Bob, the estimator; Ed, the general superintendent; Alice, the clerk-typist; Fred, the warehouseman and truck driver; and Bill, the buyer and assistant estimator.

The following list is an example of assigning the activities, using a sampling of activities from each major function of the preceding groups of activities.

Activity	Assigned to
Approving vendors' invoices for payment	Frank/Bill
Paying bills	Mary
Collecting	Frank/Mary
Depositing	Mary
Bank borrowing	Frank
Billing	Mary
Invoice preparation	Bob/Ed/Bill/Mary
Insurance reports	Mary
Bookkeeping	Mary
Posting to books	Mary/Alice
Posting to general ledger	Auditor
Reconciling bank statements	Alice
Union reports	Mary
Payroll	Mary

Preparation of management reports	Mary
Maintenance of tools	Fred
Establishing initial material requirements	Ed
Making purchases	Bill
Attending job progress meetings	Ed
Making customer contacts	Frank
Estimating	Bob
Writing proposals	Bob
Procuring insurance certificates	Mary
Management	Frank

Based on the above information, a list of activities can readily be made for each person. Below is an example of the activities for Mary:

Paying bills

Assisting in collections

Depositing

Billing

Insurance reports

Bookkeeping

Posting to books

Union reports

Payroll

Preparation of management reports

Procuring insurance certificates

The above list is Mary's job description.

When two or more people are assigned the same activity, the activity must be broken apart into additional activities in order to be able to identify one person for each activity. More than one person cannot perform the same activity. One person assists the other, however, in performing the same activity. This is necessary to prevent overlap of responsibility. The above is a representative example. Each activity includes one or more additional activities. Remember, when the activities of a company are listed, all functions should be broken down into detailed activities. When activities are assigned to individuals, each person's ability should be carefully considered and all related activities should be assigned to the same individuals, or to groups of the same individuals. When the assignment is being made, it should be written out and given to the individuals being held responsible: Also, they should be given the authority necessary to execute the responsibilities. An individual should never be given responsibility without first being given the necessary authority. If one individual is assigned activities for more than one group, the individual must understand and realize that he or she is wearing more than one hat. Communication in this area is most vital.

Facilities (space, desks, tables, typewriters, calculators, machines, pencils, paper clips, etc.) must be provided as required by the activities assigned to the individual. Management must not be penny-wise and dollar-foolish in providing these tools for support people.

The foregoing will produce the basic organizational structure. To make the groups of activities and assignments to individuals work, next the sequence of authority and the flow of responsibility, must be established. In every type of subcontracting, and for every type of job, there is a standard flow of events that occurs from the start of a subcontract through its finish. These include:

Customer contact

Sales effort

Establishing selling price, estimating

Execution of contract

Obtaining required insurance

Initiating work order

Assigning job supervision

Purchasing materials and equipment

Shop drawing and catalog submittal and approval

Job set-up

Delivery of materials, tools, and equipment

Installation engineering

Hiring and organizing manpower

Installation of work

Administration of changes, including invoicing

Monthly payout requests

Collection of monthly payouts

Finalizing work

Acceptance of work

Collecting final payout

Collecting retention

Satisfying guarantee

A successful company recognizes, organizes, and controls each event.

The flow sequence of the above major functions can best be illustrated by the old, familiar box diagram. First, the basic function boxes are arranged in the sequence of operation. Basic function flow is:

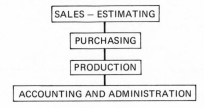

The control of all the functions is management, and so it is added to the top:

While the boxes show the sequence or flow of the functions, they do not indicate authority. If separate persons were to perform each of the above functions, most of these people would not have authority over other persons. Management (the boss, the subcontractor) controls all the functions. Thus, the sequence of authority for the functions is:

Most box illustrations are intended to show sequence of authority and are formally called "organization charts." Each box represents all the activities of the function it shows. Each box, or function, has a sequence of activity flow within itself.

After the boxes (functions) are grouped as shown, the names of the individual or individuals responsible for the function are placed in the boxes. This readily shows if a person is wearing more than one hat. Again, there is nothing wrong with this if the person wearing more than one hat is aware that he is wearing more than one. He must also know specifically *what* hat he is wearing. That is, everyone must positively know what he is responsible for, to whom he is responsible, and who is responsible to him and for what. We now have:

1. Established all the activities

2. Grouped the activities into basic functions

3. Established the sequence of flow of the functions

4. Established authority between the functions

5. Assigned people to be responsible for the functions

An organizational structure that will work has now been developed. Remember, however, that the development was by example, not sample. Each company is unique and each has its own particular activities, functions, etc. The activities, sequence of flow of activities, authorities between functions, etc., must be custom-tailored to each individual company.

There are two types of activities: one-time and repetitive. A one-time activity has to be done only once. For example, developing the organizational structure is a one-time activity. A repetitive activity is done over and over again. A good example is the payroll, which is done every week.

SYSTEMS AND PROCEDURES

To enable people to perform all the activities within each function, systems and procedures must be developed. A system is a way to perform a group of activities. A procedure is a standard way to do something. Systems and procedures are not developed for one-time or seldom-performed activities. But by all means they should be developed for repetitive activities. Here is a rule of thumb: If an activity is going to be performed 10 or more times over a year, a standard procedure should be developed for it.

Procedures for all repetitive activities are *always* developed by one of two ways:

1. By evolution

2. By design

The human being is lazy. If he did something yesterday that he is required to do again today, he will follow yesterday's basic pattern today. Yesterday's basic pattern was developed on a "do-as-you-go" basis, which may or may not have been the easiest and most effective way. Chances are that it was a cumbersome way because very little thought went into how to do it. The activity was treated as a one-time activity.

By the third time the activity is performed, the procedure for performing it has been developed. It has, however, been developed by evolution. If one were to ask a person following a procedure that was developed by evolution why he is performing obviously superfluous steps, he would answer, "I don't know why; that's just the way we do it," or he would try to justify why he was including superfluous steps by saying, "Management or accounting requires these steps for their needs."

By this time the person has no idea that he is performing an activity by following the same steps that were followed the first time it was performed on a do-as-you-go basis. All he knows is that it is the recognized official procedure and that he is expected to perform it in that manner. This is an established, officially recognized procedure that was developed without deliberate planning. It just sort of evolved.

The only way to prevent procedures from haphazardly evolving is to develop them by design. In the absence of a designed procedure an unplanned procedure will *always* evolve.

Almost everything we do in our daily life involves procedures. A procedure is simple to develop.

1. List all the steps necessary to perform the activity.

2. Arrange the steps in their correct sequence.

3. Describe each step.

4. Print (type) the procedure.

5. Explain the procedure.

Let's use the procedure of getting to work as an example. The procedure starts when we go to bed the night before.

1. Wind the clock

2. Set the alarm

3. Sleep

4. Be awakened by alarm

5. Get up

6. Wash up

7. Shave

8. Brush teeth and comb hair

9. Dress

10. Fill pockets with comb, wallet, change, keys, etc

11. Forget to kiss spouse good-bye

12. Put on overcoat

13. Raise garage door.

14. Go back and kiss spouse good-bye

15. Start car

16. Drive to coffee shop

17. Have coffee and roll

18. Continue on to work

19. Curse other drivers

20. Listen to news and weather

21. Daydream

22. Arrive at work

Many procedures within our daily lives are imposed on us. A supermarket is a good example. We automatically follow the procedures established for us to pick our merchandise, go through the checkout counter, pay, deliver our purchases to our car, and take the shopping cart back into the store. Many of us have become noncompliers to the last step and so the store has developed a procedure to cope with us noncompliers. It hires high school students to round up the shopping carts from the parking lot at regular intervals and return them to the store for reuse.

Very few procedures are independent. Most depend on other procedures, which in turn depend on them. Procedures that depend on one another form a system. The procedures within a system must satisfy the needs of their dependent procedures. There is a sequence of procedures within a system, just as there is a sequence of the steps within a procedure. There is no way to establish a useful sequence or dependence between procedures established other than by design.

Our performance of the procedure to move the food from the shelves of the supermarket to our dinner table is the last procedure in the system of procedures that moves the food from the farms to process plants, to warehouses, to retail stores, to our homes, to our tables. What would happen if each of us decided to do all the above in his or her own way? It would be one miserable costly mess. Procedures and systems provide the means for activities to be performed in an orderly manner and sequence, efficiently and effectively.

Some procedures require the use of forms. Some do not. When forms are required, they should be custom-designed for the particular procedure and need. The use of stock forms causes the procedure to be designed to satisfy the form. A form is a tool to enable the procedure to be performed with the least amount of effort and to permit ease of standardization. A form also ensures that the procedure will be performed the correct way each time. To use a stock form that is not totally applicable causes the procedure either (1) to be designed for the utilization of the form or (2) to evolve to the utilization of the form. The form is a tool to aid in the performance of the procedure. The form is *not* the procedure. Forms should be used when applicable and when they will serve a useful purpose. They should not be used when they are not needed.

Forms must be kept up to date. A form designed for today's needs will not necessarily apply this time next year. If a form is not changed, or is not officially discontinued, people will continue to use it and its information even after its need has stopped. A few years later the company is full of forms and more people to initiate and administer the forms, many of which are no longer needed. Remember:

USE FORMS WHEN THEY ARE NEEDED.

CUSTOM-DESIGN FORMS FOR A SPECIFIC NEED.

KEEP FORMS UP TO DATE.

DISCONTINUE FORMS WHEN THEY ARE NO LONGER REQUIRED.

The subcontractor is management and performs the functions of management and the manager. Management is the prime mover for the development and perpetuation of an effective organization. To contribute effectively on a continuous basis toward maintaining an efficient organization, the manager should wear as few hats as possible. In a small company the manager must perform many of the activities of the other basic functions. Unfortunately, when this occurs the management activities are neglected.

Management activities are not directly related to profit-producing activities, but they are very vital to a successful endeavor. They will directly affect the company's profitability. The major activities of management include:

1. Planning

    a. Establish long- and short-range objectives.

    b. Develop an adequate organizational structure.

    c. Develop adequate procedures, systems, and forms.

    d. Develop adequate facilities.

    e. Develop a financial structure that serves the needs of the objectives, including a source of funds.

    f. Develop operating budgets, both short- and long-range.

    g. Develop policies that will control all functions, activities, and personnel needs and behavior.

    A company is either growing or dying. Therefore, it is constantly changing, and the need to modify or change is constant and continuing. Planning must be constant and continuing for a company to survive.

2. Implementing, maintaining, and coordinating:

    a. Implement, maintain, and coordinate that which is

planned. This, too, must be done on a constant and continuing basis.

3. Controlling:

   a. The control and discipline of all activities stems from management.

   b. Functions, activities, and responsibilities are delegated; however, the control, coordination, and maintenance of discipline are management's responsibility.

4. Measuring:

   a. Management must constantly measure the results of all functions, activities, systems, procedures, forms, and personnel.

5. Communications:

   a. Management must establish and maintain effective communication between everyone in the company.

6. Manpower (personnel) development:

   a. Training of personnel is a vital function and the direct responsibility of management.

   b. Recruiting key personnel.

   c. Salary determination for all nonunion personnel.

   d. Additional remuneration determination and control for union personnel (where applicable).

7. Direct control of all legal activities.

8. Direct control of insurance activites.

9. Development and control of incentive and motivation programs.

10. Determination of gross profit markup on all jobs (consequently determining the selling price of all jobs).

11. Control of all payables (signing checks).

The size of the company determines which (if any) of the above activities are delegated. If they are delegated, management must thoroughly understand that only the performance, *not the responsibility or control,* is being delegated.

Management must be performed daily with continuity in every size company. It also must determine what type of mechanical bookkeeping systems are to be used; this decision should not be left to the bookkeeper, the accountant, or the auditor.

There are hundreds of different types of bookkeeping systems available. All can be grouped into four basic types:

1. Hand system

2. One-write, or pegboard, system

3. Mechanical or electronic posting machine

4. Computer data processing

Hand System

The hand system is an individual-oriented system that can be functioned only by the particular person involved. This system is very difficult and nearly impossible to analyze and follow except by the particular person involved. It usually is used by overly protective full-charge bookkeepers who would feel insecure if anyone else, including the subcontractor, knew how he or she operates the system. This type of person could be stereotyped as a bookkeeper with a green eyeshade and black sleeve protectors, huddled over a roll-top desk with many small drawers full of notes that no one else understands. This is a dangerous system because it depends upon one individual and the maximum capacity of that particular individual's ability, disposition, and attitude.

One-Write, or Pegboard, System

This system should be the first employed in developing an effective administrative system. It will provide the basis for the needed disciplines, standardization, and identification of all functions, activities, and subsystems. This system provides audit trails and can easily be followed by all involved because it is not dependent on any one individual. There are many variations of it; the specific one should be selected only after thorough consideration of the specific needs of the company.

Mechanical or Electronic Posting Machine

A mechanical or electronic posting machine should not be installed until after a one-write system has been developed and operated for an extended period of time. The bookkeeping and administrative system must never evolve directly from a hand system to a mechanical or electronic posting machine. *All* systems, bookkeeping and administrative, must be fully-developed *prior* to being put onto a posting machine. It is difficult and awkward to change them after they have been converted to a posting machine.

When the posting time on a one-write, or pegboard, system becomes voluminous enough to keep a person posting full-time, it is then time to transfer the system to a mechanical or electronic posting machine, and not before. A mechanical or electronic posting machine will not provide anything that a one-write, or pegboard, system won't. The posting machine will, however, require less time to post more transactions and will be more accurate. The posting machine will not correct or minimize administrative problems; it will only make the problems worse. But it will contribute to and increase the capacity of an already efficient and effective system.

Data Processing (Computer)

Data processing is the last and ultimate step in organizing, measuring, and controlling the collective efforts of many people, functions, activities, systems, and procedures. It can play an important role in a company if the company is large and/or complex enough. There is no rule of thumb for what type or size of company should use data processing. Many companies which shouldn't be are using data processing for some or all of their administrative functions. And many companies which could are not using data processing.

To use data processing for what functions and when is a decision the subcontractor should make. Remember, the companies selling data processing services and/or equipment (computers) are not really looking out for the best interest of the subcontractor. They are primarily interested in selling their services or equipment.

Data processing will *never* decrease the subcontractor's work force. Many times it will require more people. It is *not* the answer to problems. Data processing only helps a function when the function has gotten too big and complicated for a well-organized operation. If the subcontractor has a floundering function within his company, data processing will only make it worse. Data processing *will not* correct or improve a floundering function. Data processing can provide by-products only to an existing effective and efficient function that cannot be obtained otherwise. Use extreme research and care before considering data processing.

Remember, data processing is the *ultimate* means of performing an *effective* administrative function. There are many tried and proven growth means that must be utilized prior to advancing into data processing. When the time comes, however, that data processing is applicable, it is found to be wonderfully useful.

Summary

First:	DEVELOP THE ORGANIZATIONAL STRUCTURE.
Second:	CAUSE IT TO BECOME FUNCTIONAL.
Third:	ESTABLISH THE ACTIVITIES.
Fourth:	ASSIGN THE ACTIVITIES.
Fifth:	PROVIDE DESIGNED PROCEDURES TO PERFORM THE ACTIVITIES.
Sixth:	ORGANIZE THE PROCEDURES INTO FUNCTIONAL SYSTEMS.
Seventh:	MAKE MONEY.
Eighth:	PAY INCOME TAXES.
Ninth:	CONTINUE WORRYING.

We now have the organization, systems and activities, and procedures necessary to produce profit. One more important ingredient is necessary, however. It takes people to operate the systems, activities, and procedures. Effective utilization of people is necessary to put it all together and make it work and to keep it working. The manager or subcontractor cannot do it alone.

5 PEOPLE UTILIZATION

The subcontractor must utilize the resources of his company: People and money. The following chapters will relate the expertise necessary to effectively utilize the resources of money. This chapter will cover the utilization of people. The utilization of the human resources is equally important to the utilization of money. The expertise necessary to effectively utilize money can be learned and put to use mechanically with the use of systems and procedures. The utilization of people *cannot* be achieved with the use of systems and procedures alone.

People give a company emotions and cause it to be alive. A company without emotions is a dead company, doomed to failure. Utilization of people includes two separate requirements. One is psychological and the other is mechanical. We will deal with psychological requirements first.

The subcontractor must utilize people *without* the show of any adverse emotions on his part. He must, however, employ empathy (putting himself in the other person's shoes) at all times. By using empathy, he can motivate people. People must be continuously motivated. The old saying, "You can lead a horse to water, but you can't make him drink," should really be said, "You can lead a horse to water, but you can't make him drink *unless he is thirsty.*"

The construction industry differs from other industries in that the production (the work that produces profit or losses) is scattered and is very difficult to measure as to individual performance. Contrast this to a manufacturing plant where all production employees are concentrated and can be constantly supervised and measured. The construction worker is on his own to an appreciable degree. Add to this that he is earning his pay on the time he expends and not on what he does.

Tomorrow morning thousands of construction workers will report to work and all they will have to do to receive 8 hours' pay is to somehow keep breathing (stay alive) for those 8 hours. (Getting back to the horse, we can make him put his mouth into the water, but we can't make him swallow it.) Those thousands of construction workers who will report to work tomorrow are required to appear to be productive in order to be permitted to report to work the following day, but that's all. Unfortunately, that is not enough.

The subcontractor *must* have proficiency and efficiency from all his employees, both inside and outside, in order to survive. All his employees must work at their highest level of ability, with the diligence necessary to accomplish as much as they can. To accomplish this, it's like making the horse thirsty so that he will want to drink the water. Making the horse thirsty is called "motivating" him.

Everyone requires motivation, including the subcontractor himself. In fact, he must be motivated more than anyone else in the company. He is self-motivated, as Frank Cletsowitz was. That is, he has the motivation that goes along with building one's own company. Employees are not self-motivated. They must be motivated by others. Motivation of people is simple if their basic needs are recognized and satisfied.

A man by the name of Abraham Maslow theorized that the needs of a human being include:

1. Security

2. Feeling of belonging

3. Recognition

4. Opportunity

His theories have proven to be valid and necessary for everyone. The degree of importance of each varies with the individual. For example, a housewife with a family to support would have a far greater emotional need for security than the housewife with no children who is working to escape the boredom of being at home alone. An unmarried woman of 35 with no family ties, however, would feel a greater need for security than an unmarried woman who is still living with her parents.

The need for security, therefore, is dependent on the particular circumstances of the individual. The need for security, unfortunately, is a basic need for most people. The unions and welfare have provided many with a crutch-type security that dilutes the security attached to a job and employers. The unions provide a type of security to their members that causes many to feel the security of a job and a livelihood is with the union and not the employer. Of course, there is always the security of welfare that many feel they can fall back on. This gives these people a sense of independence from an employer.

The majority of office personnel and other people who are not represented by a union have a need for the feeling of security from their employer. The feeling of belonging, however, is emotionally required by everyone. This need is so great that if one cannot get satisfaction from an employer, he will seek to find it elsewhere. In the construction industry, employers have failed miserably in satisfying this human requirement. The result has been that the workmen have sought and found satisfaction for this need by belonging to a union.

A person must have the feeling of belonging not only from his employer and supervisor, but also from his peers. The separation between management and the workmen makes it difficult for management to contribute to this need for the feeling of belonging. This need is so great that if a new employee does not acquire a feeling of belonging and acceptance within a reasonable time, he will quit, regardless of the security, monetary considerations, or opportunities available. A strong feeling of belonging contributes to a feeling of security. Conversely, the lack of a feeling of belonging contributes to a feeling of insecurity. A person cannot feel that he belongs if he feels insecure. If he feels insecure, he also feels he does not belong.

The need for some degree of recognition is with everyone. Some have a greater need for recognition than others. The type of needed recognition varies from one person to the other. For some, a pat on the back is all that is necessary. For others a pat on the back is taken as being catered to and could even be offensive. To them recognition must be in the form of an award. In today's society, for most the only type of award that is accepted as meaningful is money. For still others, physical recognition is required, such as titles and publicized praise. With the exception of the few that have reward and award mixed up with recognition, satisfying this need is rather simple. As the degree of need for recognition varies with the individual, the need for opportunity varies even more greatly with each person.

Many look upon the freedom to perform within their given endeavors as an opportunity to do their thing their way. This is all the opportunity these people require. To others, unless a job is a vehicle for promotion to greater responsibilities, authority, and recognition, there is no opportunity involved.

These "people needs" present the subcontractor with some very interesting challenges. In every average-sized subcontracting firm, everybody is a key person. This is particularly true with the office and other support personnel. The average subcontracting firm usually has one of each; that is, one bookkeeper, one typist, one buyer, one estimator, one truck driver, and one field superintendent. Larger companies have assistants to most of these positions. The average-sized firm is, therefore, faced with each of these people being key personnel. Each is a major link in the chain with no links as standby. Assistants in large companies are standby links. When one of these people is ill for a day, his activities go undone that day because there just isn't anyone available to step in and pick up the slack. This causes the need for the average subcontractor to satisfy the "people needs" to be much easier. In small companies it is much easier because the subcontractor is in direct contact with everyone. In large companies it becomes a little more difficult because of the indirect control. In large companies the subcontractor must satisfy each individual's "people needs" through others.

Although the methods are very similar for both large and small companies, the following discussion is oriented to small companies where the subcontractor is in direct contact with everyone. The subcontractor must recognize and satisfy each need separately for each individual.

Obviously people are in different levels of importance to the company. As an example, the subcontractor should put more effort into satisfying to a greater degree the individual "people needs" for his bookkeeper than a clerk-typist unless, of course, she is his wife. A better example would be the difference of importance between the subcontractor's estimator and the delivery truck driver. *All* must have their "people needs" satisfied to an acceptable degree, however. Because each need must be recognized and satisfied separately on a continuous basis, the subcontractor must know them well. Again, they are: security, feeling of belonging, recognition, and opportunity.

EVERYONE IS SUSCEPTIBLE TO THESE NEEDS AND TO THE VARIOUS
MEANS OF SATISFYING THEM.

This means *everyone,* including the subcontractor himself. This phenomenon is what makes satisfying "people needs" easy. Because the subcontractor has the very same feelings as his employees, he can easily put himself in their shoes and determine how they feel toward a given situation or action.

The need for a feeling of security can be satisfied in many ways. First, the amount of pay must be relative to each employee's basic needs, to his ability to earn, and to the job he is performing (relative to similar jobs in other companies). The opposite of security is anxiety. Knowing this, the subcontractor can instill a feeling of security by preventing anxiety. He can do this by letting each employee know about matters relative to his responsibilities and the general good welfare of the company.

The general welfare of the company is very important to the feeling of security of each employee. Knowledge of losses, or any other adversity affecting the stability of the company, should be confined to the subcontractor and bookkeeper. Nothing creates a feeling of insecurity more than imagining the company is in trouble and the thought of possibly losing one's job.

A showing of continued dissatisfaction with employee performance by the supervisor or the subcontractor creates anxiety which produces a feeling of insecurity. This does not mean an employee cannot be admonished or disciplined without creating an adverse emotional feeling. Being admonished or disciplined may cause the person to become angry, but that's all. Being angry doesn't affect the normal person emotionally. An indication of being unliked will, however, create a feeling of insecurity, plus a feeling of not belonging or being accepted. To be able to admonish and discipline employees without instilling anxiety, the subcontractor must develop and maintain a consistent behavior. This behavior must be either one of warmth with firmness or one of complete neutrality and firmness. It must not change with the day-to-day changes in emotions of the subcontractor. The subcontractor must not show his changes in emotions. His emotions *must* appear to be constant at all times.

The subcontractor should never show a personal dislike for an employee. If he has an employee whom he personally dislikes, he should sever the employee in an appropriate manner. Display of negative feelings by the subcontractor toward an employee affects not only the person directly involved but also others. Other employees have a built-in concern that they may be next. This concern deteriorates the feeling of belonging. This, in turn, creates anxiety, which causes a sense of insecurity. An employee who does not feel he belongs, and feels insecure, is not receptive to motivation. The subcontractor must show feelings of security. He should never show any emotions of concern regarding the health or future stability of the company. No one wants to be involved with a losing team. Everyone wants to feel the team he is on is a winning team, one he can be proud of. This feeling of company success also instills a feeling of security. The feeling of being with a successful firm also contributes to a favorable recognition of the company by others. This favorable recognition prevents employee embarrassment and creates pride. A person's pride and ego are what require recognition.

The subcontractor must know each person's need for recognition. Some may be inclined to say that satisfying a person's need for recognition is satisfying or catering to his ego. It doesn't make any difference what it is called as long as it is satisfied. It is the foolish employer who says, "I'm not going to cater to an employee's ego." Of course, if the employer has no need for a high level of performance from his employees, he can disregard this basic "people need."

Again, the purpose of all this is to perpetuate a healthy, happy group of willing workers who are proud of their endeavors and the company for which they work. Although this is a true purpose, there is another, more important purpose. It is a requirement rather than a purpose. For a subcontracting firm to survive everyone must contribute toward an individual and collective profit endeavor. For anyone's effort to be a contribution toward profit, he must work at his peak ability. Somewhere between just breathing and working at peak ability by everyone in the company lies the difference between success and failure of the company.

It has been said that man's highest need is identity. Identity is the opposite of anonymity. Within large metropolitan areas, personal identity is absent outside one's immediate family and social circles. Lack of personal identity on one's job is one of the greatest contributors toward a halfhearted work attitude. The subcontractor *must* provide a means for identity for all his employees. Recognition contributes to individual identity.

Recognition can be accomplished in many ways. The most effective method happens to be the easiest and costs nothing. On every occasion that the subcontractor finds that an employee has satisfied a need within his responsibility over an obstacle or adversity, the subcontractor should tell the employee what a fine job he did in meeting the challenge. When this is done, the employee will go out of his way to bring his achievements to his employer's attention so that he can be given additional recognition. Many employees would feel this type of attempted recognition is false, or is beneath them, or is catering to them.

This may sound like a child bringing things to his parents so that they will tell him what a fine job he has done. It is exactly that. Our human needs are the same or greater than they were when we were children. Human emotional needs do not subside with age. If anything, they increase. The need is still there. It's just more difficult for adults to obtain satisfaction of their human needs from other adults.

The need for recognition of one's accomplishments must be satisfied by acknowledging the accomplishments. The need to be identified as an individual and with one's accomplishments must also be satisfied. The subcontractor can satisfy this need by outwardly recognizing the individual's position. That is, when introducing the employee, acknowledge his position with his name. For example: "This is Joe Motarotz, our warehouseman. He is the one who keeps the material flowing to the jobs." This type of recognition is not praise. Recognition must not be confused with praise. Praise, especially in front of others, can be embarrassing. It may appear that there is a fine line between what is right and what is wrong in handling people. This may be true, but the fine line can be easily seen if one puts himself on the other end in the other person's shoes. Just say, "Self, how would I feel in this situation when such and such was said and/or done?" The fine line won't be so fine any more. Remember, *we all* react the same to "people needs" and the methods of satisfying them.

The degree of need for opportunity must be determined for each individual. Satisfying this need can become dangerous if not handled with care and by design. Opportunity means different things to different people. Some feel opportunity is to be permitted to do their thing. That is, to perform their job their way. This does not mean outside the standard procedures, policies, or systems. It just means to be allowed to perform without a one-on-one feeling of being supervised. It means being permitted to express themselves or being allowed to do their job well on their own.

Here is a common failure with many small firms: the boss is so close to all his employees that he is able to supervise and direct their every move. They become robots. This robs them of the satisfaction of accomplishment. It has been said many times by employees, "If the boss would just let me alone I could do twice what I am doing now." Well, it is doubtful if they could do twice as much by being left alone, but in many cases they could do more, and do it better.

All this is based on the assumption that there is a well-structured organization with policies, systems, and procedures established to work with and within. People must be given the opportunity to do their job and to express themselves within their job.

The other type of opportunity is the more dangerous one. Some employees are aggressive in their ambitions and believe they can perform more and better at higher levels with greater responsibilities, authority, and recognition. These people are a great asset to a company. Opportunity can be extended to these if there are only one or two in the company. To be able to extend opportunity to this type of person requires the ability to fulfill it. That is, if the subcontractor says, "Joe, this company is going to grow and in doing so will create opportunities for you to grow too." Three things had better materialize. One, the company must grow; two, greater positions of responsibilities and authority must become available to Joe; and, three, the subcontractor's evaluation of Joe had better be such that Joe will be given the opportunity when it comes, not someone else. If the subcontractor indicates directly or by innuendo to Joe that the opportunity will come, and it does not for any of the above three reasons, the subcontractor has made a promise and broken it. Joe will no longer have any faith in the subcontractor and will either quit or become an undesirable employee.

Broken promises, whether intentional or not, are the greatest cause of mistrust between the employee and employer. This is why extending opportunity to individual employees is a dangerous practice. The subcontractor should have said, "Joe, I am very confident that this company is going to grow and I believe you have the ability and ambition to grow with it. If you prove me right, and if the company grows, you will get serious consideration toward any opportunities that may materialize." As the company grows, the subcontractor should frequently appraise Joe's growth in ability. If he is not growing, tell him, "Joe, the company is growing, don't be left behind." If Joe isn't qualified over someone else for the promotion when it occurs, the subcontractor will not have buried Joe emotionally.

IN EXTENDING OPPORTUNITY, AVOID PROMISES. PRESENT THE POS-
SIBILITIES ONLY.

There are three classifications of personnel in a construction firm. Professional, nonprofessional, and the union tradesmen or craftsmen. The professional group includes the accountant or bookkeeper, estimators, engineers, and the purchasing agent. The nonprofessional group includes clerks, warehouse personnel, delivery truck drivers, typists, accounting machine operators, etc.

Each group requires different approaches to satisfying its "people needs." Each also justifies different degrees of effort toward satisfaction. For example, the need for security from a specific company is less for an estimator than for a warehouseman; the need for opportunity, however, is greater for the estimator than for the warehouseman.

Field tradesmen feel less attached emotionally to a contractor than do professional and nonprofessional personnel. The reason for this is because of their strong emotional ties with the union. A tradesman feels he has more security from his membership in the union than from his employment with a contractor. His feeling of belonging also is with the union, and to a lesser degree recognition, and certainly, opportunity. This is not because the tradesman wants it that way, but because he has not been provided with these needs by the contractor. Two things have caused this: (1) the characteristics of the construction industry require a common labor pool that will allow the contractor's labor force to fluctuate with ease, and (2) the contractor and subcontractors have failed to include the tradesmen in their responsibility toward satisfying "people needs."

Many tradesmen would prefer to receive their needed feeling for security, belonging, recognition, and opportunity from the contractor rather than the union. This group is the backbone of the field operation. Without it, all the efficiency in the office will produce nothing. This group, with the support from the office, will produce the profit and also cause others to produce. It is, therefore, vital for the subcontractor, and *not* the union, to satisfy the "people needs" of this group.

To reach this group of extremely conscientious tradesmen is much more difficult than reaching the professional and nonprofessional groups because of the built-in wall between management and worker, the mistrust, and the erroneous belief of huge profits being made from their efforts by the subcontractor. They would prefer to be included in the company's family of permanent personnel but are very suspicious of any efforts to include them. This suspicion is caused by having had promises broken for everything, including the moon, by many contractors. To achieve this, the subcontractor must gain their confidence and respect as an individual. The best tool to accomplish this is the human need for recognition. They must be given individual and collective credit for what they are doing, that is, producing the profit for the company. The subcontractor should acknowledge to them that the success or failure of the company depends on them; he should throw the challenge down to them, both individually and collectively, to join the team to build the best construction firm in the area. They will pick up the challenge and accept the recognition because, in addition to being tradesmen and union members, they also are human and have the same "people needs" as everyone else.

There is a phenomenon between levels of personnel in *all* organizations that the subcontractor must forever be aware of: an employee can deceive up, but the employer or supervisor cannot deceive down. A subordinate can hand his boss a line, make it stick, and get away with it for long periods and frequently forever. The boss, however, cannot get away with a line that is not completely factual—even for a short period of time. The subcontractor must be completely honest with his employees. The slightest dishonesty or deception will be immediately apparent to the subordinate. A false or misleading statement by the subcontractor will immediately deteriorate the efforts of the subcontractor and develop a mistrust toward him. He will be identified as deceitful and a bull slinger and will no longer have the necessary respect of his employees.

We have now covered the psychological requirements that are necessary for the successful utilization of people. Satisfying these "people needs" is a constant endeavor. Satisfying the "people needs" today will not meet the needs a month from now. "People needs" continuously deteriorate and therefore require continuous rebuilding.

Satisfying the people needs is also the act of motivating. Motivation includes satisfying the "people needs" plus providing incentive. Providing incentive as part of motivating has its problems. In our present-day society, incentives are based on rewards of money commonly called "bonuses." Bonuses are associated with a deteriorating disease called "precedent." That is, to the employee the first bonus is looked upon as a gift in return for a job well done. The second bonus is certification that he is still doing his job well; and the third bonus is a must. The third bonus is not motivation; it is a preventor of demotivation. Bonuses that are not *directly* tied to a measurable performance soon become considered by the employee as a fringe benefit and are expected as part of their income. Bonuses must be given in a manner that does not establish precedent. The easiest way to keep them from becoming precedents is to base each person's bonus on individual performance. Unfortunately, this is very difficult in the construction industry. To tie bonuses to individual performance, each individual's performance must be measured. Measuring individual performance (with few exceptions) is next to impossible in the construction industry.

To analyze this, let's go back to our three groups: professional, nonprofessional, and tradesmen. The professional and nonprofessional people are recognized as being inside personnel, and tradesmen as being the outside, or field, personnel. Inside personnel can be associated only with the overall performance of the company. Field personnel, however, can be associated with individual jobs if the particular firm confines the job mix to large construction jobs. That is, if at the end of a year each tradesman's performance can be identified with three or four jobs, the results of the jobs can be the criteria for each one's bonus. This just won't work, though, because the tradesmen are transferred from one job to another. The job could, however, be an applicable means of measurement for foremen and/or general foremen whose activities are confined to a few jobs each year.

Unfortunately, very few small and medium-sized firms confine their job mix to larger jobs only. The majority of subcontractors have a job mix that includes jobs of the one-day-or-less size up to jobs taking several months to complete. Because of these characteristics of the construction industry, and of the wide differences in job mix and the sizes of subcontracting firms, there is no rule of thumb available for successful means to give bonuses based on individual performance for personnel on the inside or the outside. For this reason it is best to avoid bonuses as much as possible.

For the most part, tradesmen do not expect bonuses, primarily because most subcontractors do not give bonuses to tradesmen. This is because there has been no precedent of giving bonuses to field personnel throughout the industry. The professional personnel, estimators, engineers, etc., have a very good feel for whether the company is having a good or bad year. They should be given a bonus when there are good years, but they should *not* be given lesser bonuses or no bonuses when the bad years occur. The nonprofessional personnel, clerks, delivery truck drivers, etc., are tied to a precedent set by the entire business world. A small bonus is tied to a Christmas present by most companies. For this reason they expect a bonus at Christmas time. This is a Christmas present to some and a bonus to others. The subcontractor should avoid being unfavorably classified regarding the Christmas-type bonus. There is a saying in the industry that the best time to recruit capable people of the professional and nonprofessional classification is right after Christmas. That is when they have the Christmas blues from not receiving Christmas bonuses they expected.

One practical approach to giving bonuses as an incentive and staying out of trouble is to select the few key people in the company that success or failure depends on. In most firms this is only two or three people. These people should be given meaningful bonuses based on the results of the company each year. If the fiscal year ends other than on December 31, the bonus should be given at the end of the fiscal year; this will cause the bonus to be associated with the fiscal results and not the usual calendar-year-end Christmas-type bonus. All other inside personnel should be given a Christmas-gift-type bonus. One or two key tradesmen who are definitely management-oriented and have the company's welfare at heart can be selected and given a similar Christmas-gift-type bonus.

Incentive plans based on money are very difficult and dangerous for the construction industry. They must be used with great care and design in order to avoid all the potential adverse consequences.

Satisfying the "people needs" is an expertise that the subcontractor must have. This expertise is very vital to the success or failure of the firm. The second requirement necessary for the successful utilization of people is mechanical and includes facilities, tools, and direction.

FACILITIES

Facilities are classified as office and warehouse or field. Field facilities include material and tool storage and offices. Material- and tool-storage facilities vary from storage (gang or job) boxes to storage rooms within the construction facility, both temporary and permanent, to modified semi-trailers, to on-site–constructed temporary buildings. Material- and tool-storage facilities are the key to adequate flow and control of materials and tools to the work area. This flow starts at the source of procurement of the materials and/or tools, then to the curb of the construction site, then to a central storage area, and then to the work area. For small jobs the flow is from the source of procurement directly to the work area.

Regardless of the number of steps in the flow of materials and tools to the work area, storage facilities are necessary. These facilities must be adequate to provide security for and segregation of the different materials being used.

Materials handling is a major function for any trade on any construction site, be it small, medium, or large. For effective people utilization on the construction site, the material must be at the place the work is being performed. To get it there requires storage facilities and materials-handling equipment.

The construction worker must also have adequate, operable tools to be effective. Maintenance of tools and equipment is another very necessary function for proper utilization of the construction worker. Poorly maintained tools and equipment will cause the most efficient worker to become ineffective.

Other facilities required at the construction site are field offices for larger jobs. Field offices must be adequate for the size of the project and the use they will get. They must include office equipment such as typewriters, calculators, pencil sharpeners, and office supplies. For some reason it is natural for the subcontractor to look upon the field administrative needs differently than those for the home office; the need for adequate field office equipment and supplies is more acute. The salaries paid for field administrative personnel are usually appreciably more than for the home office. On many jobs, field administration personnel are tradesmen.

Communications to and within the job site also are a very important factor in control and utilization of field personnel. Communication to the job site is by telephone, mail, and hand-delivered written messages, as well as face-to-face verbal exchange. Communication within the construction site is by telephone, two-way radio, hand-carried written messages, loudspeakers, and face-to-face verbal. Whatever form of communication is most effective and efficient should be used. Whatever form is used must, however, be a result of design, not habit. The method of just letting the communication happen is not the way to effectively utilize field personnel.

A good rule of thumb to follow is that the more an employee earns, the more and better tools and equipment should be provided for him. A little further on, another rule of thumb will be given for providing the best equipment, facilities, etc., for the least paid. The two together suggest that the subcontractor provide proper equipment, tools, and facilities for all employees.

Tools and equipment for use by the construction worker are constantly being modified and improved. New tools are continuously becoming available on the market. All are improved labor-saving devices. The subcontractor must continuously be aware of the changing tools and equipment and must keep his tools and equipment upgraded at all times.

Construction site tools, installation equipment, materials, tool storage and handling facilities, and field office facilities must all be mobile, similar to a circus. All facilities must be functional, the same as permanent facilities, but they also must be portable. They must be able to be moved onto the construction site, erected in minutes, moved from location to location during construction, and then moved off overnight when the job is completed.

To best utilize field personnel, the subcontractor must provide them with the latest possible tools, equipment, communications systems, and facilities.

Home-Office Facilities

Home-office facilities include working space, desks, tables, telephones, intercommunication systems, pencils, pencil sharpeners, office supplies, and proper environment.

Adequate working space depends on the type of work being performed.

Example

An estimator who is required to mentally install the work requires working space with absolutely no distractions. To obtain this he must be alone, in a private office. A posting-machine operator requires a separate room to prevent distractions and to keep the noise of the posting machine from distracting others. The subcontractor and others involved in conversation of a confidential nature must have private offices.

Working space also includes adequate desk and/or table space. For example, an estimator, engineer, or bookkeeper needs large table spaces to spread out blueprints and books. The clerk who matches vendors' invoices with receiving tickets also needs a large table. Typists require a desk and enough room for the typewriter. Space must be provided to prevent close working conditions. This is to control socializing so that the employees' work is not affected by both errors and nonproductivity. There must be enough space to handle traffic flow in the office with minimum distraction. Office and area decor must be warm-toned to provide a pleasant atmosphere. Types of desks, files, pigeonhole organizers, trays, etc., for forms and paper work must all be designed to fit the needs of the activities that each person is performing. A good rule of thumb to follow is that the lower a person's pay, the more custom-designed facilities must be provided. This is necessary to fully utilize less capable personnel.

The warehouse must have enough bins and materials-handling equipment for the particular type and quantity of materials stocked. Hand and hydraulic trucks are necessary. Delivery trucks must meet the subcontractor's needs, and must be kept well maintained and up to date. Warehouse and delivery-truck personnel are just as important links in the chain as others and must also be utilized effectively.

The psychological "people needs" and mechanical facilities that are required for effective people utilization have been discussed. Let's stop and again remind ourselves of the purpose of all this:

PROFIT   PROFIT   PROFIT   PROFIT   PROFIT

Providing a pleasant working atmosphere, proper tools, and adequate working space, and satisfying the people needs, is not to make the subcontractor a nice guy to work for, nor to provide a nice place to work. The purpose is to obtain maximum utilization of everyone on the team to produce a profit. They are, however, desirable by-products to a profitable operation. Remember, all the by-products of a *non*profitable operation are *un*desirable.

Satisfying all the human needs, plus providing all the necessary facilities, still won't produce the desired results. All personnel must be directed. For example, a subcontractor with 20 men in the field, plus 6 people in the office, will have 26 people report to work tomorrow morning. What are they going to do? Are they going to decide what each should do themselves? The answer is obviously "No." It is equally obvious that the subcontractor cannot direct each employee individually each morning. The office personnel are automatically directed via *organized,* previously developed (we hope) systems, procedures, utilization of forms, etc. Unfortunately, the field personnel present a different situation.

Activities in the office are repetitive and are applied to repetitive needs. The field operation consists of repetitive activities, but these are applied to different needs. That is, the mechanical activities employed from time to time are similar and are frequently repeated. However, the combination of activities used for each work task can differ appreciably. Because of this, utilization of systems, procedures, forms, etc., to produce automatic direction of each individual's work tasks won't work in the field. That leaves only one method. All the work tasks must be individually developed by hand, so to speak. This is either performed by the subcontractor himself, his superintendent, general foreman, foreman, or the man who is to install the work.

When the question was previously asked, "Are the people who are going to report to work tomorrow morning going to scratch their heads and say, what shall I do today?", the answer was "No." That answer certainly indicates that the man who is going to perform the work is not the person who should develop his work tasks or work assignment. The work tasks or work assignments in the office are continuous in nature. Those tasks or assignments that have a beginning and an end are all repetitive in nature and in methods employed. For example, an estimator's work task or work assignment is that of preparing an estimate. Preparation of an estimate has a beginning and ending. Every estimate, however, is prepared using the same methods, tools, procedures, forms, etc. A purchasing agent's work assignment is continuous. He makes one purchase after the other in the same manner. However, no work assignments in the field are continuous or repetitive, requiring the same methods, tools, etc. They are all different, and all have a beginning and an end.

Each construction job, no matter how large or small, must be broken down into individual work assignments by a person as high on the totem pole as practical, the totem pole being (from top to bottom) the subcontractor, the superintendent (or estimator-superintendent), the general foreman, and the foreman. Work assignments should certainly not be developed by the journeyman. Each work assignment must include required materials, required tools, and the latest information as to location, quantity, etc. For effective utilization of field personnel all the work must be planned, prepared, and scheduled.

UTILIZATION OF THOSE WHO PRODUCE THE PROFIT OR LOSS

The characteristics of the construction industry make it difficult to successfully motivate the individual tradesmen who perform the work. Because of this, utilization of tradesmen can be achieved to a greater degree by effective planning, preparation, and timely scheduling of work. These activities must be performed by deliberate design, using established techniques. Performing all construction work includes identifying the task, planning the execution of the task, preparing, scheduling the execution of the task, executing the task, measuring the results, and recording the measurement.

The success of any task depends on the effort put into the planning and preparation. This is true for every undertaking, whether it is work, a social endeavor, or a family vacation. The more effort put into planning and preparation, the better the results will be. The time and effort put into planning and preparing for guests or a vacation always exceeds the time expended at the party or on the vacation. If there were no planning or preparation for either, neither would be successful.

Imagine going on a vacation with no planning, preparation, or scheduling. Imagine a vacation without comment afterwards as to whether it was enjoyed and without memory that can be used to improve the next vacation. Let's use a vacation trip as an example of planning, preparation, scheduling, execution, measurement, and recording.

The first step is to recognize that we are going to take a vacation trip. What type of trip do we wish to take? Before we can determine what type of a trip, we must establish our objective. What is going to be the main activity? The main activity will determine what direction the trip will take. If the main activity is to be fishing, the destination of the trip will be in an area of lakes where the temperature is not necessarily hot. If the main activity is to be golfing or swimming, the destination must be where the climate is warm. We should write to the various areas compatible to our main activity for brochures and other means that will provide us with the latest detailed information about each. We will need to know the costs involved in each of the various places offered by each area. What will be the most economical and best? An American plan, modified American plan, European plan, or no plan at all? Other cost information that we will want is the cost of driving to our destination and using our own car while there, or does the short time we have available justify flying and renting a car? We know that areas are constantly changing, and so even though we have brochures from past years with costs, we will have to obtain the latest information to formulate our plans by.

After the destination is established, the particular time must be determined. Again, the objective influences the selection of the time. The particular time of the year must be compatible with the objective. We wouldn't plan a fishing trip to Canada when the lakes were frozen. We must also determine how long we will stay. To fully enjoy our trip we should include friends. How many? If our main activity is to be golf, the number of people we invite should be in increments of four. If our trip is to include any automobile traveling, the number of people should be that which can fit into each auto comfortably.

Now that we have determined our objective, selected our destination, scheduled when we are going, and established the number of people, we can now prepare. Preparation is based on the information developed in our planning. The main activity indicates type of clothes, sports equipment, etc. The destination and length of time available for the trip will help determine type of transportation. Reservations must be made for transportation, hotels, or motels. If we are planning a fishing trip, we will need boats and perhaps a guide. If our trip is for golfing and swimming, we will have to reserve starting times. The area we will be visiting will provide things to do and see other than our main activity. We should determine these and include them in our preparation. And restaurants and evening activities will require different types of clothing. All the things we expect to do on our trip must be given thought so that we can anticipate that which will be required by each in the way of clothes, transportation, sports equipment, services, and *time*. And, finally, we must decide by what means we wish to record the trip. Movies, slides, still pictures, or just memory. Any method other than memory will require a camera and film.

Now that all is planned, prepared, and scheduled, we will wait for the time to actually take the trip or execute the activity.

Everyone who takes vacation trips goes through the above procedures. The degree of effort applied to each step varies, depending on tightness of the budget for the trip, amount of time available, and discipline of the individual. Some people perform some or most of these procedures subconsciously, while others perform each meticulously.

So far as most vacation trips are concerned, the results of either degree of effort will probably be successful. The utilization of costs and time involved will, however, vary appreciably. The meticulously planned trip will provide more for less money in the shortest time available, while the loosely planned trip will cost appreciably more, will include less, and will probably take more time.

A loosely planned vacation trip may produce an acceptable level of results for some, but a loosely planned construction job will produce undesirable results for all. Planning, scheduling, and preparation of all construction jobs must be meticulous in every detail. The construction industry includes jobs with one activity and projects with hundreds. The jobs often involve one or more trades. The simplest job involves only one trade with one major activity. Planning, scheduling, preparing, executing, measuring, and recording this type of job is simple. The main reason for its simplicity is that identification of the major work task is automatic. There is only one, and so the fact that there is a work task is obvious. The information, materials, tools, and number of men needed to perform the work task is also easy to ascertain.

Let's use a simple one-work-task job as an example. In this example the subcontractor will be the prime contractor because no other trades will be involved on this job. The job is a lump-sum contract, requiring one billing at the conclusion of the work. The costs were developed by an estimate and the job was sold competitively. Since no other trades are involved, we can schedule the job at our discretion, or in such a way as is compatible with the customer's needs. Most of the information was obtained during the estimating process. There are, however, details pertaining to equipment to be installed that must be obtained and developed prior to starting work. There is also some information that the customer was to obtain for us, and also some dimensions that must be confirmed. Our estimate indicates that the total job will take 32 man-hours. We will have to determine if the job can be done by one man in 32 hours, by two men in 16 hours, or by a combination of one man and two men. A materials list can be made up from the estimate by the person who estimated the job. The tools required can also be listed by the estimator. We have now obtained and developed all the necessary information, including dimensions, and we have established a materials and tool list and determined the number and type of men required.

The time that we are going to perform the work can now be scheduled. The materials can be purchased and/or delivered to the job site. The tools can also be assembled and delivered to the job site. A work order with all the information necessary to install the work can be written.

We have now planned, scheduled, and prepared the job. Our next step is to assign the men to the job on the day scheduled. The men report to the job site and perform the work.

Since this was a one-activity job, we measured productivity via payroll time cards from the men. The payroll time for this job totaled 36 hours. We compared this with our estimate of 32 hours and found it has taken 12 percent more labor than estimated. Upon investigation we found that the customer had requested our man to deviate from the planned method of installation. This deviation was estimated to take an additional 6 hours. When confronted, the customer readily confirmed he had requested the deviation. When we requested payment he immediately informed us that had he known there would be additional cost he would not have requested the deviation.

Our measurement and recording told us several things. Our labor units used for estimating were reasonably correct. The person who estimated the job was proficient. The method by which we had planned to install the work was prudent. The productivity of our men was acceptable. And, most important, we discovered that our man was unknowingly giving away work. Our measuring and recording had immediately indicated a discrepancy. We will now teach our man to notify the office prior to making any deviation on the job, even when he thinks there will be no additional charge. And, of course, our planning, preparation, and scheduling caused the work to be performed to the satisfaction of the customer within the time he required it.

Now that we have established that planning, scheduling, preparing, executing, measuring, and recording a small one-work-task job is simple and easy, let's apply the same principle to a large project.

All construction projects consist of many separate activities or work tasks. Each work task is a simple small job. The only difference between planning, scheduling, preparing, executing, measuring, and recording a small job and a large project is that the work task of a small job is automatically identified, whereas on a large project work tasks have to be developed. Therefore, the first step on a large project is to break the entire project into as many work tasks as possible. The work tasks should be one-man work tasks wherever possible. Each work task must be identified with a name or a number, preferably a name. The requirement of each work task must be determined. Each work task requires manpower, tools, materials, information, and a method of performing the work. Each of these requirements includes several determinations:

Number of Man-Hours. The number of man-hours required to perform each work task must be established. This can be determined from the estimate.

Manpower. The determinations required to establish the manpower for each work task are type, number, and duration.

The type of men includes capability and classification, that is, journeymen, apprentices, helpers. Does the work task require a man with special ability, or can any craftsman of that particular trade perform the work? If the work task is a two-man job, are the two men required for the total time? Or can one man perform the majority of the work while needing a hand at one or two intervals? Is the duration of the work task long enough to tie a man up for a long period? With some trades there are work tasks that run the duration of the project.

The total hours established for the work task, divided by the number of men at what duration of intervals, will determine the total elapsed time to perform the work task.

The type of tools and quantity of each type must be determined for each work task. The number of men will determine the quantity of tools required. The duration of the work task will determine how long the tools will be tied up.

Materials. The specific materials and quantities of each must be developed for each work task. On large projects, tool and materials delivery within the construction site, and tool assembly at the location of the work, may often require separate work tasks within themselves.

A work task includes (in addition to manpower) tools, materials, and information. Are the same men who perform the work also going to deliver their tools and materials to the work site area, and will they also assemble the tools? Control of manpower on large projects is lost if the men are required and/or allowed to go to a central point and obtain their tools and materials and deliver them to the work site location. The human element causes them to make many trips, whereas separate materials- and tool-handling men will deliver an entire list of materials and tools with one trip. On some large projects there are what are known as walkers. Men have been known to put an empty materials box under their arm and just walk for days without installing any work whatever. When confronted by a supervisor, they always say they are just returning from obtaining the materials they need to continue their work. This leaves the supervisor without recourse. With separate materials handlers, any men assigned to particular work tasks who are found in other areas can be disciplined. This method affords a greater degree of productivity control.

Information. The latest information in sufficient detail to perform the work task must be obtained. The method of installation must also be developed for each work task. Many work tasks can be installed in more than one way.

Example

To run a conduit from a wall switch to a wall receptacle can be either up, over, and down, or down, over, and up. One way is better than the other. The better way should be determined and be part of the information provided by which to install the work.

The work task has now been established and includes required tools, materials, information, method of installation, number of men, and estimated total man-hours. The work task must now be classified as to what type it is. That is, what is its relationship to other work tasks? A work task is either part of a series of work tasks that must be performed in sequence, or it is autonomous. A work task series may include tasks of several different trades, or it may include one trade only.

Work tasks that are autonomous can be scheduled at the total discretion of the subcontractor. This type of work task is classified as a "free work task." Work tasks that are part of a series of one trade only can also be scheduled at the discretion of the subcontractor for that trade. Each work task of this type series must, however, be scheduled to be performed in sequence with the other tasks of the series. The subcontractor is, however, in full control of the scheduling of the entire series. This type of work task is classified as a "free-dependent work task." However, work tasks that are part of a series of work tasks of several trades cannot be scheduled at the discretion of the subcontractor. They must be scheduled to be performed in sequence with work tasks of the other trades.

Example

The work task of installing reinforcing bars in a particular section of a concrete slab must be performed *after* the deck is completed and *before* the concrete is poured. The subcontractor installing the rebars has no control over scheduling when the rebars for that particular section of concrete slab are to be installed. This particular work task is dependent on work tasks of other trades and work tasks of other trades are dependent on it. This type of work task is classified as an "interdependent work task."

When a work task is within a series involving two or more trades, then the scheduling of each work task is not within the control of the subcontractor. When a work task is within a series that involves only its own trade, then the scheduling of each work task is within the control of the individual subcontractor. All work tasks are classified as free, free-dependent, or interdependent.

On all construction projects there is great difficulty in leveling the manpower requirements. This problem usually results in low productivity for the days that more men than are required are on the job. Union rules, customs, and practices don't permit the subcontractor to fluctuate the number of men on the project on a day-to-day basis. This requires the subcontractor to base the average manpower on the peak needs. Effective utilization of the classified work tasks will appreciably reduce the lost time that usually results from this practice. Peak manpower requirements are determined by the total number of men required for each work task that is being performed at any one time.

Remember, the subcontractor has no control over the scheduling of the interdependent work tasks but does have control over the scheduling of the free and free-dependent work tasks.

The free and free-dependent work tasks should be fully developed and held in abeyance; that is, all the planning and preparation of each should be completed. The method of installation must be determined, all required materials procured, the necessary tools located on the job site, all the information assembled, and the work task description written.

Within the series of free-dependent work tasks there are tasks that can be installed either partially or totally out of sequence. These should be separately identified. Then, they become similar to the free work tasks. The free work tasks, plus those free-dependent work tasks that can be performed out of sequence, will form a bank of work tasks to be used when man-hours become available in off-peak periods.

Day-to-day peak manpower requirements are primarily caused by interdependent work tasks. Scheduling all free and as many of the free-dependent work tasks as possible on the days requiring few or no interdependent work tasks will appreciably lower the average daily manpower requirements. The interdependent work tasks are performed on demand. The free-dependent work tasks are scheduled by the subcontractor to be performed on as continuous a basis as can be maintained without increasing the total manpower to satisfy the interdependent work tasks. The free work tasks and those free-dependent work tasks that can be performed out of sequence are scheduled only when man-hours become surplus to the interdependent and free-dependent work tasks being performed during any one day.

Dividing the job into individual work tasks provides not only an effective means for planning, preparation, and scheduling, but also the basis for realistic, accurate measurement of performance. Measurement of performance is vital to cost control and estimating.

The past several pages have been heavy reading. Some will say, "We've been doing that for years, but not that formally." Others will say, "It sounds good, but it's not practical."

Well, let's reestablish what it's all about:

PROFIT   PROFIT   PROFIT   PROFIT   PROFIT

Now let's look at the results of an average-sized subcontracting firm.

Based on an annual sales volume of $750,000, 5 percent net profit will equal $37,500. If, through whatever complicated system, the average labor force could be reduced by only one man (approximately $25,000 with labor burden), the net profit would be increased over 60 percent. Take the same $750,000 with a net profit of 10 percent, or $75,000. A one-man reduction of the average labor force would increase the net profit by over 33 percent. This same analogy holds true for any size company with relative labor reduction. Any method that will increase the utilization of field tradesmen is worthwhile. Utilization of field tradesmen can be effective only through the use of planning, preparation, and scheduling.

⑥ MARKETING, SALES, AND ESTIMATING

In most industries, sales are part of a marketing effort directed toward specific market areas and particular classification of customers. Marketing is directed toward the sale of a product or a service. Construction contracting is commonly defined as a service. This definition does not totally apply to a constructed building, bridge, sewer, highway, etc. Actually, a product is produced.

Manufactured single products are usually produced on an assembly line by the thousands. They are sold after they are manufactured. That is, they are developed, manufactured, and then sold. Construction is the opposite. Its product is sold, then developed, then constructed. Manufactured products are usually brought to the attention of the buyer. In construction this also is the opposite. The buyer brings the need of the product to the attention of the seller. When a facility is to be constructed it is advertised by the user (owner) to find contractors to build it. Manufactured products are advertised by the manufacturer to find users to buy it.

These characteristics cause construction marketing to differ appreciably from that of other industries. Marketing in general includes many activities: planning, research, distribution, advertising, customer relations, sales administration, sales promotion, sales management, sales, estimating, and selling price development. Not all of these apply to construction. Advertising is of little or no value to the average construction subcontractor. Sales administration, sales promotion, and sales management are all formal sales activities. Formal selling does not apply to obtaining construction sales, and so none of these have any appreciable value to the average subcontractor. All the rest of the marketing functions are highly important to construction sales.

Let's take a detailed look at these important marketing activities.

MARKETING PLANNING

If the subcontractor has any plans for the future, he *must* plan his marketing effort. This planning includes what services and what type of construction in what geographical location are going to be pursued. Within each trade there are many types of work. These include:

New residential construction

Service and repair—domestic (jobbing)

Service and repair—commercial, industrial, and institutional

Highway and bridge construction

Maintenance

Miscellaneous small construction

Institutional construction

Heavy industrial construction (steel mills, foundries, refineries)

Light manufacturing construction

Heavy manufacturing construction

Commercial construction

High-rise building construction

Power plant and substation construction

Electrical transmission and distribution construction

Pipeline construction

Commercial and institutional remodeling

Manufacturing and industrial revamping

Within these are factors that cause the method of handling the job and/or the final outcome of the job to differ. The factors are determined by type of work, geographical location, or a combination of both. They include differences in:

Methods of obtaining the sale

Methods of estimating costs

Percent of gross profit

Method of recording costs

Method of invoicing

Method of policing and causing payment

Purchasing and expediting materials, tools, and equipment

Type of customer and customer relations required

Methods used to administer the work, both in the field and in the office

Type and caliber of worker required to do the work

Type of tools and equipment required to install the work

Fixed assets (plant facilities, etc.) required to support the work

Materials installed

Type and caliber of field supervisory personnel required

Methods used to maintain and improve gross profit at the job level

Type and degree of engineering required

Ratio of material, equipment, and labor involved

Geographic location affecting logistics of materials, tools, information, and control

Geographic location involving different human attitudes, availability of experienced workmen and supervisors, customs and practices, and union jurisdictions.

The marketing plans must include the particular types of work to be pursued. The types of work must be based on the objective of the company and the ability to perform profitably. All the factors causing the differences in types of work, and the differences themselves, must be considered in the marketing plans.

Example

It would not be wise to plan to pursue work that required a type and size of organization that the subcontractor did not have. A subcontractor whose organization was capable of new residential construction would not plan to pursue heavy industrial work with the same organization. And so, the first step in the marketing plan is to select the type of work that the subcontractor and his organization are capable of performing.

Another serious consideration in the marketing plan is the geographical areas to be worked.

Example

Heavy industrial type work would not be included in the marketing plan if the area to be worked had no heavy industries. The same would hold true for high-rise building construction in a rural area.

The marketing plan would not include a type of work that was so scattered that to obtain enough to be profitable several hundred square miles would have to be covered. The costs of supply and control would absorb any gross profits that might be generated. To know these limitations for given geographic areas requires *marketing research*.

MARKETING RESEARCH

The subcontractor is his own best market researcher. Most of the time he has a pretty good feel for the market in his work area. There are, however, several factors pertaining to the markets that he should consider.

Every geographical market has a maximum amount of each type of work available each year. This amount varies with the economic activity that generates each type of work. The amount available to a given subcontractor depends on the total amount available, less the amount his competitors will get. In projecting the amount of work that can be obtained for the coming year, the subcontractor must first determine the approximate total amount that will be available. He must then say, "Self, of the total, how much can I keep my competitors from getting?" or, "Self, how much of the total can I obtain?"

Two circumstances will cause the amount possible for any one contractor to get to vary appreciably: competition and total work available.

Example No. 1

The contractor has been doing a particular type of work in a geographical area along with three other contractors. All four have been able to pretty much obtain an equal share each year. A projection of one-fourth of the total volume available in the coming year would then be realistic. However, a kink arises. A new contractor with no manners and a lot of nerve has decided he wants some of the sales volume. An evaluation must be made as to how much a newcomer to the market will extract.

The first step is to find out his past behavior on prices. Does he have a track record of low prices? If he has—and depending on his size—he could cut a swath in the total market for that type of work before reality catches up with him. Let's assume he does have a track record of low prices and that he is of substantial size and appreciable capability. In this case it is reasonable to project that he could obtain more than 25 percent of the total market for the coming year. (Remember, the customer always is susceptible to low prices. It is the naive contractor who does not recognize his competitor's ability.) If this newcomer takes, say, 30 percent of the total sales volume available for the particular type of work, that leaves 70 percent left for the other four contractors who have been getting an equal share. This would then leave 17 percent for each. It would be wise to project only 15 percent of the total sales volume available for the coming year.

Example No. 2

Let's reverse the tables. A contractor is going to break into a new market. Again, the first step is to determine how many contractors have been doing this particular type of work in this particular geographical area. The second step is to find out the past price-behavior pattern of each. A feel must be developed for how much of the total market each has been getting. If one has been getting appreciably more than the rest, a detailed study of that contractor must be made. Is he getting more than the rest because of his low prices? Or is he getting more because of his long-standing rapport with an appreciable number of the customers? Or is it because of the poor performance of the rest? Whatever the reason, it must be determined because he is the one who is going to have to be beat to establish a foothold in this new market. It is unrealistic to think that a weak competitor can be knocked out of a particular market. Therefore, to obtain sales in a new market, the sales must come from the strong, not the weak. Chances are the sales that the weak competitors have are undesirable sales. A foothold is not established in a market by taking undesirable sales.

The next step is to determine what means are going to be used to obtain the sales. Low prices? Missionary-type exposure in the area? How? Obviously, recognition must be obtained. This requires exposure. What are the total sales in the area? If 10 percent of the total sales for that particular type of work can be extracted, by whatever means are utilized, what is the 10 percent of? Ten percent of nothing is nothing. Ten percent of a lot is something. Ten percent of a whole lot is more. What is the average gross profit being realized? What are the costs that will be incurred above and beyond the costs of performing the work to get started in the area and/or in the particular type of work? Are experienced workmen for that particular type of work in that particular area available to a newcomer?

Being a newcomer into a market does not necessarily mean a newcomer to the area. For example, a contractor who has confined his work to remodeling and light commercial-type work would be a newcomer to new residential construction in the same geographical area. A contractor doing new residential construction in a given geographic area would be a newcomer for new residential construction in a different geographical area.

Assume the total sales volume available in the new market was $10 million, with an average gross profit of only 10 percent. A projection could be based on 10 percent of the total market being extracted by lowering the prices to produce 8 percent gross profit. The total projected gross profit would then be $80,000. An additional estimator-superintendent, with vehicle, would cost approximately $30,000. Sales expenses would be $5,000. General overhead of 5 percent of the additional volume from this one new market would equal $50,000. This adds up to $85,000. This represents an investment of $5,000 for the first year to break into the new market. Is there a potential for additional sales and increased gross profit from this new market? The determination of this is marketing research.

No new market should be pursued until research has been made regarding the capability requirements for that type of work in that geographical location. When this capability requirement has been established, it must then be determined if the subcontractor presently has that capability. If he has, no investment will have to be made to develop and/or acquire the capability. If he does not have the required capability, the cost and time required to develop it must be established. This cost must be included in appraising the feasibility of pursuing the new market.

The time that the subcontractor and/or key personnel will be required to expend in developing the required capability must also be considered. This is time that will be taken from existing vital functions. The possibility of neglect of these functions must be considered. Many times marketing research will reveal that the potential of the new market will not justify the monetary costs and the time of key personnel required to develop the capability requirements. Many times market research will reveal that the obtainable volume and/or gross profit are not such that pursuit of the new market can be justified.

Marketing research will reveal the requirements and potentially insufficient results when surface impressions would seem to suggest that that type of work in that area would be profitable and easy to obtain and would require no additional capability requirements.

DISTRIBUTION

Distribution in manufacturing is the process of getting the product into the consumers' hands. For a nationally used product this requires a physical distribution system, that is, a means of moving the product from the manufacturing plant to distribution depots, to wholesalers, to retailers, and finally, to the user. Distribution is a vital requirement for a manufacturer.

A good example of excellent distribution is the hula hoop. It was manufactured and distributed before national advertising was initiated. At the time sales promotion was started, the hoops were in local distributors' warehouses in great quantities and were already on the retailers' shelves. The sales promotion was highly successful. By acceleration, distribution of the hoops was immediately available to the users in the quantities that the sales promotion had caused a demand for.

There are many examples of poor distribution. For instance, almost everyone has experienced seeing a new product advertised on television, which created a desire to purchase it. However, the product was then found not to be available when the attempt to purchase it was made. In this case the advertising and/or sales promotion was successful, but the distribution had failed. This failure caused the sale of the product to fail.

Let us now relate this to subcontracting. As stated previously, there are many differences between types of work and/or geographical areas. This causes the capability requirements to differ. Distribution for subcontracting is the logistics involved in performance of the work for a particular type of job in a specific geographic area. Unlike other industries, distribution for construction contracting includes an additional vital function—control of the performance of the work must be maintained at all times. Manufacturers must satisfy the mechanics of delivery of their products to the retailers. To complete the cycle, the user must be motivated to purchase the product. The control of the quality and productivity necessary for a profitable endeavor is required at the factory. The control of quality and productivity by the construction contractor is required at the location of the user. The control of the performance of the work is at the job site. This location is always remote from the subcontractor's place of business.

Production of the product or service by the construction contractor also differs from manufacturing. The manufacturer produces his product by the thousands, each either complete or in modules. The construction contractor produces his product in ones. Each is a custom-made product or service. This causes the control requirements of distribution to be acute. The capability of the subcontractor to produce a custom-made product or service at the user's location with control of the quality and productivity is one of the major factors influencing the profitability of the particular market.

There are two concepts regarding when to develop the capabilities necessary for a specific type of work in a particular geographical area:

should the capabilities be developed *prior* to obtaining the work or *during* the performance of the work? This returns us to the age-old question: Which came first, the chicken or the egg?

The method most commonly employed by subcontractors is to first get the work and then develop the capability to perform. The capability to perform requires everything covered in this book. A manufacturer requires money, machines, expertise, a building to put his machines in, and people. He places his factory in an area where the people are available. But the subcontractor does not have the prerogative of selecting the location in which his work is to be performed. The location may or may not be where tradesmen are available.

One of the major capability requirements for a subcontractor is expertise. One of the major products of expertise is the knowledge of what is required to perform a particular type of work in a particular geographical area. With this expertise, marketing planning and marketing research of the capability requirements can be determined. To develop the capability requirements totally, prior to pursuing the market, is not completely feasible. Developing the capability requirements after the job or jobs have been committed is not feasible either. Many subcontractors have taken jobs while not having any of the capability requirements. At the conclusion of the job they found themselves still without the capabilities; however, they did have something they did not have when they started: a loss.

Somewhere between having none of the capability requirements and having all is the right answer. The right decision is dependent on the management expertise of the subcontractor. To make the right decision, the subcontractor must have the benefits of good marketing planning and research.

CUSTOMER RELATIONS

Manufacturers are several places removed from the users of their products. It is rare when a manufacturer is directly confronted by a customer. Because of this characteristic, the manufacturer's customer relations activity is primarily that of developing and maintaining a favorable image. The opposite is true for construction contracting. Not only is the subcontractor directly confronted with the customer, but he also is associated side by side in most cases with his customers while performing the work.

Architects, engineers, and general contractors are customers and are also part of the construction team. Because of this characteristic, customer relations is a vital activity of the subcontractor. Customer relations begin with the initial sales activity and continue during the performance of the job or service through acceptance and final payment. The main purpose of desirable customer relations by a manufacturer is to maintain customer acceptance of the product for additional sales. The main purpose of desirable customer relations by the subcontractor is for future sales plus many other needs. During the course of performing the work or service constant negotiations are required relative to changes, methods and sequence of installation, payout documentation, collecting, and acceptance. Customer relations by the subcontractor affect future sales plus the profitability and cash flow of sales in process. Maintaining good customer relations is the responsibility of everyone in the company. It is, however, a prime responsibility of the subcontractor.

SALES

There are two types of selling: direct selling and missionary selling. Direct selling is performing whatever sales techniques that are applicable toward a specific job. Missionary selling is exposing oneself to customers with no particular job as a target. This type selling is the type that the subcontractor must use at every opportunity. To obtain construction contracts, the subcontractor must know and be familiar (on a first name basis, if possible) with as many business people as possible. Missionary-type selling contributes to this need.

Selling construction work differs appreciably from that of all other services and products. This is because each product or service sold is unique. Construction jobs or services cannot be cataloged. Brochures provide no information regarding any particular sale being pursued. A brochure rarely contributes anything toward obtaining a construction sale. Construction sales depend primarily on the subcontractor's being personally known in the market place. Construction selling includes three steps. The first step is to be allowed to submit a bid, that is, to be placed on the bidder's list. The second step is to have the low bid. The third step is to negotiate for the job with the low figure. Unfortunately (except for public works), a low bid alone will not get the job. To get the job requires more negotiating, selling, and customer relations. Of the three steps two, on the most part, must be performed by the subcontractor himself.

There are three ways to make a sale:

Be given the sale by a personal friend.

Be given the sale as a result of a low price.

Be given the sale from selling your product or service.

To be given a sale from a personal friend is based on friendship and could or could not be a profitable sale. This would depend on the subcontractor's feelings toward his friend; that is, does he want to take advantage of his friend and make money off him, or does he want to be a hero and *give* the sale to his friend without any profit?

To obtain a sale because the competition was outsold is always conducive to producing a profit. Obviously, obtaining sales from friends, even profitable sales, cannot be the basis for a sales effort. There are just not enough friends available. Obtaining sales by outselling the competition is obviously the most desirable. Unfortunately, this does not happen very often.

The only realistic way to obtain sales in the construction industry is with the low bid. To keep this from being fatal, the subcontractor must know his costs and when to say no. The only way a subcontractor can know his costs is by proficient estimating.

ESTIMATING

Estimating is the process of finding out how much a potential job will cost. Its ultimate objective is to help establish the selling price for a job. Sales are the prime mover of the entire business endeavor. To assure this, estimating must be constant and accurate. Low estimates are bad for the company's growth and stability. Consistantly low estimates, or a low estimate on a large job, can be fatal to a company. High estimates, too, are bad for the company's growth and stability. Consistantly high estimates will prevent new sales. This will eventually destroy the company. There must be a constant flow of sales into the company that can be converted to profit. In the construction industry, estimating is the main process in obtaining new sales.

Net profit (return on the owner's investment) is the ultimate goal of the total business endeavor. It is the result of gross profit. Gross profit is the result of executed sales, and sales are the result of estimating. Net profit is, therefore, directly proportional to sales, and sales are directly proportional to estimating. Net profit is also directly proportional to estimating.

The following is an easy way to connect net profit with sales and estimating:

Each contractor has an average number of jobs awarded per total jobs estimated for each type of work. Let's say he gets one job out of ten estimated and that he does only one type of work. He averages 5 percent net profit (before taxes) on sales. Net worth of his company is $200,000. He wants to get a 40 percent return on this investment in the high-risk construction contracting business. This means he will have to make $80,-000 net profit. At 5 percent of net profit on sales he will have to sell $1.6 million worth of contracting. And so, if he averages getting one out of every ten jobs that are estimated, he will have to estimate $16 million worth of sales. This gives the required sales budget for the following year, the amount of new sales that must be estimated, the sales volume that must be executed, and the net profit objectives.

We can now establish the number of man-hours that will be needed to estimate the required $16 million, to be awarded $1.6 million to produce a net profit of $80,000. There is a specific average of sales dollars that an estimator can estimate per hour for each type of work. Assume the estimator can estimate $7,000 of sales per hour for the type of work being pursued. Based on this average, 2,286 hours will be needed to estimate $16 million of sales. This will require one full-time estimator working an average of 46 hours per week for 50 weeks.

If increased profits are desired, more sales must be obtained. More sales can be obtained by one or both of two methods:

1. Increase the average ratio of jobs obtained to jobs estimated.

2. Increase the number of jobs estimated.

The average ratio of jobs obtained to jobs estimated can be increased by:

1. Greater selectivity of jobs estimated. That is, do not estimate a job that there is little or no chance of obtaining.

2. Greater sales effort.

Unfortunately the majority of sales effort available to the contractor is the activity of getting on (qualifying for) the bidder's list. In most cases the bidder with the low bid will get the job, with or without additional sales effort. Greater selectivity of jobs estimated is then the best means to increase the ratio of jobs obtained to jobs estimated. Increasing the number of jobs being estimated requires additional estimating man-hours to be expended, increasing the cost of obtaining the sales (overhead). With this information, the cost of obtaining sales can be established. The cost of obtaining sales is made up of estimating and sales activity costs (entertainment, etc.). The subcontractor rarely considers the cost of obtaining sales.

Studies have many times shown that the subcontractor's cost of obtaining particular types of jobs exceeds the gross profit he adds to the job cost.

He therefore loses money the minute he signs the contract. Without knowing what his cost of sales is, he thinks he is making a profit on jobs when in reality he is losing.

To produce a profit, sales must be obtained. To obtain sales, estimating time must be expended. Estimating must, therefore, be recognized as a separate function and organized as such. Unfortunately, the common attitude toward the estimating process is to do it when there is time or to hurry up and do a lot of estimating as fast as possible when the work load is low. In many firms, the person who makes the estimate is the same person who purchases the job, participates in or completely directs the work, etc. When he is expending time and effort toward executing the contract he is not estimating.

Estimating, being as important as it is, *must* be done on a formal and *continuous* basis. The person who does nothing but estimate can achieve many things that cannot be achieved if he share his time with other activities:

1. He has a feel for the market.

2. He learns the price behavior of his competitors.

3. He is more proficient in the process of estimating.

4. He can estimate more accurately.

5. He can average a greater amount of sales estimated per hour (this lowers the cost of sales).

6. He does not have the opportunity to cover up his mistakes.

An estimator who also directs the installation of the work detects the mistakes in his estimate and is able to keep them from becoming known. He then is in a position of not having to answer for the validity of his estimate. When others are required to take an estimate prepared by an estimator and follow it and to execute the work by it, the validity of the estimate is well known.

Although estimating is an art, a person who specializes in estimating is able to treat it as a science. And although the mechanical details of estimating are different for each trade, there is a basic format that is common to all:

1. The amount of material to be installed must be determined. This is done by measurement and counting and is commonly called "take off."

2. Each item that has to be installed under most situations requires labor. An amount of labor is then developed for each such item. These amounts of labor (increments) are commonly called "labor units."

    The cost of each installed item must be determined. Multiplying the number of them by the cost of each provides the cost of the items. Multiplying the number of each installed item by the labor required to install it gives the cost of installing the total number of items. This process is commonly called "extending." This total process is called the "write-up."

3. The next step is to bring forth the totals of item costs and labor costs from each of the "write-up" sheets to a "summary sheet." All the cost and labor totals from each write-up sheet are added together on the summary sheet. This is commonly known as "summarizing."

4. The next step is to take the totals from the summary sheet and convert the labor hours to dollars. These dollars are then added to the materials dollars, plus any other direct job costs. This develops the total job costs.

The sheet used for this process is commonly called the "front sheet," the "tail sheet," the "cost sheet," or the "total job cost summary." In many cases the summary sheet and the front sheet are combined into one form.

The front sheet of an estimate is very frequently where losses begin. The estimator establishes the cost of material and the labor* required to install it. This, however, is not the total cost. To the cost of material and the labor* to install it must be added:

1. On-the-job nonproductive labor. This can include any or all of the following:

    a. Supervision

    b. Materials-handling personnel

    c. Clerks

    d. Engineers

    e. Draftsmen

    f. Other

*Cost of labor includes labor burden. (See Chapter 14.)

 2. Inspection fees; plan examination fees

 3. Freight and cartage

 4. Tool costs

 5. Tool and equipment rental

 6. Painting and patching

 7. Travel for field employees

 8. Field employee room and board

 9. Travel and overhead personnel

10. Room and board for overhead personnel

11. Utility company service charges

12. Temporary utilities and facility costs

13. Job-site telephone

14. Clean-up costs and charges

15. On-the-job truck costs and expenses

16. Special licenses

17. Materials-handling facilities and equipment

18. Engineering costs

19. Minority training costs

20. Bond costs

21. Special Insurances

22. Taxes

23. Personnel hoisting charges

24. Materials and equipment hoisting charges

25. Materials- and equipment-hoisting labor costs

26. Lost-time costs in hoisting productive men*

27. Overtime to satisfy job conditions

28. Overtime to attract and/or maintain a capable labor force

*Must include labor burden. (See Chapter 14.)

29. Job-site office trailer and/or office facilities

30. Job-site office expenses (equipment, supplies, etc.)

31. Labor factor

Factoring of estimated labor for a particular job includes estimated labor hours and additional labor hours to cover lost time resulting from:

a. Experienced labor not being available in the area

b. Adverse behavior of available labor in the area

c. Featherbedding clauses in the union contract and/or customs and practices in the area that reduce productivity

d. Reduced control of manpower because of the size of work force required to meet time requirements of contract

e. Reduced control as a result of inadequate supply of capable supervision in the area of the particular job

f. Anticipated union jurisdiction disputes that would affect productivity

g. Anticipated adverse weather conditions

h. Other anticipated adverse construction conditions

Labor factoring is done by adding to the labor estimated a percentage of the labor estimated. In that a labor factor is a percentage of the labor estimated, it is always a guess. A labor factor must never be used to upgrade the basic labor units used in the estimate. If the basic labor units being used are established as being consistantly off, each unit should be upgraded to be realistic. A labor factor should be used only to add labor costs to the estimated labor for specific requirements for a particular job.

DIRECT JOB COSTS

All the items listed that pertain to a particular job are *real costs* that *will* be expended. They are just as real as the material that the plans call for. A close evaluation of those items will reveal that they all mean money which the contractor will not have to spend if he doesn't get the contract. Unfortunately, many contractors either believe that these expenditures are not real and, therefore, by some magic happening will not be required, or they do not realize that these costs are part of the overhead. As a result, they do not add these costs to the material costs and labor costs to install the material. The procedure of not recognizing these costs lowers the contractor's bid and gets him the job. He later is puzzled as to why the job did not produce the anticipated profit.

Whether or not the job will produce a profit is usually established by the contractor himself at the time he develops the front sheet. An inadequate front sheet usually will produce a loss. An adequate front sheet usually will produce a profit.

The contractor is prone to say, "Self, if I add these costs to the estimate I won't get the job. If I don't get jobs I can't stay in business." Unfortunately, sales alone do not perpetuate a business. Profit, and profit alone, perpetuates a business. The fastest way to go broke is to take sales that will not produce a profit. Sales that produce profits are sales that *include all costs.* Sales that produce losses are sales that *do not include all costs.*

Contracting is a risk even with all known and anticipated costs included in the bid. Contracting is suicidal when known costs are neglectfully or purposefully left out of the bid.

PREPARATION OF THE FRONT SHEET OF THE ESTIMATE IS WHERE IT ALL BEGINS . . . OR ENDS.

7 NEGOTIATING—CAUSING THE OTHER PERSON TO DO IT YOUR WAY

Negotiation is probably the most prevalent activity of our daily living in business, vocation, and social endeavors. We are constantly negotiating a situation with someone. Driving a car in traffic involves negotiating with other drivers.

"Negotiate" may be defined as "to carry on business"; hence, to deal or treat one with another to reach an agreement. The subcontractor continuously negotiates in the normal course of the business day. In fact, everything the subcontractor does is a form of negotiating. He negotiates with employees, owners, architects, general contractors, other subcontractors, suppliers, union representatives, inspectors, banks, and purchasing agents. This means the type of negotiating that the subcontractor does daily in causing the other person to do it his way, and not the type of formal negotiating such as negotiating a labor contract.

Since this is a major function of the subcontractor's daily life, he must know *how* to negotiate. There are certain basic rules to negotiating that must be honored, and above all, not violated. There also are techniques which are used in the art of negotiation. Not all techniques apply to all negotiations, or even to the entirety of an individual negotiation. One must know the techniques and when and when not to use specific ones. It is important to use the correct technique at the correct time rather than the wrong technique—or a correct technique at the wrong time. Negotiating is an art which requires preparation, skill, and will power.

RULES OF NEGOTIATING

A. Never, never argue.

B. Do not bring up issues that are not pertinent.

C. Never allow your opponent to put himself in a position where he makes irretractable statements that would cause him to lose face.

D. Do not confuse the art of negotiation with motivation.

E. Do not confuse the art of negotiation with selling.

F. Know the disposition, attitude, intelligence, and background of your opponent.

G. Be prepared.

H. Do not set unrealistic objectives.

I. Do not alienate yourself from your opponent.

J. Avoid ending the negotiation when you don't have a winning position.

K. Always be truthful.

L. Never become greedy.

M. Never underestimate your opponent's ability and position.

N. Never negotiate when you should be selling.

TECHNIQUES OF NEGOTIATING

1. Provoke a designed argument.

2. Let your opponent do most of the talking.

3. Be a good listener.

4. Agree with your opponent on *all* unimportant points.

5. Take advantage of your opponent when he is operating by emotions.

6. Pick the right time and place for negotiation.

7. Smile.

8. Change the subject when necessary or desirable.

9. Enter into negotiations only when you have unlimited time available.

10. Use your opponent's time deadline to your advantage.

11. Cause your appearance to match the needs of your objectives.

12. Change your position from negotiating to that of selling.

13. Give in only after you are positive that your opponent won't give in.

14. Give up.

In every negotiation there is a *negotiator* and a *negotiatee;* that is, you are either on the *offense* or on the *defense.*

The most important part of negotiating is unknown, almost every time, by both parties: who is the negotiator (offense) and who is the negotiatee (defense). Both parties think they are the negotiator and are on the offense side. This automatically sets the stage for the real negotiatee to surely lose. Wouldn't it be a pushover for the offense platoon of the football team to score against an offense platoon of the other team? This is true because the offense platoon of the other team would be using offensive plays, thinking they had the ball. Wouldn't it be ridiculous to watch this type of football game when one team thought it had the ball and, therefore, was just going through the motions of offensive plays while the other team who had the ball was scoring without opposition? It wouldn't be much of a game. It would probably end up in a free-for-all. That is what happens in most of our daily negotiations. They end up in a free-for-all which we commonly call arguments.

Let's stay with the football team analogy. The team which loses the coin toss usually begins the game with its members defending their goal. To do this they use their defense platoon. The defense platoon uses defensive plays and techniques to prevent the other team from scoring until they can get into an offensive position.

Now, let's look at the other team. They start the game on the offense; however, the minute their offensive position weakens they immediately recognize it, and knowingly, by design, turn the ball over to the other team and assume a defensive position. They don't even wait for the other team to *win* the offensive position; they give it to them on the fourth down.

There really isn't anything bad, and it doesn't mean that you are going to lose, if you are the negotiatee (on the defense). It is, however, a sure thing that you will lose if you are the negotiatee (on the defense) and don't know it! You may start negotiations on the offense and then swing to the defense during the negotiation. This does not mean you have lost. If you know that your position has changed, and you change your method, you are still in control. This can, more times than not, be an asset for setting the stage to win. As in football, you may be able to gain more ground faster by swinging to the defense and holding than trying to keep an offensive position.

The negotiatee (defense) who thinks he is the negotiator usually gives himself away by arguing.

We, therefore, come to **Rule A** in the art of negotiating.

A. *Never, never* argue.

Arguing is like fighting on a football field; in no way can it contribute to winning. When both sides argue, they both have unknowingly changed to defensive positions. The result of this is a stalemate. A stalemate, unfortunately for the person who had the offensive position, is the same as losing. This is sad because if he had held his position by not arguing, he probably would have won.

Technique No. 1. Provoke a designed argument.

If you find yourself in what would appear to be a hopeless defensive position, provoke an argument *by design.* The argument *must be relative* to that which is being negotiated. Human nature will generate the emotions of your opponent and cause him to argue back. When this happens, you immediately shut up. When he stops, you will keep your mouth shut. This makes him keep the floor, which he does not want at that time because he is sure he has made his point. With your mouth still shut, he finds himself in an awkward position of not knowing whether he has made his point or not. So again, human nature steps in to help you by causing him to start over again. He now has serious doubts whether he is getting to you or not. When this happens you have gained the offensive and have a downhill road to winning.

Technique No. 2. Let your opponent do most of the talking.

Most people are poor listeners. They demonstrate this by either constant interruptions when you are talking or by not continuing on with the continuity of what you have been talking about when you finish. They pick up exactly where they left off when you gained the floor. This indicates they were not listening, but instead were waiting and thinking of what they were going to say when you stopped. This is an asset because you know what the other person knows, but he does not know what you know. You can now detect his weak areas and, conversely, he is unable to detect yours.

Technique No. 3. Be a good listener.

Most people enter into negotiations subconsciously expecting to fight and to be fought. The best way to throw your opponent off guard is to agree with him on every insignificant point he attempts to make. He feels he must build a foundation of many subpoints to support his position on the main point. By agreeing with him on all his subpoints, you let him emotionally feel that he has a downhill situation. He then relaxes and discards his calculated design for the negotiation. He then prematurely introduces the main point and his main thrust. When you flatly answer "no" to the main point after agreeing on all his subpoints, he becomes bewildered, frustrated, and confused. When he is in this emotional state you then take the offensive and conclude the negotiations in short order.

Technique No. 4 Agree with your opponent on *all* unimportant points.

The best way to take the fight out of a person is to let him win. When he wins he has nothing to fight for. In most of the "on-the-job" negotiations there are many issues that arise during the negotiations that are not necessarily pertinent to the main issue. Both the negotiator and negotiatee are inclined emotionally to throw these into the discussion to accomplish two things: (1) to take advantage of the meeting to introduce other objectives, and (2) to strengthen his position. The person doing this at a particular meeting is acting by emotions and not by design.

Introducing other objectives *during* negotiations does not contribute to the negotiation at hand, nor does it initiate the other objectives for future negotiations. The introduction of other objectives usually goes right over the head of your opponent because he is not tuned in to receive conversation not pertinent to the subject being negotiated. It will probably confuse him and deteriorate your ability to communicate effectively. The end result is that you fail to introduce other objectives and you have either confused the negotiation at hand or have led it off on a tangent.

The common belief that to point out what adversities you have endured will cause your opponent to feel sorry for you and, therefore, give in to your requests is completely false. As you are listing the adversities you have endured he is establishing the ones he has encountered. If he does not present these to you in rebuttal, he is surely thinking of them. He will, without fail, rationalize that he is the one who has suffered the most wrong. This will cause him to be more steadfast in his position. By introducing nonpertinent issues you will have failed to strengthen your position, and will probably have caused your opponent to become more unbending.

If your opponent is a prudent negotiator he will say, "It's true that you have had your problems and I am sorry about that, but I also have problems, so let's get back to the issue at hand." If he makes a statement of that nature, you had better fall back and regroup, for he is now in control and is operating by design where you have exposed yourself as operating by emotions; therefore, your position has been weakened.

Rule B. Do not introduce issues that are not pertinent.

Technique No. 5. Take advantage of your opponent when he is operating by emotions.

Actions that indicate your opponent is operating by emotions include:

1. He attempts to argue.
2. He introduces nonpertinent issues.

3. He attempts to establish the adversities he has endured.

4. He becomes vociferous (loud).

5. He says, "I don't care what you say, I'm not going to change my mind."

6. He pleads for fairness.

7. He attempts to establish all that he has previously contributed.

When your opponent becomes emotional, a very critical decision must be made—whether to continue the discussion or not. If your opponent is intelligent, with a managerial background, it will probably be wise to continue by becoming mute and letting him run down.

When he finishes, continue to remain mute, which will cause him to start over, repeating himself as described previously. After he has completely run down, remind him in a very calm, gentlemanly manner that he has become emotional and suggest that the negotiations be continued at a later date. He will then reflect and say, "No, let's get it settled." He is now in a humble state of mind because he has expressed himself in a manner that he is not proud of. Take a *very* calm, gentlemanly posture and conclude the negotiation by explaining your position and reasoning. You will find that under these circumstances he is putty in your hands. If your opponent has an argumentative attitude and has become emotional, it will be wise to terminate the discussions immediately and start over at a later time. To pursue the negotiations further with a person with an argumentative attitude while he is emotional will cause him to become more emotional and will end with his taking an irrevocably opposing position.

Rule C. Never allow your opponent to put himself in a position where he makes irretractable statements that would cause him to lose face.

Technique No. 6 Pick the right time and place for the negotiation. This is probably one of the most effective techniques.

In most cases it is better for you to have negotiations at your location (as opposed to his). A meeting at a mutually agreed to place (other than his or yours), even if you suggest the place, serves no purpose for you. If you can get him to come to your location you have gained the initiative before you begin. A meeting on the job site with the customer is not going to him. The job site is neutral territory for both of you. The job site for a field subordinate (at any level) is, however, his location, not yours. Yours is back at the office. It is easy to determine with a little thought what are his, what are yours, and what are neutral locations. The initiative is purely psychological. You are more comfortable and secure at your location, and he is less comfortable and secure at your location, and vice versa.

Rule D. Do not confuse the art of negotiation with motivation.

When trying to motivate someone, it is wise to set the stage by honoring him. The best way to honor him is to go to him. But you don't win a negotiation by motivation. You win a negotiation by *causing* your opponent to agree with you. A football game is *not* won by the winning team's having motivated the other team to lose. They won because they out-played their opponents with skill, weight, power, being prepared, knowing their opponents, outsmarting them, etc.

Rule E. Do not confuse the art of negotiating with selling.

You don't cause the other person to do it your way, nor do you win a negotiation, by selling your opponent on losing or giving in to you. You win the negotiation by *causing* your opponent to agree with you. A football game is not won by the winning team having sold the losing team on losing. They won because they outplayed their opponents with skill, wit, power, being prepared, knowing their opponents, outsmarting them, etc. The art of selling requires convincing your opponent that what you want to do is best for him. Losing, or giving in, seldom is best for the person who loses or gives in. Negotiation, or causing the other person to do it your way, requires you to win by being prepared, knowing your opponent, outsmarting your opponent, etc., not selling him.

Rule F. Know the disposition, attitude, intelligence, and background of your opponent.

As in Technique No. 5, it is vital that you know the disposition, attitude, intelligence, and background of your opponent. There are many ways to determine this. As an example, many times managers have different dispositions, attitudes, and disciplines than workmen. A man's present position is a clue and indicates whether he is a workman or a manager. Many times, however, this can be confirmed only by meeting with him. You must use techniques applicable to the person with whom you are negotiating. A telephone call to a mutual acquaintance usually is very valuable in determining your opponent's posture. Ask your mutual acquaintance, "What can you tell me about Joe Doe? I am going to have a meeting with him and I would like to know what kind of person he is." Most are prone to verbalize at great lengths about the disposition, attitudes, etc., of a person and will probably cite previous experiences with your opponent. A football team spends hours and hours studying its opponents prior to a game. It knows everything possible about them.

Rule G. Be prepared.

Preparation prior to the negotiations, as in all other endeavors, is the most important part of the total endeavor. It includes the following:

1. Determine the attitude, disposition, intelligence, and background of your opponent.

2. Establish your prime objective.

3. Determine what your opponent's prime objective is.

4. Establish your strong, positive positions.

5. Establish your weak, negative positions.

6. Determine what you think your opponent's strong, positive positions are.

7. Determine what you think your opponent's weak, negative positions are.

8. From the above, establish who has the edge.

9. From the above, establish who will be on the offense and who will be on the defense at the beginning of the negotiations.

10. Establish what are the absolute minimums you will settle for.

11. Determine what you think is the absolute minimum your opponent will settle for.

12. From the above establish a realistic, obtainable, measurable value to your prime objective.

13. Determine the location and time for the negotiation that will be most conducive to your purpose.

14. Determine what member of the opposition you should negotiate with.

15. Determine the prime objective of your opponent.

16. Evaluate all that you will lose if you win your objective. Nothing is ever won without giving up something in exchange. There is always a cost to winning.

17. Determine if time is in your favor or your opponent's.

The above requirements of preparation can either be done mentally or by writing them down. Writing them down will result in better preparation. A detailed lengthy written preparation is not necessary or desirable. An informal brief listing is the most effective. Be sure to list in detail:

1. Your strong, positive points

2. Your weak, negative points

3. Your opponent's strong, positive points

4. Your prime objective

5. The absolute minimum you will settle for

These must be fixed in your mind before entering negotiations and should be kept in your forethought at all times.

It is impossible to predesign every move you will make and every reaction your opponent will display. To do this, and then attempt to follow it, would lead you to be completely ineffective. As in football, you must call your plays as the game progresses. Your plays, however, are based on the points of your preparation.

Rule H. Don't set unrealistic objectives.

In every negotiation there is a prime objective for both the negotiator and the negotiatee. It can be measured in whole or parts of time, physical activities, dollars, material possessions, and psychological factors including prestige, honor, recognition, and reputation. Other than psychological, the prime objective can usually be converted to dollars for evaluating.

Based on evaluation by measurement, the prime objective must be based on *what you will accept, not on what you want*. Your prime objective must be within the limits of your opponent's ability to give and afterwards continue to function. If winning your prime objective would leave your opponent helpless, and cause him to fail in the endeavor of which the negotiation was a function, he would have no alternative but to fight without compromise. This would cause you to fail to win your prime objective. *What you will accept* must be based on what your opponent can and will give in to. If you can say to yourself, "No way can or will he agree to that," your prime objective is not realistic.

The two major contributing factors to failure in winning negotiations are:

1. Not knowing when you are the negotiatee

2. Unrealistic objectives

Rule I. Don't alienate yourself from your opponent.

Winning a negotiation does not include alienating yourself from your opponent and/or from the company he represents. Winning a negotiation successfully should improve your rapport with your opponent. This can be done by including the following two techniques in your negotiation: smiling and changing the subject.

Technique No. 7. Smile.

Smiling by design during the negotiation achieves many things:

1. It deters from alienating your opponent.

2. It prevents your opponent's becoming emotional.

3. It keeps the negotiation on an amiable basis.

4. It makes your final thrust and position more effective.

It is very difficult for your opponent to personally become mad at you, and subsequently your company, when you are smiling. This keeps the negotiation on a business level and reduces your opponent's tendency to be self-guarded. That is, he will feel less personally the results of losing even in situations when he would in fact be personally the loser.

There are times during a negotiation that you must emphasize your position or point by displaying an appearance of seriousness and assertiveness. If you do not smile and appear serious from the beginning of the negotiation, you have no way of indicating to your opponent your more important positions. The tone of your voice should also go along with smiling, except when you are establishing a serious point or position. The tone of your voice, and your facial appearance, are very effective tools in negotiating. Do not confuse the tone of your voice with its loudness. You cannot increase your effectiveness by talking louder.

When you are smiling you automatically hide your true emotions, thereby preventing your opponent from being able to detect your reactions to his actions. This makes it very difficult for him to determine his next defensive or offensive move. He doesn't know whether he is effective or not. Your facial expression, as in poker, must be constant. By smiling you satisfy this requirement, and you also avoid alienating your opponent.

Technique No. 8. Change the subject when necessary or desirable.

As stated in Technique No. 5, when the person you are negotiating with becomes emotional, you should stop the negotiation. Do this in a manner that will not alienate him so that you can renew the negotiation at a later date. The best way is to abruptly change the subject. Your opponent will attempt to continue the argument. However, you must persist with other subjects. This technique is valuable during any negotiations. Successful negotiations are kept on an amiable basis by not allowing your opponent to become tense. To prevent him from becoming too serious, which will lead him to becoming emotional, introduce levity, intermittently. The best levity is pertinent to your position. That is, make fun of your position, your unbending nature, and, at times, compliment him in a joking manner on his ability as an unbending negotiator.

Interject intermittently completely unrelated subjects by abruptly asking your opponent how his family is, or how is his golf game, something that you know is of prime interest to him. He cannot say, "Never mind how my family is." He is required to answer your question by referring favorably about his family. That automatically breaks the tension. If he is on the offensive, abruptly changing the subject as suggested above will break his continuity of thought and will prevent him from pursuing his point. After the superfluous talk is concluded, it is difficult for your opponent to pick up where he left off; he now has neither continuity nor momentum. When you are on the offensive, the same technique is effective in making it difficult for him to defend his position.

Rule J. Avoid concluding the negotiation when you do not have a winning position.

This is an obvious rule. Never allow the negotiation to end if you haven't won. Unlike a football game, there is no time limit set by the negotiators. This is the reason that the person who has the most time available for the negotiating meeting, and who can afford to prolong the ultimate conclusion the longest, has the greatest edge.

This rule does not apply when you have truly lost. When you have, in fact, lost, lose gracefully and admit that your position wasn't as valid as your opponent's. Congratulate him on his ability to negotiate and on his being right and your being wrong. Be a hero. These acts will be tremendous assets in future negotiations. If, however, you haven't truly lost, and there is still validity to your position, and time is in your favor, don't allow the negotiations to be concluded. End the meeting gracefully and tactfully and resume the negotiations at a later date. During the interval between meetings, take another look at your positive and negative points and prepare for the next meeting.

Technique No. 9. Enter into negotiations only when you have unlimited time available.

Negotiations *must* be allowed to take a natural course. If one of the negotiating parties is short of time and attempts to force a conclusion, timewise, all his opponent has to do is slow down and wait. He will then win by default.

One of your greatest assets is time. It is also an asset if your opponent knows that you have all the time that may be necessary. Conversely, it is a serious detriment if your opponent knows or even suspects that you are short of time. Always schedule the negotiations at a time that will not interfere with other commitments. Critical negotiations should be the last activity scheduled for that day.

Another technique relative to time is to schedule the negotiations at a time when you know that your opponent will be short of time. This will force him to take shortcuts in both his offensive and defensive moves. If he has a designed plan for presenting his position, he will forfeit his plan in favor of his limited time.

Another time-related technique is to announce at the beginning of the negotiations that you must leave by such and such a time. Your opponent will then change his technique to take advantage of this limitation. Allow him to have the floor as much as possible. At the time that you were supposed to leave, announce that you have missed your commitment and now have all the time in the world. Your opponent will have already presented all his strong points, which you now know. To further his offensive or defense he must now resort to repeating. If you wait long enough, he will repeat himself into a defensive position. At this time you can introduce your strong points. You will also be in a position to quote him to his detriment.

There is another important time factor. In most situations requiring negotiations something is being either held up (stopped), or delayed, is proceeding, will be held up (stopped), or delayed, or will proceed. These represent a point in time that affects, or will affect, one of the parties adversely. The person that the above will not affect can gain the offensive by causing the delay of starting negotiations until there is little or no time left before the other party is affected. The other party cannot be as independent to his opponent's negotiating technique as he could if he had no deadline for a conclusion of the negotiations.

Rule K. Always be truthful.

There is no situation that will justify anything but the truth. The minute you lie you will surely lose. Being truthful doesn't mean you have to tell all there is to tell. It does mean, however, that everything you say must be fact and the truth.

When you lie there are two very basic laws of nature that keep you from being successful in negotiations:

1. For mechanical or scientific situations there is the fact that 2 + 2 = 4. It can be either proven or disproven.

2. For nonmechanical situations there is the law that everything is relative.

If you introduce a nonfactual point you will eventually lose because your negotiation was without foundation or because you just plainly did not know what you were talking about. If you use a falsehood flavored with true statements, it will eventually present itself as such because it cannot be relative to the truth. For a false statement to be worth anything, your entire negotiating position would have to be completely devoid of any true statements. True statements and false statements are not relative and will not mix successfully. If an entire negotiating position were based on false statements, it would be a hoax. A successful hoax does not exist in the construction industry.

Rule L. Never become greedy.

Greed is an emotion. It is one of the emotions that affect our daily activities the most. It is also one of the emotions that get us in the most trouble. Greed is brought into many negotiations by the negotiator when he realizes he is winning. Although he has based his objectives on what he will accept and not on what he wants and, as a result, is about to obtain that objective, he often cannot resist the emotion of greed to go for more. Don't forget, the success of the negotiation is based on obtaining the objective without alienating your opponent, not on how much you can extract from him at any price. Most situations in the construction industry require the parties to continue to work together after the negotiations. There is an old saying that goes, "Take a lot, but leave some for the other person." In negotiating, an attempt to take it all will probably allow the other party to win the negotiation.

If you realize you are about to win the negotiation, let it continue to its conclusion, pick up your marbles, and go home. Don't get greedy and put new demands on your opponent that will require him to reassess his position and reevaluate the cost of losing. When this happens, your opponent will probably dig his heels in for a long battle which you may lose. Win when you have won.

Rule M. Never underestimate your opponent's ability and position.

Failure to employ this rule is what causes the actual negotiatee to enter a negotiation thinking he is the negotiator. It is natural and human to confine your evaluation and preparation to your position and objective. Unfortunately, this is fatal. No opponent is without some ability, or without some positive positions. If he didn't have either there would be no negotiation. Evaluating your opponent's ability and positive position is more important than evaluating your own. You are aware of yours without formal evaluation. You must, however, research and analyze your opponent to determine his.

It is common to look upon your opponent as stupid, weak, wrong, etc. If he is all these, chances are you are also, because he is at a level that requires you to negotiate with him. It would serve your best interests to look upon him as smart, strong, and with a lot of positive points. This would cause you to better prepare yourself.

Rule N. Never negotiate when you should be selling.

It is very simple to determine whether you can negotiate or whether you must sell. In preparing for a negotiation, list your strong and weak points and your opponent's strong and weak points. If your strong points *won't* cancel your opponent's strong and weak points, or if your opponent's strong points *will* cancel your strong and weak points, you are *not* in a position to negotiate. You must sell.

The art of selling is completely different from negotiating. If you are in a position that will allow you to negotiate and you use selling techniques, you will lose. If you are in a position that requires selling and you attempt to negotiate, you will lose.

Technique No. 11. Cause your appearance to match the needs of your objectives. Your appearance expresses the tone of your position. It is, therefore, very important that your appearance express the tone that will strengthen your position.

Appearance includes:

1. Type of clothes
    a. Work clothes
    b. Casual clothes
    c. Business clothes
    d. Mixed-up
2. Personal
    a. Shaved

b. Unshaven

c. Clean

d. Dirty

Appearances provide first impressions. Always remember that if your opponent has not yet met you. You can control his impression of you simply by your appearance.

Appearance can establish either a warm or a cold tone between you and your opponent. A warm tone makes it difficult for your opponent to be uncooperative; a cold tone makes it easy for you to be uncooperative. It must be determined which is best. A cold tone can be established by dressing the opposite to your opponent; a warm tone can be established by dressing the same as your opponent.

If a manager is going to negotiate with a worker and desires a warm tone, he will take his tie off and roll up his sleeves. This causes the worker to feel more comfortable and, therefore, more cooperative. If the manager wants a cold tone and desires his authority and managerial position to contribute to his negotiating position, he will wear his tie and coat.

But do not confuse establishing tone with motivating your opponent.

If your opponent is on the same level and normally wears the same clothing as you, you can change the tone by removing your coat and tie and rolling up your sleeves. When you do this your opponent will probably say, "I wasn't aware we were going to use boxing gloves!" You have now set the tone of the negotiations to that of a very serious and uncooperative attitude on your part. You have also notified your opponent that you have dug your heels in for a long session. This is a good technique to mislead him when you are actually short of time. Remember! The appearance you select for the negotiation should be well thought out as to what it will do to strengthen or weaken your position. Your appearance will work either for or against you.

Technique No. 12. Change your position from negotiating to that of selling.

If you know you are losing the negotiation and still desire to *cause the other person to do it your way,* try selling him. This decision must be made *prior* to losing the negotiation because you must switch from negotiating to selling before the negotiation is concluded. You then lose the negotiation in a graceful and humble manner that will set the stage for selling.

Technique No. 13. Give in only after you are positive (by trying him) that your opponent won't give in.

Many negotiations have been lost only because the would-be winner gave up just short of winning. The classic example of this was in World War II. Hitler had England on her knees with his air strikes. It has now been accurately established that had Hitler continued his massive air raids for 2 more weeks, England would have crumbled.

You never know whether your opponent is ready to give in until you test him. You can test him by:

1. Calling his bluff by actually allowing him to start his available course of action

2. Establishing and maintaining a mute and unbending position

It is like buying an automobile. You never know whether the salesman has offered his lowest price until he lets you walk out of his show room. When he lets you leave, you then know that his last offer was his last. You can then go back in and accept his last offer knowing it was his best. After you have tested your opponent and factually established his final position, you can then use the technique that is always available to you and will always work.

Technique No. 14. Give up.

This technique also is called:

Acquiescing

Giving in

Compromising with your opponent's terms

Giving up is the most positive and effective technique of the art of negotiation. It always, without fail, works. It is so positive that it will work no matter when you use it. It will work whether you use it at the beginning, at the would-be middle, or at the end of the negotiation. It is so powerful that when you do use it, it immediately concludes the negotiation.

Unfortunately, giving up is the most advantageous technique you can use for your opponent, for it always causes or allows him to win. Because of this, and the fact that it will always work no matter when you use it, never use it except as a *last, last, last* resort. No matter what you do during the negotiation you *always* have this technique as your ace in the hole to conclude the negotiation. This being true, isn't it logical to avoid using this technique until you are *very, very* sure that you have lost the offensive forever? You never know whether you have really irretrievably lost the offensive until you let your opponent start whatever unfavorable recourse he has available to him as a result of your refusing to give in. More often than not he will be the one to give in if you wait him out. If he does start his available negative course of action, you can always give in, in which case he will immediately stop.

After knowing all this about the art of negotiating, you may be inclined to say that it all has validity; however, many people in the construction industry also have the same know-how of the techniques and rules as you. As a result, will it be of less value to you? Not so. All football teams are sharp in all rules, techniques, and knowledge of their opponent. But there are very few ties; most football games have a winner and a loser. The same holds true with proficient negotiators. The person who is better prepared, knows his opponent better, and uses the techniques more effectively *wins*. Nowhere has it been said that you can win as a result of your opponent's stupidity. In fact, it is impossible to negotiate successfully with a stupid person. A stupid person will never react logically to designed action on your part. The more knowledgeable your opponent is, the better your chances of winning by calculated design.

⑧ CONTRACTS

Contracts are the basis by which construction jobs are awarded, performed, paid, and accepted upon completion. A contract is the agreement and understanding of the commitment between the owner, or owner's agent, and the contractor. The name "contractor" is derived from the word "contract." A contractor is a person who performs a service in accordance with a contract. The contract (agreement) is that which governs—or perhaps could be said controls—the contractor's performance and course of action. The contract (agreement) is a legally binding commitment which the contractor must honor and satisfy. He must also comply with all its provisions and requirements. Because the contract is a legally binding commitment, it influences the actions of the construction firm more than any other single aspect.

Contracts (agreements) are either written or verbal. Both are legally binding on both parties. The difference between a verbal contract and a written one is that a verbal agreement is much more difficult to verify or prove if there is a dispute between the two parties. For a verbal agreement to be meaningful and to be able to be proven or verified, there would have to be a witness with a very keen and accurate memory.

The most simple agreements relative to construction projects involve many requirements and commitments by both parties and cover many many details. It is rare when the details of an agreement are so simple and small in number that a verbal contract left to memory is of any value. For this reason, with few exceptions all agreements, understandings, and commitments should be in writing, forming an official contract between the parties involved.

Because a contract is an irreversible commitment by the subcontractor, he must know all the aspects of contracts, including the legal ramifications. The subcontractor must be, in fact, an expert on construction contracts.

There are two types of construction contracts, prime contracts and subcontracts. A prime contract is a contract directly with the owner. A subcontract is a contract with a general contractor or with another subcontractor.

It is common for a subcontractor to perform work for:

1. An owner, under a prime contract

2. A general contractor, under a subcontract

3. A subcontractor, under a subcontract

The basic difference between a prime contract and a subcontract is that the subcontract includes provisions that transfer certain responsibilities, obligations, and requirements from the general contractor to the subcontractor or from one subcontractor to another subcontractor.

Contracts are created in one of two forms:

1. A proposal which becomes a contract when accepted. This is called a "proposal-contract."

2. A formal contract.

The use of the proposal-contract form is confined to small and domestic work. With the exception of the proposal-contract, construction contracts are prepared by the owner or by the general contractor. They are not prepared by the subcontractor. Formal contracts can be either of two types: (1) a purchase order issued by the customer and accepted by the subcontractor or (2) a document written in a form which is unique in all respects to the particular job involved.

The construction contract usually is prepared by the buyer and not by the seller. This puts the subcontractor (seller) at a disadvantage because contracts are written for the protection and advantage of the buyer (owner or general contractor). There is very little a subcontractor can do to change or alter a contract to his advantage and/or protection. Construction contracts are usually based on take the job—subject to the buyer's contract provisions and terms—or leave it.

Contracts are made up of words intended to convey a specific commitment by one of the two parties to the contract. The sentence structure, number of words, and type of words used in contracts are employed to attempt to prevent misunderstandings or misinterpretation of the intent. This is why such words as whereas, heretofore, shall, thereof, etc., are used. This also is why words which describe or identify are repeated for each separate sentence. Many refer to this type of writing as legal mumbo-jumbo, fine print, etc. Anyone with the level of intelligence necessary to be a subcontractor can read, understand, interpret, analyze, and evaluate every word in a contract. Contracts are worded in such a way that there are no meanings or intents implied or left for "in-between-the-lines" interpretation. *Every* word in a contract is put there for a specific reason and has a *logical* meaning.

THE SUBCONTRACTOR MUST KNOW THE REASON AND MEANING OF EVERY WORD IN EACH CONTRACT HE SIGNS.

Interpreting, analyzing, and evaluating a contract is an activity that the subcontractor himself must perform, not his lawyer. A lawyer cannot do this because he does not have the first-hand knowledge required. A lawyer, without exception, will advise the subcontractor not to sign the contract. The only portion of a contract that the subcontractor should delegate to outsiders for interpreting, analyzing, and evaluating is the insurance provisions part. If a subcontractor does not understand a provision in the contract, he should seek help on *how* to understand the provision. He should never delegate this understanding. If the subcontractor fails (after help) to understand the contract (that which he is committing his resources to) *he should not sign it.*

All contracts are made up of provisions, each covering a specific requirement or establishing a specific condition or recourse. The subcontractor must realize that every provision in the contract is for the benefit and protection of others. To avoid the pitfalls of these circumstances he must *know* how and to what extent each provision affects the specific job involved. The format used for contracts divides the contract into groups of paragraphs which are identified by title and/or number. Each identified group of paragraphs covers a provision. All the provisions in a contract are part of basic provisions.

The basic provisions of a contract include:

1. Project data

2. Mechanics

3. Insurance

4. Time limitations and requirements

5. Legal recourse

6. Payment

7. Waivers of lien

8. Changes

9. Guarantees and warranties

10. Governmental requirements

11. Special

Each of the above basic provisions is described in detail below.

I. Project Data

The project data is the physical data pertinent to the particular project. The data include the following:

A. Identification or name of the project

B. Legal description of the entity whom the contract is with, either the owner, general contractor, or others

C. Legal description of subcontractor

D. Date of the contract

E. Type of work (electrical, plumbing, painting, plastering, etc.)

F. Source of funds (bond issue identification, government appropriation number, etc.)

G. Contract number

II. Mechanics

The mechanics of the contract are:

A. Reference to that which the contract is based on, such as identification of plans by sheet, date of each, date of specifications, letters, addenda, and other documents indicating the work to be installed, and how

B. A list of addenda to specifications

C. The amount of the contract which is either a lump sum and/or a list of unit prices, time and material, or cost plus fixed fee, etc., and a list of alternates with amounts of each.

III. Insurance

The insurance provisions of a contract include a detailed description of insurances and insurance limits required to be carried by both parties. Insurance requirements can include any or all of the following:

A. Workmen's compensation and employer's liability

B. Comprehensive general liability

1. Operations—premises liability

2. Elevator liability

3. Contractor's protective liability

4. Completed operations liability

5. Contractual liability

6. Special requirements

   a. Property damage, including explosion, collapse, or underground (XCU)

   b. Property damage—care, custody, and control

7. Comprehensive automobile liability

8. Hold harmless

(See Chap. 18.)

IV. Time Limitations and Requirements

This provision establishes when the work is to be completed. Many times this provision puts a daily penalty beyond the date of completion established by the contract.

V. Legal Recourse

Legal recourse provisions are established by the contract to protect the owner or general contractor. These recources are established against.

A. Delay of work by subcontractor

B. Bankruptcy by the subcontractor

C. Nonpayment of bills owed by the subcontractor

D. Recourse by the subcontractor against the owner or general contractor

E. Installation of faulty materials and/or equipment by the subcontractor

F. Poor workmanship by the subcontractor

G. Disputes

The recourses* made available to the owner or general contractor are:

A. Termination of contract

B. Backcharging the subcontractor

---

*Note: It is rare when a contract includes *any* recourse by the subcontractor to the general contractor and/or owner.

    C. Withholding of payments due the subcontractor

    D. All or any combination of the above

  VI. Payment

The payment provisions of the contract include:

    A. Amount and method of retention

    B. Schedule of payment as to method, frequency, and forms to be used

    C. Final payment requirements and when they must be made

  VII. Waivers of Lien

The contract's waiver of lien provision includes a detailed description of types of waivers of lien required for interim payouts and final payment. Some contracts include the provision which waives all lien rights upon acceptance of the contract by the subcontractor. (See Chapter 12.)

  VIII. Changes (Extras)

The contract's provision covering changes includes:

    A. Authority of the owner to order changes, deletions, and additions

    B. Who is authorized to order changes, deletions, and additions

    C. Method of payment

    D. Permissible percentages for overhead and profit

    E. Type of documentation and substantiation required (see Chapter 9.)

    F. Method of approval of changes

    G. That which constitutes a change that affects the amount of the contract

    H. That which will not be considered an addition to the contract

  IX. Guarantees and Warranties

This provision covers the guarantees and/or warranties that the subcontractor is required to honor, and how long he is to honor them. This is usually for one year after the completion date. The completion date usually is established when the general contract has been satisfactorily completed and accepted by the architect or owner. Under these circumstances the completion date is left to the discretion of the architect or owner. The termination date of the guarantee period, therefore, is controlled pretty much by the owner and/or architect. The guarantee usually covers poor workmanship, faulty equipment, etc.

X. Governmental Requirements

This section commits the subcontractor to all the governmental requirements that are imposed on the project, which include when applicable:

A. Occupational Safety and Health Act (OSHA) requirements

B. Minority participation requirements (Equal Opportunity Act)

C. Local, state, and federal code requirements

D. Minimum wage requirements (Davis-Bacon Act)

E. Local, state, and federal tax requirements

F. Local, state, and federal workmen's compensation requirements

G. Local, state, and federal unemployment compensation and Social Security Act requirements

H. Local, state, and/or federal permit requirements

I. Governmental audit requirements relative to costs and profits (national and defense contracts)

J. Government price-control requirements

K. Copeland Anti-Kickback Act and Regulation requirements

L. Federal executive order compliance

M. Compliance with Department of Health, Education, and Welfare standards

N. Local, state, and/or federal code requirements

XI. Special

This provision includes all the specific project details agreed to by the subcontractor which are not included in the plans or specifications. This provision also is used to assign to the subcontractor responsibilities originally assigned to the owner or general contractor by the specifications and/or plans. These include:

A. Temporary facilities

B. Excess facility charges

C. Performance bond requirements and who pays for the bond

D. Utilities charges: water, gas, electricity, telephone, etc.

E. Special agreements

F. Accepted alternates

This provision also includes a description of what is not included.

When reading a contract, the subcontractor must readily identify each paragraph as being part of one of the *basic provisions.* Dividing the contract into the above basic provisions provides the subcontractor a standard method to "interpret, analyze, and evaluate the contract." The subcontractor must evaluate whether his estimate, prior agreements, and understandings meet each provision. If there are discrepancies, he must:

1. Correct the discrepancy *before* signing the contract

2. Refuse to sign the contract and forfeit the job

3. Prepare to abide by the provisions

Following are standard evaluations relative to each basic provision that the subcontractor must check for accuracy *before* signing.

1. Data

All the data listed in the contract must be checked for correctness of:

a. Name of project

b. Division of work (electrical, plumbing, etc.)

c. Address of project (legal description)

d. Legal description (name) of subcontractor. The correct address and legal description are very important if it becomes necessary to place a "claim for lien" on the project. (See Chapter 12.)

e. Date of contract. The correct date is very important if the contract has a time limitation. It also is very important if there is no time limitation in case there is an unusual delay. The owner may sue the contractors for undue delay. The subcontractor may want to sue other contractors for undue delay.

f. Source of funds. Government-funded and many financial institutions identify the project with a number and/or name. Again, this identification must be accurate in case it becomes necessary to place a *claim for lien* on the property.

g. Other data. All other data must similarly be accurate for logical reasons.

2. Mechanics

a. Identification of plans and specifications must be accurate. Each sheet of the plans must be listed by sheet number, original date, and date of latest revision. The date and page No. ————— through No. ————— of the specifications also must be listed.

The subcontractor must check the listing of each sheet of the plans to make sure they are the exact plans the estimate was taken from. He must be particularly alert to revisions. That is, are the revisions listed in the contract for each sheet of the plans the same as those listed on the sheets used to estimate the job?

b. Addenda to the specifications must be checked, both by identifying number and word for word, to make sure they are the exact addenda received prior to completing the estimate. They must subsequently be included in the estimate.

The specification page numbers must also be similarly checked. The subcontractor very frequently is required to initial each sheet of the plans and each page of the specifications.

c. The amount of the contract must obviously be correct. If the contract is a lump sum, the amount must be accurate to the penny, including all alternates. The amount must be broken down, showing the amount of the base bid, plus identification and amount of each alternate included in the contract.

If the contract is based on unit prices, *each* unit price must be identified and the amount listed in the contract.

If the contract is "time and materials," the *exact* hourly labor rate must be listed, along with the percentages of overhead and profit which are to be added to material costs. The source of materials costs should also be listed. That is:

(1) Actual invoices

(2) Accepted pricing service (If so, what column or percentage of discount from list price can be expected?)

(3) One's imagination

Hourly labor rates can be listed as a lump sum: $15.18; or they may be shown broken down:

Journeyman's hourly scale	$10.00
20% Labor burden*	2.00
15% Overhead	1.80
15% Profit	1.38
Total hourly rate	$15.18

If the contract differentiates between apprentices and journeymen, each apprentice scale also must be listed by either lump sum or a breakdown as shown for the journeymen.

*See Chapter 14.

If the contract is for a "cost plus fixed fee" or "cost plus percentage," the definition of costs must be listed in *infinite detail*.

3. Insurance

It is vitally important for the subcontractor to make sure the insurance provisions in the contract are the same as those listed in the specifications. If there is a discrepancy, the discrepancy must be corrected or the contract must indicate which has precedence—the contract or the specifications.

The contract's insurance provision is the only provision for which the subcontractor should rely on outsiders for interpretation, analysis, and evaluation. He should submit the insurance provisions of the contract and the insurance section of the specifications to his insurance agent for interpretation of the coverage and limitations required. The insurance agent should advise the subcontractor if the contract requires insurance coverage and/or limitations that the subcontractor does not normally carry. The subcontractor must keep in mind at all times that the provisions of the contract are for the protection of the buyer, not the seller.

The contract's insurance provisions require the subcontractor to carry insurance for the protection of the owner and/or general contractor. The coverage may or may not also protect the subcontractor to the extent of the exposures relative to that specific job.

The subcontractor should describe to his insurance agent the characteristics of the job and mutually evaluate if there will be any unusual exposures related to the job. Unusual exposures are any exposures not covered by the standard insurance carried by the subcontractor and exposures not encountered on the type of work normally performed by the subcontractor. (See Chapter 18.) The insurance analysis should be done while the estimate is being prepared. The costs of any additional coverage required should be included in the cost of the job.

Some contracts reserve the right of owner or general contractor to procure any or all of the required insurance. The contract may include payment of the insurance procured by the owner or general contractor or may require that the subcontractor pay directly to the insurance carrier, that he be backcharged, or that the amounts be deducted from payouts when they become due. When this provision is included in the contract, the subcontractor must establish as soon as possible whether the owner or general contractor is going to exercise this right, and if so, to what extent. This is necessary so that the subcontractor can cancel the coverages being procured by the owner or general contractor that the subcontractor normally carries to prevent duplication of coverage and premiums. Before any coverage is cancelled, such as workmen's compensation, etc., the subcontractor should obtain a certificate of the coverage from the owner or general contractor. (See Chapter 18.) This should all be performed through the subcontractor's insurance agent.

4. Time Limitations and Requirements

If the contract includes a time limitation, the subcontractor must establish his ability to satisfy the time requirements. Many contracts have unrealistic time requirements. Many contracts include a penalty clause against the subcontractor in the time limitation provision for liquidated damages.

A contract does not have to include a time limitation penalty clause to force the subcontractor to perform his work. All contracts include a recourse provision against delays by the subcontractor. The recourse available to the owner or general contractor allows each to use the necessary forces to meet the time requirements and to backcharge (deduct from monies due) all costs involved.

Many contracts include a requirement that the subcontractor comply with any progress (work) schedule furnished by the owner or general contractor. This is a dangerous provision and should be contested. If the owner or general contractor insists on this provision's remaining in the contract, the subcontractor should insist that the progress (work) schedule be made part of the contract. The word "any," as related to progress (work) schedule, should be removed from the contract.

The subcontractor must realize that to satisfy an unrealistic time schedule he must do one or more of the following: generate additional work hours by working overtime; increase the size of the work force; install work out of normal construction sequence. All these add appreciable costs.

a. Work overtime. It has been factually established that productivity decreases proportionately with the number of days overtime hours are worked. For example, the productivity of a 12-hour day worked repeatedly will deteriorate to 25 percent. Overtime costs the subcontractor the premium time rates, plus the loss of productivity, plus the additional finance to pay the increased payroll.

b. Increase size of work force. Every job has a normal construction sequence for all trades. Within this normal construction sequence there are normal work tasks for each trade. Each normal work task requires a specific number of men. Each job has a normal period when there are a maximum number of work tasks being performed at the same time. This period is called the "peak." That is, it is the time that the maximum number of men are employed. When the time schedule is shorter than the normal time requirements, the "peak" (maximum number of men) is increased by the number of men employed and in length of time; that is, the duration of the "peak" period is increased. An average "peak" period may require 20 men for 2 weeks; a shortened time schedule for the same job may require a "peak" period of 35 men for 6 weeks. There is a saying in construction, "The way to make money on a job is to get in and get out." This saying is true to the extent that the sequence and number of men employed are *controlled*.

The subcontractor is prone to say that if the length of the job is shortened, more money will be made. He will say the shorter the job, the less supervision and other job overhead costs that will be incurred. This is also true to the extent that the sequence and number of men are *controlled*.

The key to a prudent, realistic increase in number of men employed in a longer peak period is *control*. The number of men employed and the length of peak period can be increased to the point that *control* can be maintained. When that point is passed, several things which appreciably increase costs occur:

(1) The ratio of nonproductive labor to productive labor increases.

(2) The quality and effectiveness of supervision decreases.

(3) Productivity decreases.

(4) Logistics of materials and tools is adversely effected, which further deteriorates productivity.

The increased costs resulting from the above *will not* be offset by the savings of nonproductive and job-overhead costs realized by a shorter time schedule.

The subcontractor *must* know at what point the *control* of men employed will start to deteriorate. Any time schedule requiring the peak to be beyond the point of *control* is unrealistic. Additional compensation to the subcontractor should be included in the contract to cover increased costs for an unrealistic time schedule.

    c. Install work out of normal construction sequence. In many accelerated time schedules, the general contractor will schedule the work of other trades out of normal construction sequence. In an accelerated time schedule environment, the subcontractor is prone to schedule his own work out of its normal construction sequence with other trades. Any work installed out of normal construction sequences generates additional costs. These costs are incurred by:

(1) Not being able to conclude work tasks. This causes loose ends to be left to be completed at a later date, on a hand basis as opposed to a production basis. These are called "go backs."

(2) Work tasks of other trades having been concluded ahead of normal construction sequence. Additional work is then required to perform the work task that would normally follow. This is called "being covered up."

If the subcontractor commits himself via contract to an unrealistic or abnormal time schedule, he must either have the costs included in the estimate or be prepared to absorb the cost from the gross profit of the job.

5. Legal Recourse

The legal recourses established in the contract are made available on the most part to the owner and/or general contractor in event of specific failures by the subcontractor. The subcontractor must prevent these recourses from being executed by preventing the failures. To prevent the failures, he must be aware of the legal recourses available to the owner and/or general contractor. When evaluating the contract, the subcontractor should make a list of all these legal recourses and a list of the legal recourses available to him against others. The subcontractor must realize that all the provisions of a contract have, at one time or another, been legally enforced against some other subcontractor and that he is not immune from such enforcement. He must be prepared to prevent or defend himself against all the legal recourses established in the contract.

6. Payment

The payment provisions consist of: amount and method of retention; schedule of payment: method, frequency, and forms to use; final payment requirements, including when payment is to be made.

a. Amount and method of retention. Retention is an amount deducted from each payout and held in escrow until the total contractual commitment has been satisfied. The money that has been retained can be used to satisfy contractual commitments that the subcontractor has failed to perform.

The amount of retention is a percentage of each payout, usually 10 percent. Most contracts permit the retention (upon request by the subcontractor) to be reduced to 50 percent of the original amount after substantial completion. For example, a retention of 10 percent could be reduced to 5 percent after substantial completion. A retention of 15 percent could be reduced to 7½ percent after substantial completion.

There are two types of retention. Assume the retention to be 10 percent.

(1) 10 percent of each payout is withheld as retention

(2) 90 percent of payment for work installed is paid for each payout period (monthly)

Although the amount of money withheld is the same for each type, there is a significant difference. When 10 percent of each payout is withheld, the owner has paid 100 percent for the work installed to date. He therefore accepts and assumes certain responsibilities to the work installed to date. When 90 percent is paid for the work installed to date, the owner has not paid for the work. He has merely made a payment toward the work installed to date. He, therefore, has not in any way accepted any portion of the work installed to date. If a catastrophe should occur, the above could be the determining factor regarding who is responsible for the replacement of the work installed to date. (See Chapter 12.)

There is very little a subcontractor can do to change the contract in his favor. The subcontractor should be aware as to which one of the above types of retention is included in the contract. If the retention is based on 90 percent of the value of the work completed to date, the subcontractor should investigate whether the builders' risk insurance (actually carried by the owner) covers all catastrophes, including acts of God such as floods, etc. If the builders' risk insurance does not include *all* possible catastrophes, or if there is no builders' risk insurance carried on the project, the subcontractor should discuss the potential exposures of that job with his insurance agent. He should think about getting high-deductible catastrophe-type insurance coverage for that project.

b. Schedule of payment: method, frequency, and forms to use. This provision spells out in detail the frequency of payouts and methods of measurements on amount of work installed. It also tells whether materials and equipment on site, not installed, will be included in payouts. This provision is very important because it will have a heavy effect on the cash flow of the job.

If payouts are to include only work installed, and not materials and equipment stored on site, the amount of money required to finance the job will be greater (depending on the ratio of labor to materials and equipment). Some contracts provide for full payment (less retention) for materials and equipment stored on site. Other contracts provide for either no payment or a percentage of the value (less retention) of materials and equipment stored on site.

Final payment requirements and when payment is to be made. This provision details the requirements necessary for final payment. The subcontractor must pursue diligently all the requirements in the contract for final payment. Release of final payment varies with the financial structure of the project. There are financial structures that motivate the owner to finalize the project as soon as possible.

Example No. 1

The interest on construction loans is usually greater than on mortgages. The project must be complete, with all payouts finalized, before the property can be mortgaged. The mortgage is required to pay off the construction loan. The owner is, therefore, motivated to close out the job as soon as possible.

Example No. 2

When there is no construction loan, or if the interest on the construction loan is less than the long-term mortgage, the owner is motivated to delay final payment and release of retention. Public projects that are financed from the sale of bonds are conducive to delay of final payment and release of retention. When the bonds are sold, the cash is invested. The longer payments and retention are delayed, the more income is earned from the short-term investment.

Many contracts indicate specifically the number of days after completion of the job that final payment will be made. When contracts require final payment and release of retention to be made within a specific time after completion, and the owner desires to delay finalizing the project, he will delay final acceptance. The subcontractor must be aware when this situation exists. The final payment and release of retention provision in the contract, plus the financial structure, will clearly show the probable course of action that the owner will take at the project's conclusion. When the circumstances influence the owner to delay final payment and release of retention, the subcontractor must pursue completion and acceptance with *diligence and forcefulness.*

7. Waivers of Lien

The waiver of lien provision is, many times, included in the payment provision. There is one main commitment that the subcontractor must be alert for regarding this provision. The waiver of lien provision in many contracts waives all lien rights to the project, contractually. That is, the contract binds the subcontractor to relinquishing all lien rights to the project at the time the contract becomes effective. He must fully realize that this provision destroys the most valuable, and in many cases the only, recourse available to force payment.

Before a subcontractor signs a contract which includes a provision that waives all lien rights to the project, he must know in detail:

a. The owner's payment behavior

b. Sources of construction funds

c. Finance structure for the project

The owner's payment behavior can be determined from other contractors who have had experience with him, and through the various credit reporting institutions. The subcontractor should *never* assume the payment behavior of an owner to be desirable when the contract includes a provision that relinquishes lien rights to the project. The source of funds should be known to the subcontractor for *all* contracts. It is *imperative* to know that the funds have been arranged for, and from what source, and the structure of payouts, when the contract includes a provision that relinquishes lien rights to the project. (See Chapters 12 and 13.)

8. Changes

This provision details the procedure and type of authorization required for payment of changes (extras). The details of this provision *clearly* indicate that *no* payment for changes will be made unless authorized by the owner or his agent in writing. This provision is one of the few that protect the subcontractor. Unfortunately, many subcontractors violate it.

Virtually no job (of appreciable size) exists that does not have changes. Changes are the greatest source of losses to the subcontractor even though *all* contracts provide a vehicle for payment of all authorized changes (extras). The changes provision also details the gross profit that may be added to the costs of changes and credits. It is imperative for the subcontractor to follow the procedure and abide by the requirements of this provision. The subcontractor must be thoroughly familiar with *all* the details of this provision and forward copies of it to *all* job supervisors. (See Chapter 9.)

9. Guarantees and Warranties

This provision gives the subcontractor certain responsibilities to the portion of the project installed by him for a period of time after completion. Under certain circumstances the implications of this provision could be severe to the subcontractor. All projects are subject to abuse. It is important that clear differentiation be made between what the guarantee covers and abuse and acts of God.

The guarantee period starts on the established date of completion or acceptance. Most owners want to delay this date for two reasons:

a. The guarantee period is prolonged.

b. The period of time that the subcontractor is responsible for mainenance is extended.

The subcontractor must aggressively pursue acceptance (completion) as soon as possible. Most contracts indicate the requirements for acceptance in the "final payment" provision. The subcontractor should satisfy these requirements as soon as possible to permit final payment and release of retentions and to allow the guarantee period to begin.

The guarantee includes all equipment furnished by the subcontractor. The guarantee period by the manufacturer to the subcontractor usually begins on the date of delivery. This causes the guarantee from the manufacturer to the subcontractor to be either expired or nearly expired at the time that the guarantee period for the subcontractor to the owner begins. This causes the subcontractor to be without recourse to the manufacturer for part or all of the guarantee period of the contract. The severity of this exposure depends on the specific equipment and costs involved.

The subcontractor must be aware of exposure to the elements of equipment that he will be required to guarantee after the manufacturer's guarantee expires. Many times, circumstances over which he has no control expose equipment to weather, abuse, etc., that could affect the performance of this equipment during the guarantee period. When this occurs, the subcontractor must, at that time, document the circumstances and, if possible, have the guarantee waived for the equipment involved.

The guarantee and warranty provision of a contract should never be taken lightly. The subcontractor should know exactly what he is contractually committed to guarantee.

10. Governmental Requirements

There are many and varied types of governmental requirements imposed on construction contracts. Many of them are somewhat of an automatic activity which are part of the normal course of doing business as a subcontractor. There are a few, however, that can have an appreciable effect on the project as to costs and mechanical restrictions on the installation of the work.

During the estimating period, the subcontractor should determine what governmental requirements will be imposed on the project and what effect they will have on costs and methods of installation. These costs must be included in the estimate of costs. The subcontractor must be *thoroughly* familiar with all the governmental requirements that apply to the job. He must be prepared to install the work in compliance with them. He must also be prepared to satisfy all governmental requirements not related to installation of the work. If he is not prepared, or does not desire to comply with these requirements, he should *not* sign the contract.

11. Special

The special provisions of a contract are agreements that are pertinent to the specific job. The commitments included in the special provisions are usually job-related as opposed to administrative. Special provisions indicate in detail who is to pay and be responsible for what and to what degree.

The special provisions agreements include the agreements that were negotiated after the bid was submitted. These provisions often also include responsibilities that were not negotiated or previously agreed to. These provisions are where the owner, architect, general contractor, etc., slip into the contract "gotcha"-type responsibilities not necessarily normal to the subcontractor. Many of these gotcha-type responsibilities are potential; therefore, the subcontractor disregards the implications. The subcontractor must assume that the potential gotcha responsibilities *will* occur or knowingly gamble that they will not occur. The gamble must be the result of knowing *all the details,* related costs, and odds of the potential responsibility.

Example

In a subcontract for the electrical work on a building the following special gotcha provision was included:

All work claimed by the electrician shall be part of this contract and the responsibility of the electrical contractor.

The electrical contractor construed this to be relative to composite crews and other insignificant trade-jurisdictional requirements. The general contractor elected to use the permanent boiler and heating system to provide temporary heat. The Steamfitters' Union agreement required a standby steamfitter around the clock. The Electricians' Union agreement required a standby electrician when a standby steamfitter was required. The overtime rate was double time. The cost to the electrical contractor was $2,200 per week for 22 weeks, which totaled $50,000. This represented the entire gross profit for the electrical contract.

When gotcha provisions are included in a contract, they usually are for a specific purpose known to the person who wrote the contract. Before signing the contract, the subcontractor should also know the specific purpose of the gotcha provision.

Special gotcha-type provisions usually cover responsibilities whose costs cannot be estimated. They should not be included in the subcontract. Special provisions should also include a description of work normally related to the specific trade that is *not* included in the contract. The subcontractor should insist that a description of all related work not included be listed in detail in the special provisions section of the contract.

CONCLUSION

All words, phrases, etc., in a contract have a specific meaning and are put there for a specific reason. The subcontractor must *know* all the ramifications of every provision in the contract. He must always be aware of the fact that the contract is written for the protection and advantage of others and that upon signing the contract he must be prepared to abide by all the provisions.

The subcontractor must communicate, via work order, all the administrative and mechanical requirements of the contract to the following persons:

1. Insurance agent

2. Person responsible for invoicing (billing)

3. Person responsible for purchasing

4. Job supervisor

⑨ CHANGES (EXTRAS)

The construction industry is plagued with changes to original contracts. Almost all new construction jobs include changes. This fact is recognized by owners, architects, and engineers. Provisions for recognizing, establishing the cost of, approving, and paying for changes are included in most specifications and in many contracts. The rules for establishing the cost, approving, and paying are set forth by the customer.

The following is an actual sample of a formal set of rules set forth in the general conditions section of specifications. These rules were written by the architect for the benefit and protection of the owner.

GC-123. CHANGES IN THE WORK:

a. The Owner may make changes in the work of the Contractor by making deductions or omissions therefrom, without invalidating the Contract, and without releasing or relieving the Contractor from any guarantee given by him pursuant to the Contract provisions, and without affecting the validity of the guarantee or performance bond, and without relieving or releasing the surety or sureties of said bonds. All such work shall be executed under the conditions of the original contract. The Contractor shall submit to Architects "As Built" or revised drawings clearly showing the revised work, all as required by Section 1-7 of the Technical Specifications.

b. Except in an emergency endangering life or property, no change shall be made by the Contractor unless he has received a prior written order from the Architects, approved on its face by the Owner; and no claim for an adjustment of the contract price or time of performance shall be valid unless so ordered in writing.

c. The Contractor when ordered in writing shall proceed promptly in accordance with said order. The adjustment of the contract price therefore shall be determined by one of the following methods:

1. Method 1—Unit Price and/or Lump Sum Adjustment.

   (a) The Contractor shall submit promptly to the Architects for their approval and for the acceptance of the Owner his written proposal for changes in the work. Such proposals shall be based upon agreed upon unit prices or in their absence on a detailed estimate of the cost of the changed work. If after receipt of the Contractor's proposal, the parties can agree on an equitable lump sum adjustment of the contract price, a change order shall be issued establishing such adjustment.

   (b) Where the change in the work involves items for which agreed upon unit prices have been established and where the net aggregate quantity of such items is in excess of the contract requirements, payment for such items shall be at the established unit prices. Where the net aggregate quantity is less than the contract requirement, the credit shall be the established unit price less 10 percent. Where the "agreed upon unit price" is a unit price bid on estimated quantities, then the Owner may at his option demand a readjustment of such "agreed upon unit price" in any case where the requirements for the particular unit price item exceeds 125 percent of the estimated quantity bid.

(c) Where the change in the work involves items for which agreed upon unit prices have not been established the Contractor's proposal shall be based upon the estimated fair cost of the Contractor's labor, material, equipment, insurance and applicable taxes. In submitting such proposal, the Contractor shall use his ability and buying power to obtain the best possible prices from suppliers of material and equipment and from subcontractors consistent with his general responsibility for the performance and completion of the work. To his end, the Contractor, when submitting such a proposal, shall be deemed to have represented by the submittal that he has used the lowest prices obtained or obtainable by him from his suppliers of material and equipment and from his subcontractors and that he has added nothing to such prices unless in the proposal or billing such contrary fact is specifically set forth. Should the Contractor at any time, without disclosing the fact, add any amount to the bill or proposal of any supplier of material or equipment, or to the bill or proposal of any subcontractor, and should the Owner act on the same or make payment on any work covered by such proposal or billing, then and in that event the Owner shall have the right to recover from the Contractor any such amounts as may have been so added and not disclosed. Such recovery may be made by deducting the undisclosed additions from any payments due the Contractor, or by any and all other means available to the Owner.

(d) To the Contractor's proposal of cost for items of work not covered by agreed upon unit prices shall be added, for additional work ordered, overhead of 10 percent and profit of 10 percent. For deleted work, the price shall be net cost. Where the items of work involved in the change are performed by a subcontractor, the cost thereof shall be similarly established, to which cost, as approved by the Architects, the subcontractor shall add ten percent (10%) for overhead and ten percent (10%) for profit. To this total shall be added only ten percent (10%) to cover both overhead and profit for the General Contractor. If more than one level of subcontractor is involved, the subcontractor performing the work shall add to cost ten percent (10%) for overhead and ten percent (10%) for profit, and each other subcontractor involved and the General Contractor shall add only ten percent (10%) each to cover both overhead and profit. For deductive changes the cost shall be net regardless of the Contractor or subcontractor performing the work.

(e) The overhead and profit changes referred to above shall constitute full reimbursement for all costs of supervision, engineering, field and main office expense, premium on bonds, small tools, and incidental job burdens.

2. Method 2—Cost Plus Fee Adjustment.

(a) Where the change in the work involves items in whole or in part for which a unit price determination cannot be made under Method 1, and where the parties are unable to determine and agree upon an equitable lump sum adjustment of the Contract price for such items, a proceed order shall be issued, and the Contractor shall proceed with the work thereof on a cost plus fee basis. Cost shall mean the Contractor's actual cost of labor, material, equipment, insurance, and applicable taxes, as approved by the Architects. To the Contractor's cost so computed shall be added overhead and profit as defined under Method 1 above.

(b) The Contractor and subcontractors shall keep and present in such form as the Architects may direct a correct accounting of the costs of all labor, material, equipment, insurance, and applicable taxes, together with supporting vouchers, receipts, and payroll records.

(c) Upon completion of the change and determination of the cost plus fee price thereof, a change order shall be issued establishing the adjustment of the contract price.

The above actual sample is quite lengthy and formal. It is rare when a specification does not include provisions and conditions for changes. The provisions and conditions for changes in specifications run from the above lengthy and formal type to a one-paragraph provision. Regardless of the formality and length of the provisions in specifications and/or contracts, they all say the same thing:

1. No claim for charges for changes (extras) will be recognized without WRITTEN APPROVAL PRIOR to the changes being made.

2. Payment will not be made without documentation of the costs.

The architect who wrote the above actual sample in the specifications also required the general contractor and all subcontractors to administer the project by procedures, forms, etc., established by him. The procedure that the architect set up to handle changes in accordance with the specifications is described next.

When it was established that a change was required, the architect would issue a "field order." The field order was a formally printed form. The data on it included the name of the subcontractor to whom the change order was directed, the date, the number of the field order, project name, address, description of change, reason for change, and a place for the signature of the architect's field representative, who was authorized to issue the field order. This type of formal field order would appear to be very acceptable to the subcontractor. A formal order of this type would certainly appear to be sufficient authorization to permit the subcontractor to proceed with the change with confidence that he would be paid for the costs involved plus the 10 percent overhead, plus 10 percent for profit, as spelled out in the sample specifications.

Well, unfortunately there was more to it. The FIELD ORDER included one more *printed* paragraph not mentioned in the above data: "YOU ARE HEREWITH DIRECTED TO PROCEED WITH THE FOLLOWING CHANGES, SUBJECT TO AN EQUITABLE ADJUSTMENT IN THE CONTRACT AMOUNT AND/OR PERFORMANCE TIME."

What this really says is, "We authorize you to go ahead and install the extra work and sometime later we will argue with you as to how much we will pay. If you don't agree with what we want to pay, we will hold your final payment and retention until you do agree to accept what we decide that we want to pay." It is rare when that which is equitable for the architect and owner is also equitable to the subcontractor. In this particular case the architect was not following his own specifications by using the field order with the above qualifications. The subcontractors collectively refused to accept this field order, and so the architect agreed to change the specifications to read, "YOU MAY PROCEED WITH THE FOLLOWING CHANGES. ADJUSTMENT IN THE CONTRACT AMOUNT AND/OR PERFORMANCE TIME WILL BE MADE IN ACCORDANCE WITH CHANGE ORDER PROPOSAL NUMBER —————— DATED ——————."

This qualification was acceptable because it made the change order proposal a part of the field order. The change order proposal included the amount of money for the change as prepared and submitted by the subcontractor. Acceptance of the qualification's wording change, however, was a compromise. The architect should have written the paragraph: "You are authorized to proceed with the following changes. The contract amount shall be increased (decreased) by $————."

The subcontractor must be very alert and make sure that the rules, procedures, customs, and practices established by the customer for changes are not to his detriment.

Changes to a contract can be a liability or an asset, depending on how effectively the contractor handles the changes. Changes should be considered a profit center and treated as such. Properly administered changes are a great source of gross profit. Improperly administered changes are the greatest contributors to job losses. There are three types of changes:

1. Additions to contract

2. Deletions from contract (credit)

3. Relocation of items with no quantity change

There is no such thing as a "no charge" change. There is a cost incurred in establishing that there is no cost involved in the change. The owner should pay for this service.

Additions to the contract should include gross profit. Deletions from the contract should generate gross profit. Credit of bare costs without overhead and profit should only be returned to the owner. The previous actual sample of specifications covering changes provides for this.

Satisfying a change entails administration of the change, performing the additional work involved, or not performing the work deleted. Other than administration, satisfying a change involves the mechanics of installation. Administering the change requires a work order system.

The work order is the first step in converting the costs of jobs to cash. It triggers all the activities required to satisfy the contractor's commitment to the customer. Every company has a work order system. For those contractors who would contradict this statement, their work order system consists of a series of verbal instructions and happenings. The verbal instructions are given to field personnel to perform the work. The accounting system receives news of the job either verbally or as a result of costs appearing in the form of vendor invoices and/or payroll (happenings). Because the work order system triggers the expenditure of money and resources it should be formalized, even in the smallest of companies. The work order system must satisfy the needs of the following functions:

1. Field (installation of work)

2. Changes to contract

3. Purchasing

4. Accounting (job costs, etc.)

5. Billing

The work order system provides a means of communication of the contractual commitment, detailed instructions to the field, purchasing, accounting, etc., and the monetary structure of the job (job budget).

Unrecorded changes represent costs of work installed that are given to the customer at a 100 percent loss. Recorded and properly administered changes represent a source of sales without competition, and therefore should produce a very desirable gross profit.

To enable the field (and all others) to recognize a change, the description of the contractual commitment *must* be *all*-inclusive on the work order. This is necessary to assure that everything included in the contract is satisfied in its normal sequence of construction. What is *not* included in the contract is equally important and must also be included in the work order. This is necessary to assure that work *not* contractually committed is recognized as a change and treated as such.

Changes are the result of one of three situations:

1. Changes necessitated by structural and/or mechanical requirements

2. Owner's desires

3. Code requirements

The first two situations are always the responsibility of the owner. Responsibility for the third could be either the owner's or the contractor's, depending on the contract. Changes necessitated by structural and/or mechanical requirements usually originate in the field at the installation level. Changes resulting from the owner's desires usually originate at contract management level. Changes resulting from code requirements not shown on the drawings or included in the specifications usually originate at the contract management level. This, then, reduces the origin and characteristics of changes to two categories:

1. Field—on-demand changes

2. Office—deliberate changes

Field-type changes originate during construction and must be started and satisfied immediately to satisfy construction sequence on demand.

Office-type changes are introduced well ahead of the time when the change must be performed and, therefore, are deliberate and can be scheduled. These time characteristics establish the method of payment for the changes. Field, on-demand-type changes automatically can only be on a time and material basis. The office-type changes, because of the available time, can be by lump sum or time and material.

Lump sum–type payment obviously requires the sum to be established, accepted, and agreed to by the owner before the changes are performed. This method is more desirable for both the contractor and the owner. A lump sum, accepted and agreed to *prior* to the change being performed, eliminates disputes about costs of the changes. Prices based on unit prices should be avoided whenever possible because it is seldom that unit prices are totally applicable to changes.

One of the most dangerous types of contract to control additions to a contract based on time and material not to exceed a maximum amount. The work under this type of contract is based on time and material. The amount of the contract is the amount of the labor plus material if it turns out to be less than the maximum amount. If it is more than the maximum, the maximum becomes the amount of the contract. The dangerous characteristic of this type of contract is that everyone, including the subcontractor himself, looks upon the job as a straight time-and-material project. When changes are made they are made without identifying the change as a change to the contract. No written authorization is obtained and no documentation of the costs of the change is initiated and developed.

If there had been a possibility at the beginning of the job that the time and material would be less than the maximum, the unrecognized changes would cause the final costs to exceed the maximum. Of course, the amount over the maximum is at the expense of the subcontractor. Changes to contracts based on time and material not to exceed a maximum amount must be treated exactly like a lump-sum contract. All changes to this type of contract must be authorized in writing prior to the change being performed, documented, and immediately billed separately.

The specification and/or contract spells out the rules, procedures, required authorization, and documentation for both of the two categories of changes; field (on-demand) and office (deliberate). The documentation for office (deliberate) changes range from requiring the subcontractor to submit his complete estimate and summary sheet showing all material and labor costs and mark-up, to no documentation at all. The end result of the documentation for office (deliberate) changes is a proposal for the change with a fixed lump-sum amount. The documentation for field (on-demand) changes requires *in all cases* a daily work record, listing the names of the men who worked on the changes and the hours each worked and a description of that which was performed. The daily work record must be signed by an agent of the owner signifying agreement that the indicated number of hours were expended, performing that which was described and authorized. This procedure is a must, whether it is required by the specifications or not. The subcontractor must protect himself from challenges by the owner when it comes time for him to pay for the change. Material charges for field (on-demand) changes can always be authenticated. Labor expended cannot. The end result of documentation for field (on-demand) changes is an invoice to the customer. It is the rare exception when a customer will accept an invoice for a field (on-demand) change based on time and material without proof of the costs. An invoice reading: "Labor and material to install such and such ... $100" will not be accepted.

An invoice reading:

Install such and such.

4 hours labor	$50.00
Material	50.00
Total	$100.00

will not be accepted without proof that 4 hours actually were expended. The proof that the labor was expended is the documentation. This documentation is usually required to be sent with the invoice.

Changes generate hidden costs that are very difficult to recognize and/ or justify. A good example is the additional field personnel time that is required to handle changes. If the change is a field (on-demand) type, it takes time for the supervisor to recognize the requirement as not being included in the contract. It takes time to bring this to the attention of the architect, owner, or whoever else may be responsible. After authorization is confirmed, it takes time to establish and obtain the required material. It takes time to schedule and direct labor to perform the work, and it takes time to initiate and administer the daily documentation that is required (daily work record) to prove the costs involved.

Many owners and architects will argue that these costs are part of the subcontractor's overhead. No field expenditures are part of overhead. All field expenditures are direct costs to the job.

Many times additional work causes other work tasks to be installed out of sequence, causing additional hidden costs to the subcontractor. Changes involving appreciable additional man-hours frequently cause the total number of men on the project to be increased and/or require overtime to be expended on basic contract work. Additions to the contract should always extend the time allotted to complete the contract. Frequently a single subcontractor may be required to install appreciable additional work that has no effect on other trades. This slows the progress of the single contractor while the rest of the project progresses as scheduled. This causes a hardship on the single contractor to keep up. To keep up, the subcontractor experiences additional costs that are difficult to recognize as being caused by the change order.

All the above activities are additional costs to the job that would not have been incurred if the particular change had never occurred. These costs must, therefore, be identified, included, and invoiced as part of the costs of the change. It is difficult, however, to determine exactly how much these costs are for each particular change. Experience has indicated that the nonproductive field labor required to handle a field (on-demand) change is at least 25 percent of the expended productive labor. To recover this, the subcontractor must add 1 hour of supervision labor to each 4 hours of productive labor to all the documentation, daily work records, etc. The other hidden costs must also be charged in the form of additional labor. These charges are many times challenged. The subcontractor should, therefore, avoid whenever possible field (on-demand) or any other type of time-and-material arrangement for payment. The contractor can always realize a greater gross profit from a lump-sum change than from a time-and-material change.

Field (on demand) changes require field personnel to:

1. Recognize that the work being requested or required is not included in the contract and that it therefore constitutes a change.

2. Obtain proper authorization by a person duly authorized to approve changes.

3. Initiate and record approved documentation of labor expended and material installed.

The above require field personnel to perform administrative activities for which they do not appreciate the need and of which they are not capable.

Analysis shows that a job supervisor who is skilled in directing the work is usually not capable of performing administrative activities effectively. Conversely, a job supervisor who is skilled at performing administrative activities effectively is often not capable of directing the work proficiently. Job supervisors who are capable job administrators, but who do not direct the work effectively, are known as "profit killers." To the contractor they appear to be effective supervisors because their paperwork is excellent. When the costs versus gross profit become known to the contractor, he refuses to accept the reality that he has a man who sounds and looks good, but cannot produce a profit. The job supervisor who does not perform the paperwork efficiently, but produces a desirable gross profit, looks bad and aggravates the contractor. Gross profit is the objective, *not* good paperwork. Adequate paperwork is a necessary function to realize the objective; it is *not* the objective. Because the job supervisor who can produce a desirable gross profit usually is deficient in administration (paperwork) activities, it would be wise to minimize his required paperwork.

Effective administration of changes is a must, but it involves paperwork. Because of this, the job supervisor should *not* be required to start the paperwork required to authorize and document changes. The job supervisor must, however, recognize and establish that the work involved is not part of the contract and, therefore, is a change. The basic work order should enable the job supervisor to know what is part of the contract and what is not part of the contract. After recognizing that the work is not part of the contract, the job supervisor's responsibility should be limited to informing the owner or his representative that the work involved is not part of the contract; therefore, he cannot install it without authorization from the subcontractor (his employer). This requires the *owner* or his representative to contact the subcontractor and authorize him to proceed with the change. This requires the subcontractor to issue a work order covering the change. The supervisor receives his authority from the subcontractor (his employer). This is a simple way to prevent changes from being installed without payment. The discipline of the supervisor is reduced to one requirement:

INSTALL ONLY THE WORK AUTHORIZED BY A WORK ORDER ISSUED BY HIS EMPLOYER.

Authorization for a change is the key to payment for extras.

As listed before, there are three types of changes:

1. Additions to the contract

2. Deletions from the contract

3. Relocation of items with no quantity change

Written authorization is vital for all types of changes.

Recognition by the owner that the change involved constitutes an addition to the contract is necessary to assure payment for the change. Written authorization for a change that either deletes something that was included in the contract to be installed and/or a substitution, happening, or anything else that generates a credit to the contract is very important. If something is deleted, or a substitution is made without authorization by the owner, the subcontractor can be forced to install that which was deleted or substituted. Without authorization for a deletion or substitution the owner can require the subcontractor to install that which was contracted for as per the specifications and location shown on the plan. Installing an item in a different location requiring no additional cost or credit without written authorization is dangerous. The owner can require the item to be installed in the location shown on the plan after the job is completed at the expense of the subcontractor when written authorization has not been obtained.

A good example of the dangers involved is this true story of an electrical contractor's experience:

The project consisted of 78 five-room town houses, each with a basement. The plans showed a ceiling outlet with a porcelain socket and wall switch at the top of the stairs to the basement. Adjacent and back-to-back to the stairs was a closet. There was no light shown in the closet.

The electrical code required a light in the closet, but did not require the light at the top of the basement stairs.

The owner was made aware of this by the electrician before the rough work on the first town house was started. He immediately said, "Let's make a trade. Let's install the ceiling outlet that is shown to be installed at the top of the stairs 2 feet over in the closet. You can put in a pull-chain porcelain socket without a switch."

The electrician felt that was a good trade because it would require less material and one less outlet. And so the 78 town houses were installed with no light at the top of the basement stairs but with one in the closet.

The project was financed by the FHA. During final inspection it was noted that there was no light at the top of the basement stairs as was shown on the plan and which was a requirement of the FHA.

The electrical contractor was confronted with the logical question: Why was the light and switch at the top of the stairs left out when it plainly showed them on the plan?

After asking the same question of his electrician he found out about the super trade that had been made. The owner was confronted with the sad news and as a compromise paid for the light in the closet at a price based on new construction. The electrical contractor installed at his own expense, based on remodeling costs, 78 ceiling outlets and wall switches at the top of the stairs as was originally shown on the plans.

If the owner had been required to authorize in writing the deletion of the ceiling light and wall switch the problem would have been his, not the electrical contractor's.

Proper authorization must be given not only in writing, but also by a person in a position to authorize changes. Accepting the signature of a project superintendent or manager has cost many subcontractors untold dollars. The owner has the authority to order changes to the contract. He may delegate this authority to others. This authorization must *also* be in writing. Before accepting authorization from anyone other than the owner, the subcontractor must be sure that the person authorizing the change is in a position to do so. It would be wise at the beginning of each project to obtain over the owner's signature a list of the names of those who have the authority to authorize changes to the contract. When this is done the owner must honor the signatures of those so authorized.

The best authorization for a change to a contract is a purchase order issued by the owner prior to the change being made, which includes a description of the change with the price.

The subcontractor is always committed in writing (via contract) to install that which has been specified in the quantities and locations shown on the plans. Any and all changes to these commitments must be authorized in writing before the change is made.

If the subcontractor issues a work order directing the installation of additional work without following through by obtaining proper authorization for this change, and subsequently fails to obtain payment, it is he who failed, and not the field personnel. If the subcontractor is going to give work away, he should be selfish and retain the thrill for himself. The job supervisor does not get a thrill from giving his boss's money away.

Most lending institution payout forms provide a means for the contractor to include the amounts of the changes. If the lending institution is made aware that changes exist, they will assist in assuring payment prior to closing the loan. When construction loans are established, contingencies are provided for. If changes are allowed to lay uninvoiced, the source of funds is depleted, requiring the owner to provide the money from other nonexistent sources. When this occurs, collecting for changes becomes very difficult and, in many cases, impossible.

After the change has been invoiced and included in the payout request, collection must be pursued aggressively. The administration of changes is not over until the money involved is in the subcontractor's bank. The ability to collect for changes, even though they have been officially approved, documented, etc., deteriorates every day the changes continue to be unpaid. (See Chapter 13, section on Collections.)

There are definite steps required of the subcontractor in order that he be paid for changes:

1. He must recognize that the work requested is not part of the contract.

2. He should obtain written authorization from the owner to install or delete the work involved. The only foolproof type of authorization is a purchase order or directive to proceed written on the owner's letterhead and signed by him.

3. The terms of payment and amount *must* be established *prior* to, and be a part of, the purchase order or letter to proceed.

4. If payment is to be based on time and material, means to establish and document the hours expended and material installed must be initiated and approved by the owner or his *authorized* representative. This documentation becomes an integral part of the invoice.

5. The subcontractor must prepare an invoice to match the purchase order or letter of direction. The price is based on lump sum, as per purchase order, letter of direction, or if on a time and material basis, the documentation.

6. An invoice should be included with the *next* payout request. If possible, the amount of the invoice should be made part of the payout request, thus changing the contract amount.

Changes *must be invoiced* as soon as possible. *Never, never* should the subcontractor wait until the end of the job to invoice changes.

Effective handling of changes and extras is one of the eight basic requirements for a successful subcontracting business.

10 MATERIALS AND TOOLS MANAGEMENT

For most trades, materials and tools represent an appreciable portion of the total costs of a job. For some trades, the costs of materials and tools equal, and frequently exceed, the cost of labor. Labor is totally dependent on materials and tools. As a soldier in combat is powerless without guns and ammunition, so too the construction worker cannot work without materials and tools. No matter what the ratio of materials is to labor, labor is still dependent on materials and tools. If materials and tools represent only 10 percent of the total cost, labor is still dependent on materials and tools—without them, nothing happens. This dependence makes materials and tools pretty important. They are, however, of no value to the construction worker unless they are in the right place at the right time and in the right quantities. The process of doing this is called "materials and tools management."

Management of materials and tools involves several major functions. These include purchasing, warehousing (shop inventory), distribution, job storage, care and maintenance of tools, and materials management administration. This chapter will cover each of these separately.

PURCHASING

Most purchases by the subcontractor are for materials and equipment to be installed on the job and for tools. Purchases of services of other contractors are rare. These are discussed in Chapter 19. The following pertains to purchasing material and equipment to be installed on jobs, and tools, only.

The purchasing process is divided into two categories: "buying" and "delivery." Buying consists of major (one-time) purchases and day-to-day buying of sundry items. Delivery includes:

1. Establishing delivery dates.

2. Establishing method of delivery (vendor's truck, contractor's truck, air freight, etc.).

3. Establishing type of packaging (cartons, pallets, etc.).

4. Establishing methods of receiving; that is, how are items going to be handled when received? By hand? Mechanically?

5. Expediting.

6. Back-order follow-up.

A source of profit is the savings generated by buying the required material and equipment for less than was estimated. This activity makes purchasing a profit center. Buying at the lowest possible price is achieved by:

1. Research of equal substitutes

2. Pursuing competitive quotations

3. Prudent analysis of quotations

4. Effective negotiation of purchases

The above applies to both major (one-time) purchases and day-to-day (sundry) purchases.

Major (one-time) purchases include all the major items required for the job. There are two types:

1. Items in known and fixed amounts

2. Items in approximate amounts

For the known- and fixed-amount items, the purchase is for so many widgets for so many dollars to be delivered at a predetermined time in a specified manner. For example, the purchase order would state, "183 Type A fixtures," or "92 toilets," or "143 Type B air diffusers," or "1 switchboard," or "1 boiler," or "1 chiller." For approximate amount items the purchase is based on price per unit for an approximate number of units to be released for delivery in many and various order sizes throughout the job. For example, the purchase order would merely state: "conduit," or "pipe," or "paint," or "concrete."

As many items as possible should be purchased under the major-purchase activity. There is less purchasing power, negotiating, and subsequent price reduction available by the day-to-day procedure. For example, assume a plumbing contractor needs 10,000 feet of ½-in. water pipe for a job. He can get a better price by buying the 10,000 feet on a single purchase order to be released for delivery throughout the job than by buying the 10,000 feet on many purchases each time a delivery is required.

Day-to-day purchases should be confined to those items that cannot be bought ahead of time for later release and amounts that do not justify purchasing in advance.

Purchase Orders

Every company must have a purchase order system. It should allow *no* purchase to be made without issuing a purchase order. The purchase order system will accomplish the following:

1. Back-order control

2. Effective cost control

3. Costs of all materials being included in invoices to customers

4. Preventing overbuying

5. Preventing underbuying

6. Delivery control

7. Effective vendor-invoice processing

8. Job inventory control

The basis of the purchase order system is the purchase order form. This form should contain the following information:

ABC CONSTRUCTION CO.		
Job Name_____ Purchase Order No._____		
Job Address_____ Date_____		
Vendor's Name _____		
Delivery Instruction_____		
Quantity	Description of Item	Price

The above is a standard heading for a purchase order form. The purchase order may contain additional information as may be required by the individual subcontractor. Additional information could include:

   Name of field person requesting the material

   Date and time order was placed at supply house

   Name of person at supply house who took the order

Some contractors have elaborate legal clauses as a part of their purchase orders. These mean nothing for most purchases, except for services, which include both labor and material. (See Chapter 19.)

Written confirmation of acceptance by the vendor should be obtained for all major (one-time) purchases. Day-to-day purchases rarely need confirmation. In most cases, when the order is phoned to the vendor it is meaningless to send the vendor a copy of the order. Research shows that he does nothing with it.

Purchase orders should be identified by numbers. A purchase order numbering system should be used. Its purpose is to assure that all costs are charged to the proper job or overhead expense account, to prevent duplicate payment for the same items, and to provide a means for easy reference. To enable the costs for each purchase order to be charged to the correct job or expense account, the purchase order number should contain the job or expense-account number. To prevent duplicate payments, each purchase order must be numbered differently. A single job may have many separate purchase orders. To use the job number only as the purchase order number would cause all purchase orders to have the same number with no means of identifying one from another. To prevent this, an additional set of numbers must be used. For example, assume the job number is 126. The first purchase order number for that job could be 126-1; the second, 126-2; the third, 126-3; and so on. Another effective numbering system is to prenumber purchase order forms, using the numbers 0001 through 9999. For each order written, the job number would be written in as the prefix—for example, #126-0001. This latter system is easier. There is no need for the last group of digits to be related to the job because the first group is the job number. The last group identifies the individual purchase order from all others. The first method requires a record of numbers for each job; the second method eliminates this need.

Back Orders

Back orders are common, and if not properly policed and expedited, they can cause costly delays in installing the work. A system must be developed by the subcontractor that will notify him immediately when a back order exists. It also will initiate expediting of the back-ordered item, including possible substitution or canceling and placing an order for the item elsewhere. Effective vendor invoice administration will prevent duplicate payment of items originally back-ordered. (See Vendor Invoice Administration, later in this chapter.)

Preparing for the Major Purchases

Effective preparation for the major purchases includes authenticating the quantities. Items purchased as one-time, or major, purchases are usually custom-built for the job or are catalog items that will be manufactured on order. In either case, the time to manufacture, and deliver, requires what is called, "manufacturer's lead time." The quantities ordered for this type of item *must* be accurate to the single unit. The estimate will indicate the quantities established by the estimator's takeoff. The takeoff should never be used to establish quantities for items with a long manufacturer's lead time. The unit cost for these items usually keeps the purchaser from overbuying. With the long lead time, the number of units purchased must not be less than needed. The length of the lead time and the unit cost of the item determine the trouble the purchaser should go to in ordering the correct amount.

To utilize the purchasing function as a profit center, less costly, but equal, substitutions should be researched. It must be remembered that *all* substitutions *must* be submitted and approved *prior* to committal to purchase. A substitution should never be made without prior approval. Because of this, the savings generated by the substitution must be great enough to allow a credit to the customer with enough left to make the substitution profitable to the contractor. The credit to the customer is usually necessary to get him to accept the substitution.

Potential substitutions should be carefully examined to see if they will give a worthwhile savings. Savings can many times be developed on custom-built equipment by prudent internal design changes (which must be approved prior to purchase).

All purchased items must meet all applicable codes. To assure this, the purchase order should be worded to say that the purchase is based on all items meeting all applicable codes; the wording should also put the responsibility for all necessary approvals from inspection bureaus on the supplier and/or manufacturer.

Most job specifications require submittal and approval of catalog cuts and/or shop drawings for certain materials and equipment. The purchase order covering these items should be worded to state that it is good only if the items are as specified and approved. Custom and practice require the contractor to receive, submit, and obtain approval of manufacturers' catalog cuts and shop drawings. The catalog cuts and shop drawings *must not* be sent for approval without close inspection by the subcontractor. This inspection is necessary to assure the contractor that the items are going to be manufactured in the best way for ease of installation.

Example

Large equipment must be manufactured and shipped in sections whereby the size and weight of each can be economically received and set in place. Only the contractor is concerned with this requirement. The owner is concerned only with that which he is ultimately buying, installed. This involves installation engineering and the field conditions. The person developing and administering the purchase must have a close connection and/or be involved with both.

The activity of ordering items to be delivered in specific sections, sizes, weights, packages, etc., affects the costs of receiving and installing. This is another area that will generate profits. The purpose of purchasing should *not* be to merely buy and cause delivery of materials, equipment, and tools to the job to satisfy the contractor's responsibility. The purpose of the purchasing function should be to buy all required items at the lowest possible price and to design and schedule delivery in a manner that will generate the least possible installation and delivery costs. Under this policy, purchasing becomes a profit center.

WAREHOUSING (SHOP INVENTORY)

There are three ways to look at shop inventory of materials:

1. Stock all staple items (items not custom to specific jobs) in the contractor's warehouse.

2. Stock nothing.

3. Stock a few hard-to-get staple items.

The correctness of these ideas has generated many pleasant discussions among contractors for years. Obviously none of them is wrong. What is wrong for some subcontractors may be right for others. There are, however, certain facts that should be recognized when maintaining a stock. Costs to keep stock should be established. Stock comes from direct purchase or from items returned from completed jobs.

Items purchased directly require labor to:

1. Remove the items from the shipping cartons and place them on the warehouse shelves.

2. Assemble the items and pack them for delivery.

3. Deliver the items to the job on the contractor's truck.

4. Unload the items at the job site.

5. Price and extend the items on a material requisition form.

Items returned from completed jobs require labor for the above plus:

1. Deliver the items from the job to the contractor's warehouse.

2. Sort, separate, and shelve the items.

For the items returned from completed jobs, the cost of handling, storing, administration, and delivery to other jobs very frequently exceeds the cost of the item. The handling, storing, administration, and delivery of both direct-purchase items and items returned from completed jobs often requires one or, if the volume is great, two additional overhead personnel.

The following are the steps involved in satisfying an order from the field when the subcontractor has a shop inventory:

1. An order is placed from a job to the buyer for five widgets.

2. The buyer, being familiar with his stock, *thinks* he has three in stock.

3. He leaves his desk, goes to the warehouse and determines factually that he indeed has three widgets in stock.

4. He returns to his desk and initiates two orders:

   a. A material requisition order for three widgets from stock

   b. A purchase order to a supply house for two widgets

5. The three widgets are packed and delivered to the job on the contractor's truck.

6. The buyer places the order for the two widgets with a supply house by phone. The order is delivered to the job on the supplier's truck.

7. The buyer obtains the unit price of the widget from a trade price publication and prices the material requisition. He then multiplies the unit price by three.

8. The invoice is received from the supply house listing the two widgets.

9. The invoice is approved for payment (see section on Vendor Invoice Administration, p. 172).

Following are the steps involved in satisfying the same order as above when the subcontractor has no shop inventory.

1. An order is placed from a job to the buyer for five widgets.

2. The buyer places the order for the five widgets with a supply house for delivery to the job on the supplier's truck. truck.

3. The supply house delivers the five widgets to the job.

4. The invoice is received from the supply house, listing the five widgets.

5. The invoice is approved for payment (see section on Vendor Invoice Administration, p. 172).

The main difference between the two examples is:

1. Additional time for the first example is required to:

   a. Check inventory.

   b. Initiate two orders in lieu of one.

   c. Price and extend the material requisition.

   d. Assemble, pack, and deliver by the subcontractor.

2. Additional cost is incurred by:

   a. Delivery cost (truck and driver).

   b. Warehouse personnel and upkeep costs.

   c. Additional administration of the material requisition.

It is impossible to avoid filling the order from two sources unless no stock is returned to the warehouse from completed jobs. This, unfortunately, is an appreciable source of warehouse stock. It also is the reason many subcontractors have a shop inventory. If no stock were returned from completed jobs, many subcontractors would be without justification for a shop inventory.

It is a fallacy to justify the delivery costs by saying, "We have to have a delivery truck available to go to the jobs anyway to deliver tools." If an accurate analysis is made by the subcontractor, it would show his tool delivery needs represent less than 20 percent of the total delivery trips. Most contractors, no matter how small, who maintain a warehouse with material stock, have a truck with driver on the street full time. The contractor may also have a full-time buyer. For the small contractor, if no stock were maintained in the warehouse, perhaps the buyer could also be the truck driver, with 80 percent less delivery trips. For the larger contractor, fewer trips, less trucks, and/or no warehouse personnel are required when no stock is maintained in the warehouse. A warehouse is necessary for tools and as a holding point to store items received before needed, for security, and/or for storage space if it is not available at the job site.

A subcontractor can be more effective and efficient at contracting if he confines all his effort to contracting. When a subcontractor maintains a stock in a warehouse, he has diluted his efforts of contracting with those of the supplier. How many suppliers also are contractors? This combination is almost nonexistent. There must be a reason.

There are some subcontractors, however, whose type of work and mix of jobs require a warehouse with shop inventory. Some of the requirements that justify a shop inventory are:

1. The geographic market area of the subcontractor is remote to a supply house with adequate stock.

2. The delivery capabilities of the supply houses cannot meet the needs of the types of jobs. If the subcontractor's mix of jobs includes an appreciable number of small jobs, requiring delivery by 8 A.M. and/or to the job prior to the tradesmen being there, delivery by a supply house would not be dependable or feasible.

3. Many of the items required by some subcontractors are of a special nature and are not stocked by local supply houses and/ or the lead time required for delivery is great. If items of this nature are frequently used, shop inventory is necessary.

4. When the quantities required for each delivery are too small to justify the supply house making delivery and/or administering a separate invoice, the subcontractor must warehouse a shop inventory and make his own deliveries.

Subcontractors who confine the majority of their work to small, short jobs must maintain a shop inventory and make their own deliveries to hold down the initial costs of the material and the costs of the deliveries and to make sure the deliveries are timely.

The savings obtained by buying in huge quantities as opposed to normal quantities are not that great. The costs of handling the material into the subcontractor's warehouse, storing, handling, interest on the money, and tying up needed capital usually is as great, or greater, than any savings on volume buying.

For the small-job contractor there are other considerations. For small orders a premium price usually is paid for the material even if the material is delivered by the subcontractor. For the subcontractor whose type and size of jobs are such that the jobs can be supplied directly from the supply house, a warehouse with a shop inventory is an expensive, ineffective luxury. For the subcontractor whose jobs are small and/or the type of material used requires a long lead delivery time, a warehouse with a shop inventory is necessary and justified.

Remember, effective delivery capability is an absolute necessity if a shop inventory is maintained.

DISTRIBUTION

Remember, two of the basic requirements of materials and tool management are that the materials and tools must be at the right place at the right time. This requires their adequate and timely distribution. Distribution starts with determining what is required, and when. After this is done the materials and/or tools must be assembled and scheduled for delivery.

Distribution includes two or three stages, either together or separate, beginning with the subcontractor's initial source of the material and/or tools. This source is either a supply house or a manufacturer's plant. The final destination is the point where each item of material is to be installed. Between the initial source and the final destination are points of distribution. The characteristics of the job or work task and the type of work determine the flow and number of distribution points.

Figure 1 shows some of the various sequences of material flow from initial source to final destination.

As Figure 1 shows, some sequences include only one, some two, and some three stages. Because materials and tools are so important, the distribution should not be allowed to just happen. The subcontractor should know exactly what method of distribution is being used, and the method should be identifiable.

Each of the distribution sequences in Figure 1 applies to certain types and sizes of jobs. If the subcontractor's job mix runs from service calls to medium-size jobs to large jobs, he will be using all the sequences. If the mix is confined to one type and size of job, perhaps only one will be used.

MATERIAL FLOW DIAGRAM

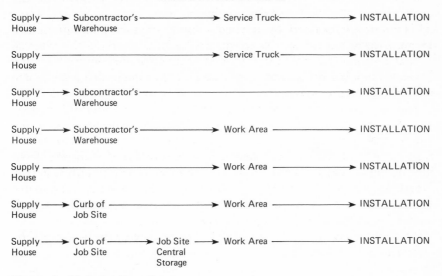

Figure 1 Material flow diagram.

NOTE: A subcontractor whose jobs are all small would probably use one or all of the first four sequences. He would never use the last one. Conversely, a subcontractor who was doing only large jobs would never use the first three. He would most likely use the last three.

The subcontractor should be aware of all the various sequences and use the most applicable ones for particular jobs or groups of jobs.

JOB STORAGE

The effectiveness of job storage and handling of materials and tools depends upon the methods used and facilities provided by the subcontractor. Custom and practice in the construction industry has established four methods of on-the-job materials and tool handling and storage. These are identified as the "corner method," the "gunny sack method," the "trunk method," and the "shanty or trailer method."

Corner Method

The corner method is simple, although very costly. When the material is shipped to the job, the journeyman in charge selects a convenient corner that will not affect other trades. He then proceeds to pile the material in the selected corner, keeping the items segregated in their original cartons and paper or plastic bags. Of course, this segregation lasts only a few hours, for as the bags and cartons break, the pieces of material soon become one large pile of scrap. At this stage the journeyman no longer knows what he has on the job or where to find it.

The following is an old familiar story that describes this situation:

While the job is being estimated, care is taken to note that a particular item will be required. When the job is awarded and the work order and initial materials list are written, further care is taken to assure that this particular item is delivered to the job. The materials and tools are delivered to the job and the tradesman assigned and scheduled. The subcontractor meets the journeyman on the job and explains the installation to him in detail. The subcontractor leaves the job feeling confident that everything is rosy and that this job will produce a profit. After a few hours of work the journeyman reaches the point where the particular item of material is needed. Being one of the subcontractor's better men, and very conscientious, he does not immediately initiate a search into the pile of material in the corner. He still has a copy of the original list of material shipped to the job, and so he looks on this list to determine if the boss has, as usual, forgotten the item. Well, for once he gives the boss credit, for there it is on the list. He now launches the search; confident that somewhere in that pile it is there. After considerable wasted time he decides that whoever packed the order failed to include it, and so he calls the subcontractor and informs him that the particular item is not there. The subcontractor is fit to be tied because he knew that it was included in the estimate, work order, and initial list of material. The subcontractor's stock man or supply house is called in and the roof proceeds to be raised. The subcontractor is promptly told that the item was indeed shipped because the man being verbally beaten states he personally packed the order. The subcontractor cools down a bit and realizes that the problem isn't who is to blame, but "to get another one to the job" as fast as possible, so off goes the particular item on another order. While all this was going on the journeyman was instructed to go for coffee until the particular item arrived.

What happened to the original particular item? Well, many things could have happened to it. Chances are when the job was over and the leftover material picked up, it would turn up. Or another tradesman could have been passing the corner being used for material storage and spotted the particular item and immediately found a need for it in his basement. It doesn't really make any difference what happened to it. What really matters is that the journeyman could not lay his hands on it when he needed it, and by not having it the work was stopped. In this case the subcontractor was fortunate that someone did not take a liking to the tools stored in the corner.

Gunny Sack Method

The gunny sack method is similar to the corner method except that the items of material are shoveled into the gunny sack at night and spread out on the floor during the day. This method has its advantages over the corner method in that no effort whatever is exerted to segregate the material in cartons or bags. By spreading all the material out on the floor in one layer, one could probably find what is needed a little sooner than searching through bags or cartons; that is, if enough floor space is available.

It is obvious that neither the corner nor gunny sack method provides any security.

Trunk Method

The trunk method repeats the inefficiencies generated by the corner and gunny sack methods, plus a few more. With it, everything is piled one on top of the other in a trunk-type storage box. Consequently, the journeyman must take everything out of the box each morning and spread it out on the floor as in the gunny sack method and then dump it back in at night. After one day of this, it would be wise to provide a scoop shovel, for by the second day the journeyman is no longer handling items of material but just a mixed-up box of junk.

This type of storage box can never be used to any degree of success, for its size is always limited to two factors: it must always be small enough to pass through doorways and it must be at least light enough for four men to carry. When any storage box is limited in size, then the items must be packed one on top of another, thereby permitting no segregation. Adequate storage *must* provide segregation of the materials with security for both materials and tools.

Storage boxes are a necessity during the last stage of distribution at the work area. These boxes must, however, be large enough to provide complete segregation of the various items of material, plus security. Heavy-duty casters can help eliminate the problem of weight when the box becomes too heavy for one or two men to move. Casters, unfortunately, decrease the security of the box. The box can be long and high, but must be limited in width to that of a doorway. The familiar piano box has proven to be applicable when large enough to provide segregation by shelves and bins inside.

Many types of boxes are available to the subcontractor. The criteria for selecting or designing a storage box should be segregation, volume (that is, is it large enough to be worth while?), and security.

Shanty or Trailer Method

The shanty or trailer method is only effective as central storage on larger jobs. As was pointed out under distribution, the last stage of storage must be at the work area. Use of a shanty or trailer as the last stage, or the last point of storage prior to installation, is very ineffective and becomes the most costly method of storing materials and tools. The tradesmen cannot be allowed to leave their work area and go to a shanty or trailer on a demand basis for their material and tools. Lack of control of the workmen, plus the costs of walking, cannot be accepted.

When the job is large enough to require a shanty or trailer for materials and tool storage, then additional storage depots with adequate facilities must be provided at the various work areas. No tradesman should have to walk farther than 200 feet, or one story, for his materials and tools.

When a shanty or trailer is used as central storage, it must have adequate shelves and bins. The corner or gunny sack method must never be used in the shanty or trailer. This same requirement holds true for trucks (such as a service truck) when they are used for material storage. Trucks, too, need shelves and bins to segregate the material.

No matter what sequence of distribution is used, adequate storage facilities must be provided at each point of distribution within the sequence. The sequence, number, and types of distribution points are determined by the size and type of job. The type and size of storage facilities are determined by the method and type of distribution. Both must be by thoughtful design. No method, type, or sequence of distribution and storage should be allowed to just happen. The subcontractor must *cause* it to happen in the most effective manner and with the most applicable storage facilities.

CARE AND MAINTENANCE OF TOOLS

Except for those trades employing operating engineers and those which use large engine-driven equipment, the care and maintenance of tools and equipment is probably the most neglected important activity of the construction business. Remember, tools and equipment to the construction worker are like guns and tanks to the combat soldier. Without guns, tanks, etc., the combat soldier cannot fight, and without tools and equipment the construction worker cannot work.

The characteristics of the construction industry, plus the human element—that is, out of sight, out of mind—makes it very conducive for the subcontractor to grossly neglect the care and maintenance of tools and equipment. Tools are transferred from job to job and seldom come home. This makes it difficult to maintain and repair the tools. The costs incurred by lost time that are caused by poorly maintained tools are hard to identify. That is, when a tradesman works with a dull drill or spends time to makeshift a repair or to get the equipment to run, no bells ring and no red flags go up. This type of lost time is identified as poor productivity.

There is no magic solution or suggested method for effective care and maintenance of tools and equipment. Each subcontractor must develop his own system, methods, administration, or whatever is required to keep his tools and equipment in good, sharp, working order. About the only thing that can be done by someone outside the subcontracting firm is to impress upon the subcontractor not how much he is going to make from good care and maintenance of his tools and equipment, but how much he is going to lose by allowing his tradesmen to work with poorly maintained tools and equipment.

Tools and equipment must be cleaned, sharpened, tuned, lubricated, and worn parts replaced on a regular, repetitive basis. And they must be replaced when they become obsolete and/or irreparable. Irreparable would be taken to mean both mechanically and monetarily. Tools reach a point when the cost to repair and keep them operable exceeds replacement costs.

An effective tool and equipment care and maintenance program will include a system to: sharpen all tools periodically; lubricate as required on a regular, repetitive basis; clean, paint, and inspect tools; replace worn parts periodically; immediately repair a tool when it becomes inoperable; and replace a tool when it becomes obsolete or irreparable. The subcontractor must develop systems and methods to cause this to happen.

MATERIALS MANAGEMENT ADMINISTRATION

Materials and tool management involves six steps: procurement, distribution (delivery), storage, submitting and obtaining approval of what is to be installed, approval for payment of the costs involved, and preparation of the costs for distribution to the various job records. Materials management administration involves the last three steps.

Submitting and obtaining approval of that which is to be installed involves securing required manufacturers' catalog cuts and shop drawings, submitting the cuts and/or shop drawings for approval, and obtaining the approval. Approval for payment of the costs involved and preparation of the costs for distribution to the various jobs are activities of vendor invoice administration.

VENDOR INVOICE ADMINISTRATION

Vendor invoice administration is a very necessary function of the total business endeavor. It also is a profit center. The money recovered from the suppliers for items not shipped, but invoiced, correction of arithmetical errors, duplicate billing, and improper prices is appreciable. The recovery of this money is the same as earning it. This is especially true for the mechanical subcontractor.

This simple function involves these activities:

1. Determining whether the invoice is for costs to be charged to a job or to an overhead expense account.

2. Determining what job the costs are to be charged to if the invoice covers a job cost.

3. Determining what overhead expense account the costs are to be charged to if the invoice covers an overhead expense cost.

4. Determining whether the costs are for material or are miscellaneous direct job costs if the invoice covers a job cost.

5. Checking and making sure that all items listed on the invoice have been received. These include services or products not covered by a shipping ticket. The person who orders and/or receives these products or services must do the checking.

6. Checking the multiplication and addition shown on the invoice.

7. Checking whether the prices shown on the invoice are correct and/or match the purchase order.

8. Initiating a back charge to the vendor in the amount of discrepancies determined by the above activities.

9. Recording on the purchase order each item that was received and invoiced.

10. After *all* the above activities are completed, the invoice can be approved for payment.

After the invoice is approved for payment, its payable cycle must be established. The payable cycle would be immediately, 15 days, 30 days, or 60 days.

The vendor invoice activities must be satisfied as follows:

Activities No. 1, No. 2, and No. 3

These must be done by a person who accurately knows the job that needed the purchase or the particular use other than on a job. If the item of service was for a job, that job's identification must be shown on the invoice. The same should be done for a product or service for other than a job. The amounts of these invoices are then charged to overhead accounts for measurement, capitalization, etc., of overhead expenditures. The invoice must be checked to be sure it is for the proper company. Many times invoices are sent to the wrong company.

Activity No. 4

If the invoice is for a product or service required on a job, it must be decided whether the product or service is to be measured for cost control as "material" or "miscellaneous direct job costs." This is then shown on the invoice. This decision must be made by a person who accurately knows where the invoiced products or services will be used.

Activity No. 5

This is accomplished by:

1. Matching the invoice with the shipping ticket. For material shipped to the job the shipping ticket *must* be forwarded to the office. If any item shown on the shipping ticket was not received, the job supervisor should indicate that the item was not received. For items shipped to the subcontractor's warehouse or office, the shipping ticket is available there.

2. For invoices covering products or services, wherein shipping tickets are not used, the actual person receiving the product or service must authenticate receipt of that which is being invoiced.

Activity No. 6

This requires actual duplication of the multiplying and additions necessary to compute the total of the invoice.

Activity No. 7

When a purchase order system is being used, many times the prices are shown for each item on the purchase order. To determine if the prices are correct, the invoice prices should be matched with the prices on the purchase order. When the prices are not shown on the purchase order, they must be checked by a person who accurately knows prices and/or agreed-to price schedules.

Activity No. 8

This corrects discrepancies discovered in the invoice by the above activities. Correction of the invoice should not be attempted. Rather, a back charge should be issued to the vendor in the amount of the discrepancy; this amount is then deducted from the next payment to the vendor.

Activity No. 9

Most purchases include:

1. More than one item.

2. Items that are part of a lot purchase wherein the price of all the items was a lot price. Many times, delivery of the various components or items is in many shipments, each generating a separate invoice.

To prevent duplicate billing, each item on each invoice to the purchase order should be recorded as having been invoiced.

For purchases which include many items, back orders are frequent. Vendors have been known to include back-ordered items on an invoice. They also have been known to submit a duplicate invoice. When each item on the invoice is recorded to each item on the purchase order as having been invoiced, the duplicate billing is immediately recognized.

For purchases of many items or components under a lot price to be delivered by many shipments and subsequently invoiced by the shipment, the amount of each invoice must be recorded on the purchase order. This prevents the total of all the invoices from exceeding the lot price.

Activity No. 10

Payment must not be approved until *all nine* activities have been completed. These activities are necessary to the total business endeavor. They allow costs to be distributed (charged) either to jobs for cost control or to overhead expense accounts to establish overhead costs. They also prevent overpayment.

To satisfy all the activities of vendor invoice administration, a rubber stamp like the one shown here is suggested.

EXP. # JOB #	*1 2 3 4*
MATERIAL	✓
DIRECT EXPENSE	
RECEIVED	*F. B.*
EXTENSIONS O.K.	*J. B.*
PRICES O.K.	*F. B.*
APPROVED FOR PAY	*F. B.*
BACK CHARGE ESTABLISHED	*J. B.*

The stamp is stamped on each original invoice. As each activity is completed, it is initialed by the person completing it. When all the activities have been so initialed, the invoice is ready to be paid and recorded as a cost to the particular job record involved.

Preparation of cost for distribution to the job records includes vendor invoice administration as described above, plus administration of the other job costs (other than labor). Job costs other than labor, and those invoiced by vendors that must be administered, are cost of materials from the subcontractor's warehouse; subcontracts; and small, miscellaneous job costs.

Materials shipped to a job from the subcontractor's warehouse must be recorded on a shop material ticket or material requisition (or whatever the subcontractor wishes to call it) similar to a purchase order. The administration of a shop material ticket is similar to that of a vendor's invoice. The job that the items were shipped to must be identified. The items must be priced, extended, totaled, and then checked. The checking of the prices and arithmetic should be done by a different person, if possible, than the one who made out the ticket. A stamp similar to the one used on vendors' invoices can be used.

JOB #	*1 2 3 4*
SHIPPED	*J. R.*
EXTENSIONS O.K.	*J. B.*
PRICES O.K.	*F. B.*
APPROVED FOR RECORDING	*F. B.*

The stamp is stamped on the shop material ticket. Each activity is initialed as having been completed. When all the activities are initialed, then the total is ready to be recorded as a cost to the particular job record involved.

Subcontracts are similarly handled. Subcontracts are based either on an agreed-to lump sum or on a time-and-materials basis, based on agreed-to labor charges and percentages of markup for material. Preparation for distribution to particular job records of the costs invoiced for subcontracts includes making sure the invoice is in accordance with the purchase order as to amount and/or quantities agreed to. When this is confirmed, these costs are approved and ready to be recorded as a cost to the particular job record involved.

Vendor invoice administration and preparation of costs for distribution to the jobs are vital to the subcontractor's billing process. If possible, the person in charge of vendor invoice administration should also be responsible for the preparation of costs for distribution to the job records.

The ideal situation which is possible and proper for a small operation is for the same man to wear all the hats: purchasing, vendor invoice administration, and preparation of costs for billing. When the operation is too large for one man to wear all three hats, the responsibilities should be separated, with the billing and invoice administration either performed by the same person or directed by the same person.

Materials and tools management begins with procuring the materials and tools and ends with approving payment and recording the costs involved to the particular job record for billing.

11 BILLING (INVOICING)

Profit is the ultimate objective of all companies. Therefore, the activity that initiates the realization of profit is vital.

Gross profit is earned by doing a job for less money than is received for doing it. The profit, however, has no real value until it is converted to cash. Every job, no matter how profitable, will be a 100 percent loss unless the sale is converted to cash. The conversion process is initiated by issuing an invoice and is concluded by collecting and depositing the money into the company's bank account. No money will come into the company without an invoice's having been issued. The importance of invoicing cannot be overemphasized. No matter how efficient and effective all the other functions of a company are, without effective and timely invoicing the company will either struggle in a state of mediocrity or fail.

Construction billing is a major function within itself. It is *not* part of the accounting function. Early in this book it was stated that construction is mechanically simple and consists of very similar mechanical functions. This is true for all the functions and activities of subcontracting except billing (invoicing). Subcontracting billing is unique to all other industries, complex, and intricate. Unfortunately, billing in most subcontracting firms is recognized and treated as a routine and subordinate activity. The results of this lackadaisical attitude are:

1. Work is performed that is never billed.

2. All costs are not included in billing.

3. The quality of the billing is such that it allows the customer to challenge or totally disregard the invoice and/or permits delay in payment.

4. The lack of timely billing destroys collecting activity recourse.

5. The wrong type of billing is applied to the specific type of work.

6. Cash flow is adversely affected.

The first step in the billing process is to establish that which can be billed. There are three types of billings:

1. Basic job billing

2. Interim (partial) billing

3. Changes (extras) billing

177

The contractor who is billing out all the jobs (contracts) he performs is rare. The contractor who is billing out all the work he is performing (extras) is nonexistent. This is a bold statement because it says that no contractor is billing all his work. Unfortunately, it is true; and because of the characteristics of contracting, it will always be true.

It is impossible to establish control that will prevent work that is not included in the original contract from being installed without an extra being established. For this reason, billing starts with the original contract. The original contract provides the basis for billing that particular job and with that particular customer. The type of contract determines the method of payment, which can be one of the following:

1. Time and material, based on predetermined percentages.

2. Time and material, based on the contractor's discretion. (usually confined to one-time services).

3. Time and material not to exceed a maximum. This involves a specific amount of work predetermined by either agreement or plans and specifications with agreed-to percentage of charges over costs for labor and material, with a limit on the total amount that can be charged.

4. Lump sum (contract) involving monthly draws against completed work to date, usually with a percent of retention.

5. Lump sum (contract) involving one billing at the conclusion of the work.

6. Payment on account, as agreed to with customer, such as a 60- or 90-day payment arrangement.

7. Cost plus fixed fee. This involves billing all costs for all items and services agreed to, plus a fixed amount (fee) (not a percentage). Costs plus a prorated portion of the fixed fee are usually billed monthly, or if agreed to, weekly.

8. Cost plus percentage. This method is the same as cost plus fixed fee except that the gross profit is based on an agreed-to percentage of the costs.

9. Unit price. This method is based on a contract to install certain items of material and/or equipment with an agreed-to selling price established for a unit of each item. Amount of billing is based on quantity of units installed, extended by the price for each individual unit. This requires physical mea-

surement of items installed. Billing for this type of arrangement can be on a weekly, monthly, or one-time basis as agreed to.

The person responsible for billing must, therefore, be privy to the contract as soon as possible. He must know how to interpret the contract relative to:

1. Method of payment

2. Frequency of payment

3. Limitations of recourse against nonpayment or untimely payments established by the contract

4. Partial and final lien waiver requirements and specific waiver of lien forms required to be used

5. Latitude available to the contractor of any or all of the above

6. Amount of contract, if a lump-sum contract or "time and material not to exceed a maximum" contract

7. Rates, when method of payment is based on rates

8. Rates for changes (extras) for lump-sum contracts

9. Other information required to develop invoices in accordance with the contract

In addition to the payment information in the contract, there are several other requirements pertinent to the particular contract and/or customer which must be established so that the invoice can be developed. These include:

1. Invoice format

2. Support-document requirements

3. Types of forms for support documents

4. Type and degree of breakdown

Determining all this is many times neglected because it requires personal contact with the customer or his payable personnel. This information is usually determined on a trial-and-error basis, which requires several submissions and rejections of invoices.

The person who is responsible for billing should have a rapport with the customer or his payable personnel and be knowledgeable of the billing requirements. Personal contact is very desirable. It permits the person responsible for billing to accurately learn all the requirements, personal desires, customs, and practices of the customer. Direct liaison and an amiable rapport with the customer's payable personnel is conducive to timely payments, and if a shortage of money develops, a personal rapport usually causes payment prior to others.

Invoices that are not partial payment requests, or are not for a job for which a formal contract or purchase order spells out in detail the required billing format and procedures, require a particular expertise. The customer's administrative structure must be well known to the subcontractor. Is the invoice handled by clerks in an automatic manner, or does the customer personally go over every invoice and approve for payment? If the invoice is handled by a clerk using automatic procedures to approve payment, the invoice must be based strictly on the mechanics of the costs. The invoice will have to include a breakdown of hours and previously approved rates with a definitive description of the work. It will also have to include documented authorization for the work performed and the costs being invoiced. If the invoice is to be personally approved for payment by the customer, all the above may be required, plus an elaborate description of the work performed, justifying the amount being invoiced. This is where the expertise is required. A short story describing the work must be part of the invoice. The story can be written in a manner that will indicate to anyone that the amount of the invoice is reasonable and should be paid. A poorly written story for the same work and the same amount will cause the invoice to be rejected by all involved as representing an unreasonable charge for the work described.

The following are examples of two stories for the same work.

Example No. 1

Repair light

2 hours labor @ $25	$50
Materials	40
Total	$90

Example No. 2

Light in entry was not working. Removed light fixture, tested circuit conductors, removed cover from branch-circuit distribution panel, and tested branch circuit breaker. Replaced one circuit conductor by removing defective one and pulling new conductor in existing conduit. Replaced branch circuit breaker that was damaged as a result of the faulty conductor having shorted out. Cleaned light fixture, replaced lamp, and reinstalled on ceiling.

2 hours labor @ $25	$50
Materials	40
Total	$90

It is obvious which of the two invoices will be paid without challenge.

To forward an Example No. 1 type invoice and then, after having been challenged by the customer, produce the true story as in Example No. 2, will always cause the customer to be skeptical as to what really was required to repair the light. The subcontractor needs to be paid while at the same time retaining the good will of the customer. Both can be achieved with a good story of what was performed as part of the invoice. The story is especially important on invoices for time and material extras.

No subcontractor should allow the invoice function to become an automatic operation. Every invoice should be handled as a separate activity and recognized as being the vital factor in collecting the money for each particular job. The subcontractor should personally see all invoices before they are forwarded to the customer. He should double-check the costs, the gross-profit markup, the description of the work, and the neatness of the invoice. Many times the subcontractor can add his knowledge of the job, hidden costs, and other characteristics to the invoice, thus increasing the gross profit and causing the invoice to be accepted and promptly paid. Final checking of all invoices should not be delegated. Neat, accurate, and timely use of proper forms, procedures, etc., are necessary to ensure timely payments. It also is one of the best public relations activities available to perpetuate the contractor's position with a customer.

The customer sees the contractor through two sources:

1. Field performance

2. Administrative documents he receives

Effective field performance is what the customer buys and expects. Therefore, it does not impress him. When he flushes a toilet it flushes; when he pushes a switch the light comes on; when he looks at a wall it is the color he selected. In most situations the customer (who is the user) is not qualified to determine the difference between high-quality and mediocre field performance.

Administrative documents must be administered to some degree by the customer. Their quality enables the customer to process them either with ease or with difficulty. Since the industry standard for documents received from contractors is usually of poor quality, the customer is impressed with the contractor whose documents are of high quality. As a result, the impression a customer forms of a contractor is not based on his ability to mechanically perform on the job, but on the quality and timeliness of his paperwork. The paperwork that the customer receives from the contractor falls into three categories:

1. General correspondence

2. Proposals for additional work, shop drawings, and manufacturers' catalog cuts

3. Invoices and support documents

High-quality general correspondence can be achieved with a neat-appearing letterhead and well-structured sentences making up the communication. General correspondence seldom requires administrative disposition by the customer. Low-quality or mediocre general correspondence has little or no effect in impressing the customer. Proposals, shop drawings, and manufacturers' catalog cuts are received by representatives of the customer. They do, however, reflect the contractor's ability and generate a favorable or unfavorable impression on the customer. The one thing the customer is always directly involved with is money. He is directly exposed, therefore, to the quality of the invoices and the support documents.

Invoices and support documents are required to be combined with those of other contractors for forwarding to the lending institution for partial and final payouts. Subcontractors are evaluated against each other by the customer. Obviously, the contractor who is always on time with his payout request and who is always in strict accordance with the customer's procedures, customs, and practices, is the one with whom the customer will be impressed.

A subcontractor with a fair or poor field performance, but with excellent paperwork and administration, will always make a favorable impression on the customer. A subcontractor with an excellent field performance, but with poor paperwork and ineffective administration, will always leave a poor impression with the customer.

PREPARING THE INVOICE

No matter what the method of payment, or type of work, preparation of the invoice should start with developing the costs to date for the job. This includes:

1. Determining labor expended to date, including labor burden
2. Materials and equipment invoiced to date
3. Materials and equipment received but not invoiced to date

For time-and-materials and cost-plus types of payments it is an absolute must to develop these. For lump-sum-type billing it is possible to start an invoice without developing the cost. When the subcontractor fails to develop the cost, he violates the purpose of being in business, that is, making a profit.

Every invoice, without exception, includes a gross profit or a loss. The contractor must know this. Knowing the gross profit or loss of the individual invoice gives the contractor the day-to-day information necessary to run a profitable business. It is knowing *all* the costs that ensures to the best possible degree that all which can be billed is being billed.

Establishing the costs is a vital activity of billing. Therefore, the person who is responsible for billing becomes the watchdog of the company. The person who is responsible for billing should be responsible for the following allied activities:

1. Vendor invoice administration
2. Pricing of material and equipment used on time-and-material work
3. Evaluation of costs reports as to required productivity
4. Work order administration (see Chapter 9)
5. Contract administration (see Chapter 8)
6. Collection of receivables on or about due date (see Chapter 13)
7. Policing lien expiration dates
8. Administration of waivers of lien and lien administration (see Chapter 12)
9. Billing forecasts (this differs from sales forecasts)

It should be obvious that many vital functions are centered around billing. Remember that billing is the first step of conversion of investment into cash. Success of all following steps in the conversion process depends on the quality, completeness, and timeliness of the billing. Like the vital organs in the human body, in business billing is a vital procedure which *must* function effectively.

12 LIENS, WAIVERS, AND PAYOUT DOCUMENTS

One of the most difficult requirements in subcontracting is collecting payment of money lawfully and morally due.

Subcontracting in any trade and for any size company is highly competitive. It is the rare exception when a subcontractor is in a noncompetitive market. This characteristic of the construction industry is well known to the subcontractor and his customers. Customers (including architects and general contractors) appear to have the feeling that if one subcontractor does not perform in the manner expected, and many times abusively demanded, they will get his competitor to do the work. Included in that which is expected is not to request or expect payment. It seems that when the subcontractor requests payment he becomes the bad guy and the customer puts on the holier-than-thou white hat. By innuendo and silent behavior the customer lets the subcontractor know that if he isn't a good guy and doesn't go along and finance the job, he will not even get to bid the next job.

Because he is in a highly competitive business, the subcontractor needs every customer and every job he can get. He cannot afford to alienate any customer. This puts the subcontractor in a compromising position because he also cannot afford to continue to do work without payment. There comes a point, however, for each job and for each customer when the subcontractor must put collecting that which is owed above the future good will of the customer. About the only way to force a customer to pay is with a mechanic's lien on the property where the work was performed.

There are laws that help the seller of goods or services to collect money due from the buyer. Manufactured items such as appliances, autos, etc., can be repossessed. The seller, in cooperation with the lender, places a lien on the item at the time of purchase, which remains in effect until full payment is made. The recourse to the seller is the legal right to repossess the item. Contracts for various services, such as membership in a health club are prepared by the seller and include a judgment (confession) clause which permits the seller to go into any court at the buyer's expense and obtain a court directive for the buyer to pay. If he does not pay, his assets (bank account, wages, etc.) are then attached, requiring the employer or bank to withhold from the buyer the funds involved and pay directly to the seller. Repossession or attaching assets both require legal activity by an attorney.

Construction contracts do not include judgment (confession) clauses (because the buyer prepares the contract), and the installation cannot physically be repossessed. From the mechanical aspect, a plumbing contractor could repossess by removing toilets, sinks, etc.; however, he could not repossess the cost of labor to originally install them. The cost of the labor to remove that which was installed would exceed the value of the item being repossessed. It would be mechanically impossible for a painter to remove the paint from the walls, or an electrician to remove the conduit embedded in the concrete floors. The mechanical inability of the seller (contractor, suppliers, etc.) of construction materials to repossess the items requires a completely different type of recourse. Laws to assist or provide the legal base for recourse must be, and therefore are, completely different from all others. The laws which legal recourse is based on for the contractor to force payment are called "mechanic's lien laws." Mechanic's lien laws, unfortunately, are state laws; therefore, they differ from state to state.

Most contractors confine their market to one state. Therefore, they must be familiar with the mechanic's lien laws of that state. A contractor must, however, be familiar with the mechanic's lien laws of any state he is working in. Lien laws in the various states range from very good, in favor of the contractor, to very poor. Because the lien laws do vary from state to state, the descriptions outlined here are general rather than specific. Again, the contractor *must* become completely familiar with the lien laws of the state where the job is. When and whether to start a lien is strictly a judgment decision by the contractor. Effecting the lien is a legal procedure that should be performed by an attorney specializing in liens. An attorney or anyone else cannot make the decision as to when and whether to use the lien laws as recourse against the customer. The only recourse available to force payment after the job is completed is through the lien laws, or suit without lien. (See Chapter 13, "Cash Flow.") Suing without a lien seldom brings satisfactory results.

Lien laws in all states include time. That is, there is a specific limitation of the number of days that the contractor has to start lien action after the work is substantially complete. (See Chapter 13, "Collecting.") A lien in itself does not force the customer to pay. It does several things which, in most states, include:

1. Establishes the contractor's claim of debt legally.

2. In effect puts the property in escrow pending final disposition of the claim. If the claim is ultimately recognized by the courts, the courts can (if necessary to satisfy the claim) force the property to be sold to generate the money to pay the claim.

3. Stops payouts (if any are still due) to all contractors on the job by the interim lending institution.

4. Prevents any further financing or refinancing of the property, including the improvements (buildings). This prevents sale of the property.

5. Places a legal encumbrance on the property that could adversely affect the owner in other ways.

The owner can provide a bond that will satisfy the courts as to the potential claim. This will remove all the above encumbrances against the property. The bonding company will then be responsible for the debt if it is proven.

The lien consists of three actions by the Contractor:

1. Notice of lien

2. Effecting the lien

3. Suing for the amount involved

Each of these actions is required to be done within a specific time from substantial completion of the job. A job does not, however, have to be completed to permit the contractor to effect a lien.

The number of days to file notice of lien is different for a prime contractor than for a subcontractor. A prime contractor is a contractor who has a contract directly with the owner of the property. A subcontractor is a contractor who has a contract with the contractor who has the contract with the owner. A contractor who is normally classified as a subcontractor (plumbing, electrical, heating, or other) very often is a prime contractor. That is, his contract is directly with the owner and not with a general contractor or another contractor. A subcontractor usually has less time to file notice of lien than a prime contractor.

Example

A prime contractor may have 120 days after substantial completion of the job to file notice of lien, while a subcontractor may have only 90 days.

Notice of lien is serving notice in writing to the owner of the contractor's intentions of filing a lien. It can be prepared and served by the contractor (it is not required that an attorney perform this function, but it is advised). Notice of lien is usually a letter from the contractor or his attorney to the *person* who owes the money (which is not necessarily the owner) *and* to the owner, stating the details and amount of the debt and the intentions of placing a "claim for lien" on the property in a certain number of days (usually 10) if the monies due are not paid.

Within a specified number of days after notice of lien has been established, the lien must be effected. The lien is effected by filing a claim for lien with the recorder of deeds and/or registrar of titles for the county in which the property is located. A sample claim for lien is shown in Figure 2.

After the claim for lien has been recorded on the title to the property,

---

STATE OF ILLINOIS ）
                    ） SS
COUNTY OF WALACUTY ）

In the Office of the Recorder of Deeds,

Walacuty County, Illinois

Motarotz Contracting, Inc.	）	
	）	
Claimant,	）	Claim for Lien in the amount of
	）	
v.	）	$1,031.10
	）	
PATRICK J. CLETSOWITZ and	）	
	）	
Defendants.	）	

The Claimant, Motarotz Contracting, Inc., of Chico, County of Statower, State of Illinois,

hereby files a Claim for Lien against PATRICK CLETSOWITZ (hereinafter "OWNER"), having

property in Walacuty County, Illinois, and states:

1. On or about January 15, 1982, and at all times subsequent thereto, Owner owned real

property at 15 Sermony, Penadry, Illinois (hereinafter "Property"), the legal description of which

is lot 82 in Samen Forest Unit Seven, bng a sub of pt of Sec. 29-43-3.

2. On or about January 15, 1982, Claimant made a contract (hereinafter "Contract") with

Owner to perform construction work and install construction equipment for certain facilities on

the Property.

3. Claimant has fulfilled its obligations under the Contract by completing all work contracted to be performed on January 20, 1982.

4. To this date, Owner has not fulfilled its obligations under the Contract by paying the charge of $ 1,031.10.

WHEREFORE, Claimant claims a lien against the Property and all improvements thereon, in the amount of $1,031.10 against all persons interested, together with interest and costs.

Motarotz Contracting, Inc.

By: Joseph M. Motarotz, President.

STATE OF ILLINOIS   )
) SS
COUNTY OF STATOWER   )

Joseph M. Motarotz, being first duly sworn, on oath deposes and says that he is an officer of the above named Claimant, that he has read the foregoing Claim for Lien, knows the contents thereof, and that all the statements therein contained are true.

Joseph M. Motarotz, President.

Subscribed and sworn to before me this 22nd day of May, 1982.

Michelle Bitsko
Notary Public.

Figure 2   Claim for lien.

the contractor must start suit (within a particular period of time) against the owner for the amount claimed to be due. The time period between filing the claim for lien and starting the suit in most states is 2 years.

The suit is tried in court the same as any other suit. The contractor is required to prove to the court that the monies claimed are in fact owed. If the contractor fails to prove that the monies claimed are owed, the suit is dropped and the contractor does not collect the money. If the contractor proves that the monies are in fact owed, the court directs the owner to pay. If the owner does not pay as directed, the courts will then cause the property to be sold, to generate the money to pay the amount owed.

When the contractor has been paid, or otherwise satisfied, the lien must be released. This is done by filing a "release of mechanic's lien" with the recorder of deeds and/or registrar of titles. There are stock release of mechanic's lien forms available where legal blanks and forms are sold. Again, an attorney should handle this for the contractor. "Release of lien" is a requirement of the owner. The contractor does not have to worry whether this is done. The owner will make positively sure this release is started, executed, and recorded. When this document is filed, the property becomes free of all lien encumbrances from that specific contractor.

Costs of establishing notice of lien and filing claim for lien vary with the charges of the attorney and the time it takes to establish the legal description of the property. Attorney's fees for lien services range from $20 to $50. Most charges are less than $50. There are firms which specialize in preparing liens whose charges are less.

Caution is advised against having anyone prepare the lien who is not an established attorney and who is not motivated to represent the contractor in his best interests. Many of the firms specializing in mechanic's liens are primarily collection agencies. They are motivated to use whatever means, in whatever manner necessary, to obtain payments. (They usually are paid a percentage of the amount recovered.) When collecting on percentage, the agency could expose the contractor to adverse actions by the persons whose property is being liened. A good example is the necessity of making sure the exact property involved is the one on which the claim for lien is based. If the legal description of the property is incorrect, or the wrong property or incorrect owner is listed, the contractor is exposed to possible suit against him and/or the claim for lien will be invalid.

Liens should be used by contractors to protect their interests and to force collections. All activities relative to notice of lien, claim for lien, and release of lien should be performed by an attorney. The only activity that the contractor should perform is to exercise *judgment* as to *whether* and *when* liens should be used.

WAIVERS OF LIEN

Waivers of lien play a vital role in the lien process and are important to the billing function. There are two types: partial and final.

Partial waivers of lien are required by owners and lending institutions when partial payouts are being made during the job's construction period. If the job is a one-time-billing job, partial waivers are not used. Contrary to many contractors' belief, partial waivers are very meaningful. Flagrant issuance of partial waivers of lien can be the determining factor on the ability of the contractor to collect. It is common practice to issue partial waivers of lien without concern or without even being aware of the amounts the partial waiver of lien is for. The construction industry is plagued with "sharpie" developers who are working on a shoestring. These developers manipulate the funds of the lending institution to provide the cash flow for the project, including the cost of the land.

Contracts are offered to contractors contingent on the contractor's giving the developer a partial waiver of lien in advance for an appreciable part of the contract. This allows the developer to collect money from the lending institution illegally for work not installed. It also legally establishes that the contractor has forfeited all rights to the property for the amount of the waiver, an amount that the contractor did not receive. Also, the contractor has joined in a conspiracy with the developer to defraud.

The contractor assigns little or no value to the partial waiver of lien, thinking that as long as he does not issue a *final* waiver of lien he still has a hold on the property. The contractor has mechanic's lien rights against the property in the amount of money that he has not issued partial waivers of lien for. If the total amount of partial waivers of lien issued exceed the amount of the contract, a mechanic's lien would be of no value. The owner could readily prove that the contractor had waived his mechanic's lien rights to the amount claimed due.

For the foregoing reasons the contractor must be extremely careful that partial waivers of lien are for the amount being received, *not including retention.* Many times the amount of the partial payout paid to the subcontractor is less than the amount of his partial payout request. Reasons for the difference include:

1. Correction of arithmetical mistakes on the partial payout request

2. Backcharges deducted from the partial payout payment

3. Reduction of the partial payout request based on work claimed to be installed being disputed

4. Other

PARTIAL WAIVERS OF LIENS MUST BE FOR THE EXACT AMOUNT OF THE CHECK BEING RECEIVED.

There is always the age-old problem of giving partial waivers of lien before payment to permit the general contractor, or the owner, to obtain the money required to pay the subcontractor. Without the partial waiver of lien from the subcontractor, the lending institution will not release the funds for payment.

Industry custom and practice is such that it is common to give the partial waiver of lien prior to receiving the payment. Practicality requires some feasible means for the exchange of the partial waiver of lien and the check without physically trading one for the other. The question is who trusts whom. Does the subcontractor trust the general contractor, developer, or owner and issue the partial waiver of lien before receiving payment, or does the general contractor, developer, or owner trust the subcontractor and issue the check prior to receiving the partial waiver of lien?

A practical and equitable solution is for the lending institution to release the first partial payment without requiring partial waivers of lien. The second partial payout would be withheld until the partial waivers of lien are received for the first partial payout. The third partial payment would depend on the partial waiver of lien for the second payout, etc. Final payment would be withheld until partial waivers of lien for the last partial payout *and* final waiver of lien for the final payment are received. This method has been used and been proven to be successful. The subcontractor should insist on this method being used. If this method is not being used, the subcontractor places his mechanic's lien rights in jeopardy every time he issues a partial waiver of lien prior to receiving payment.

The subcontractor is usually at the mercy of the prime contractor, developer, owner, and/or lending institution. Therefore, his ability to demand the above procedure is limited.

If partial waivers of lien are required to be issued before payment is received, the subcontractor can reverse the procedure. That is, *do not issue partial waivers of lien* before getting paid for the previous payout request. This *steadfast* position could delay payment of the payout due at that time. It is imperative, however, to expose an adverse payment behavior or money problem as soon as possible. For small jobs requiring only one or two partial payouts, and for customers in whom there is the *slightest* indication of an adverse payment behavior, THERE IS NO SUBSTITUTION FOR PHYSICALLY TRADING THE PARTIAL WAIVER OF LIEN FOR THE PARTIAL PAYOUT CHECK (currently dated).

Many different types of partial waivers of lien forms are being used in the industry. There are standard stock forms printed by business forms printing companies. There are custom forms provided by the architect, owner, lending institution, developer, or general contractor. The type of form used has little or no effect on the subcontractor. The specific wording used on the partial waiver of lien form *is very important* to the subcontractor. It should read:

THE UNDERSIGNED, FOR AND IN CONSIDERATION OF $——————— AND OTHER GOOD AND VALUABLE CONSIDERATIONS, THE RECEIPT WHEREOF IS HEREBY ACKNOWLEDGED, DOES HEREBY WAIVE AND RELEASE ANY AND ALL LIEN OR CLAIM OR RIGHT OF LIEN UNDER THE STATUTES OF THE STATE OF —————, RELATING TO MECHANIC'S LIENS, ON THE ABOVE-DESCRIBED PREMISES AND IMPROVEMENTS THEREON, AND ON MONIES OR OTHER CONSIDERATIONS DUE, OR TO BECOME DUE, FROM THE OWNER, ON ACCOUNT OF LABOR OR SERVICES, MATERIAL, FIXTURES, OR APPARATUS HERETOFORE <u>FURNISHED TO THIS DATE</u> BY THE UNDERSIGNED FOR THE ABOVE-DESCRIBED PREMISES.

The important words in the above are "FURNISHED TO THIS DATE." These words are what make a partial waiver of lien different from a final waiver of lien. In a final waiver of lien the words "FURNISHED TO THIS DATE" are replaced by "FURNISHED OR WHICH MAY BE FURNISHED AT ANY TIME HEREAFTER." All other wording on both the partial and final waivers of lien are identical.

On many stock-type waivers of lien forms the title of the form will read "Waiver of Lien to Date," or "Waiver of Lien—Partial," or "Partial Waiver of Lien," or "Final Waiver of Lien." Unfortunately, on many custom combination-type payout forms which include a waiver of lien section, there are no titles indicating whether it is a partial or final waiver of lien. The contractor must be alert at all times to be sure that it is, in fact, a partial waiver of lien and not a final waiver of lien.

There are lending institutions who have custom payout forms, which include the alleged partial waiver of lien section, in which the structuring of the wording is such that upon signing and accepting the first payout the contractor waives all lien rights in the same manner as if it were the final payout. This type of combination "payout-waiver-affidavit" form does not distinguish between partial or final as to payout or waiver of lien by title or otherwise. That is, the same identical form is used for partial payouts and partial waivers of lien as is used for final payouts and final waiver of lien. Subsequently, the wording of the waiver of lien section is the wording for the final waiver of lien: "FURNISHED TO THIS DATE, OR WHICH MAY BE FURNISHED."

A note of warning to subcontractors: Refuse to sign or accept the payout subject to the above type waiver of lien. As in contracts, *every word* is meaningful and must be respected by the subcontractor. The words mean exactly what they say, nothing more and nothing less. In all legal writing, every attempt is used to prevent misinterpretation of the intent. This is why legal writing is full of whereas, heretofore, hereby, shall, any and all, etc. As in contracts, when the contractor signs a waiver of lien, partial or final, he commits himself irrevocably to *exactly* what the document says.

Contractor's Affidavit or Sworn Statement

The contractor's affidavit or sworn statement is nothing more than a statement which the contractor has sworn to as being true regarding the payout. The payout request is the breakdown of the contract on which the payouts are based. That is, at the beginning of the job the subcontractor and/or owner, or others, break the total amount of the contract down into measurable parts. The payouts are based on the amount of each measurable part furnished and/or installed to that date.

The contractor's affidavit or sworn statement also is a statement which the contractor has sworn to as being true regarding the contract to date and payout request. The payout request, or application for payment, always includes a section which includes:

Amount of original contract

Extras to contract

Credits to contract

Total contract to date

Total retained to date

Amount previously paid

Net amount of this payout

The "extras to contract" portion is very vital. Amounts of *all* extras incurred to date *must be* shown. Frequently, the subcontractor waits until the latter part of a job to bill the extras. He therefore fails to include the amounts on the payout request at the time the extras occurred.

All projects are financed during the construction period either by a lending institution or from the working capital of the firm purchasing the work. In either case the money to finance the construction during the construction period has been either appropriated or borrowed (construction loan). The amount appropriated or borrowed is the amount of the contracts, plus an amount for contingencies. Many times, the amount budgeted for contingencies is not enough. When this occurs, there is no source for funds to pay for extras not recorded. This causes the owner to provide the money for the extras from nonexistent sources. He is forced either to attempt to deny payment of part or all of the amount claimed for extras or to delay payment for long periods until the project generates a return on the investment. This may take years, or in many cases, it may never occur. To prevent this, the subcontractor *must* invoice the extras immediately and record them on the next payout request. The lending institution will then be aware of the total commitment being made to the subcontractor.

Many contractors refuse to accept final payment (which does not include the extras that are due) because they do not want to sign the final waiver of lien, thinking this will prevent the owner from obtaining the mortgage. (When the mortgage is obtained the construction loan is paid off.) All the owner has to do to close out the construction loan and obtain the mortgage is to put the amount shown as due on the contract in escrow with the title guarantor. If the subcontractor has not included all the extras in the payout requests, the amount required to be put in escrow will not include the extras. This leaves the subcontractor at the mercy of the owner and without recourse unless the lien period has not expired.

Partial waivers of lien and payout requests *must* be administered accurately to the nth degree. Both are a vital function of billing. The waiver of lien, contractor's payout request, notice of mechanic's lien, and the lien itself are the most powerful tools the subcontractor has to obtain payment. They should all be used when necessary without reservation. A customer who does not pay his bills is of no value.

The laws governing notice of lien, claim for lien, release of lien, and partial and final waivers of lien vary appreciably from state to state. These laws also are continuously changing. For example, just because a subcontractor performs work on a particular property, he does not necessarily have the right to place a claim for mechanic's lien. Repair to existing equipment does not establish the right to lien.

Subcontractors should not be a "do-it-yourselfer" in understanding and exercising lien laws. An attorney knowledgeable in the latest lien laws for the particular state must be consulted for each requirement.

13 CASH FLOW AND CASH MANAGEMENT

It has been established that the subcontractor must have knowledge of, and possess an expertise in, many different fields. It has also been established that the two resources of a company are *people* and *money*. The rest of this book is related to the resource of people and how to administer and control the expenditures of money. This chapter will cover the management of money. Human resources are very important and vital. The management and control of the actual cash of the company is equally vital. The subcontractor *must* have a personal expertise in cash management and knowledge of cash flow.

The monetary functions of a construction company are related to costs of obtaining sales, committing funds for installing the work, payment of commitments, and conversion of results of it all to cash. The major activities of costs of obtaining sales include estimating, making the sale, obtaining the contract, and ordering the work (work order). Committing funds for installation of the work includes purchasing and installation (utilization of labor). Payment of commitments is the act of releasing the money to satisfy the commitments. These activities represent investing the cash. Converting the investment back into cash includes invoicing, collecting, and depositing.

CASH FLOW

"Cash flow" in the construction industry is the movement of money through the organization. The control of cash flow is cash management. Cash flows through a company in two directions: in and out. The cash flow cycle is in, out, and back in. All businesses start with cash (how much the owners have put in). The cash is invested into fixed assets, jobs-in-progress costs, and overhead costs. The jobs in progress generate receivables (invoices) which, when paid, go back to cash. The cash is then reinvested into jobs-in-progress costs, fixed assets, and overhead costs. The cash flow cycle is then started again and repeated over and over for the life of the company. The conversion of cash to investment to cash is profitable when the converted cash exceeds the invested cash or when the "in" cash exceeds the "out" cash. Cash comes into the company from receivables, invested equity, and loans. Cash goes out of the company through payables,* loan repayments, return of owner's original investment, dividends to owners, and taxes.

*Payroll is one type of payable. The term "payable" includes payroll.

Cash management includes:

Providing the cash to pay payables*

Scheduling and controlling the payment of payables*

Controlling the entire receivables function

Administering surplus funds

Controlling bank balances

No matter how efficient the company is in terms of performing the work, if there isn't an effective and timely cash flow the company will surely die. This means if there is no effective means to convert the efficiency into cash, the efficiency has no value.

The cash flow cycle consists of two parts: (1) the investment process and (2) conversion of the investments to cash.

The investment process includes two major activities:

1. Commitment

2. Payment

The commitment activity includes:

1. Purchasing the materials

2. Hiring and utilizing labor

3. Purchasing and utilizing fixed assets

   a. Tools

   b. Trucks

   c. Office facilities and equipment

The payment activity is the paying of costs created by the commitment. After the costs are committed, they are invoiced by the vendors.** These costs are then called "payables." Costs created by labor also become a "payable." However, the paying process for labor is commonly called

---

*Payroll is one type of payable. The term "payable" includes payroll.

**The vendor is the supplier, person, or firm providing the material, equipment, supplies, or service purchased.

"payroll." It is, however, a payable due on a specific day, the same as a vendor's invoice.

The second part of the cash flow cycle involves converting the investments back into cash. This includes invoicing and collecting. The efficiency of the investment process determines the degree of profit. The effectiveness of converting investments to cash determines the realization of profit.

With the exception of a few legal activities, all the activities of a company are related to either the profit-producing endeavor or cash flow. Since the investment process is also the profit-producing endeavor, details explaining these activities, except paying payables, are covered in other sections. This chapter will cover converting investments to cash, cash management, and the paying of payables. The invoice is the final step necessary to start payment (conversion back to cash) before the *cash receipts functions*.

Before the invoice is made up, the following activities, which are explained in detail in other chapters, are done:

Work order administration

Vendor invoice and payables administration

Materials cost recording and reporting

Miscellaneous job-cost recording and reporting

Payroll distribution

After the invoice is submitted to the customer, the "cash receipts functions" come into play. These functions actually convert the investment back to cash. They include collecting, recording, and depositing:

COLLECTING IS VITAL TO CASH FLOW.

Recording the payment is done in the cash receipts journal, the customer's accounts receivable ledger, and other ledgers that may be used to police collections. The third function is depositing the payment into the company's bank account.

CASH MANAGEMENT

Cash management is the process of controlling the cash flow of the company. Remember, cash flow is the flow of cash in and cash out. Management of *cash in* is the control of all the activities that bring cash into the company. These include:

1. Development of contract payout-breakdown schedule, including format and criteria for each new contract

2. Control of the amounts to be added to or deducted from costs of jobs in progress for each month's payout requests

3. Control of amount of markup for overhead and profit on all noncontract invoices

4. Control of all collection activities

The control of cash in (other than collection) begins with developing the payout form. What it says depends on the customer. Some customers require practically no information; others want specific forms with specific items of breakdown of the contract. What is on the payout form usually is dictated by the lending agency. The items of the contract breakdown are usually the prerogative of the contractor. With the exception of FHA-guaranteed loans, the amounts of the items of the contract breakdown are always left for the contractor to determine. It is common practice for the contractor to establish, above costs, the amounts for those items that will be completed first. This allows him to draw more than his costs for those items completed first. This is commonly called "front-loading." The theory of front-loading is to extract from the job as soon as possible enough funds to finance the job. The job then produces its own financing. Front-loading works fine in theory and is considered good, practical cash management. For the company that does not have sophisticated management in all areas: that is, in accounting, cost control, cost reporting, and cash management, *front-loading is a very dangerous practice*. It may result in:

1. Insufficient funds to finance the last few months of the project

2. Distorted gross profit reports for the particular job

3. Distorted gross and net profits shown on profit and loss statements

The greatest of these dangers is that front-loading creates a deficiency of funds during the last part of the job. The result is that the contractor is without enough funds left to be drawn from the contract to cover the costs expended during the last 2 or 3 months of the project. The techniques of cash management presented here are based on a policy of *not* front-loading.

Remember, the control of cash in begins as soon as the invoice becomes due. That is, control of cash in starts for the jobs-in-progress-type billing at the invoice level and for all other types of billings at the time the invoice becomes due. The reason for this difference is that the amount of the billing for jobs in progress, including gross profit, is for the most part at the discretion of the subcontractor. That is, the amount of cash taken by each payout from a job in progress is at the discretion of the subcontractor. This puts the subcontractor somewhat in control of the amount of cash in for jobs in progress. This is not true for other jobs or for the final payout of a job in progress. For these jobs the amount of the invoice is determined by the lump sum of the contract (for one-time billing jobs), or by the costs plus percentage of markup, not by the subcontractor. The control of the cash in for this type of billing, therefore, begins when the invoice becomes due.

For the jobs-in-progress-type billing, the amount of the billing is determined by adding to, or deducting from, the cost incurred on the job during the period being invoiced (1 month). This amount is determined by the percentage of gross profit or loss expected at the end of the job. This requires a firsthand knowledge of the progress and efficiency of the job. The percentage of expected gross profit or loss that should be added to, or deducted from, the costs for the period will fluctuate from month to month. The amount of gross profit or loss not only fluctuates from month to month, based on each separate month's results, but also fluctuates from the start of a job to any given date.

Example

Assume the entire job was expected to produce a 10 percent gross profit. The work during the first 3 months earned 15 percent above costs. The amount to be added to costs for these periods would theoretically be 15 percent. The work during the next 3 months earned only 5 percent. The amount to be added to costs for these periods would theoretically be 5 percent. This is impractical for most trades because of the inability to measure accurately what has been installed for the costs incurred in a given period of time. The practical method is to determine the productivity status of the job from the start of the job to date. This is done by:

1. Spot-measuring the profit centers that will appreciably affect the outcome of the job

2. Considering verbal reports from supervisors

3. Personal observation

4. Analyzing cost to complete reports

5. Past experience

6. Prayer

From these, the cash manager can acquire a fairly accurate feel for the productivity status of the job. He should know very accurately the results of the purchasing.

If the job is slipping, a lower-than-expected percentage must be added to the costs incurred for the period. If the job has slipped, and appears to be a loser, a deficit must be built into the monthly payout requests. If a job is going to be a loser, it is best to recognize this as early in the job as possible. The more months across which the cash manager can spread the expected loss, the less effect the loss will have on the cash flow of the company.

Many times the productivity appears, early in the job, to be very good. Based on this, and the need for cash, the cash manager takes additional profit, only to be disappointed during the completion stages. He then has to put the profit back by requesting less than costs on the last several payout requests. If the job appears to be exceeding the expected gross profit, it is wise to limit the percentage added to the costs incurred for the month to the original expected gross-profit percentage.

The percentage of completion profits from jobs-in-progress-type billings is completely controlled by the cash manager. If most of the total sales are from jobs-in-progress-type billings, the cash manager can control the profits shown on monthly statements. The cash manager must, therefore, be very realistic in determining the amount to be added to, or deducted from, the costs incurred for the month. To be other than realistic will produce an erroneous profit and loss statement for the month and will generate serious cash flow problems later.

The third function of cash in management is control of all collection activities.

Collecting

The receivables collecting process is divided into two categories:

1. Collection on or about due date

2. Collection of past-due receivables

Every customer has a payable cycle, which is the subcontractor's receivable cycle for that particular customer. The subcontractor, therefore, has a receivable cycle for each customer. The receivable cycle is the number of days from the date the invoice is forwarded until the date payment is received. On projects where the money is put up before the job (construction loan, bond issues, etc.), the receivable cycle is usually based on the administrative cycle of the lending institution. This cycle can be factually determined, even before bidding the job. It includes an agreed-to cutoff date to submit the payout request to the general contractor or the architect. After submittal it takes a specific number of days for the request to be administered by the various departments until final approval and payment is made. For projects financed internally by the customer, a specific receivable cycle exists, again based on the particular administrative cycle. Smaller projects which are paid directly from the customer's day-to-day cash flow have a receivable cycle based on the payment behavior of that particular customer. This is the most precarious type of customer when it comes to collections.

Payment behavior of a customer can be determined only by his past payment performance. If he is a customer whose work has been performed previously, his payment behavior is known by experience. If work has not been performed for that customer previously, a check with other contractors and/or firms who *have* had experience with him is vital. The receivable collecting process includes one or both of two processes: collection on or about due date or collection when the invoice is past due.

Collection on or about the due date involves knowing in advance the receivable cycle and payment behavior of the customer. With this knowledge a date can be determined when payment can be expected. Most payments are received within 3 working days of that date. If payment is not received within this time, an immediate effort to determine why must be initiated. A phone call will usually reveal why the payment has not been received and when it will be made.

Many situations and reasons hold up payments. These include:

1. Discrepancy in the payout request.

2. Costs on which the payout was based were not authentic.

3. Work not completed.

4. Payout request submitted after cutoff date.

5. Invoice not properly documented.

6. Invoice or payout request not in accordance with customer's forms and procedures.

7. Customer's administrative ability and/or procedures do not match lending agency's requirements.

8. Money has not been appropriated.

Correction of many of these is within the subcontractor's control. Unfortunately, it is rare when the customer will call and inform the subcontractor that he has made a mistake, and consequently payment will be, or is being, held up. A phone call by the subcontractor is necessary and will reveal that which must be done to allow payment to be made. Therefore, the first activity in this case is to *investigate what is holding up the payment.* Correction on the subcontractor's part, or aiding the customer's personnel, will cause payment to be made in a few days. If payment is not made in a few days following the established receivable cycle for that customer, then the activity becomes *collection of past-due receivables.* A receivable (invoice) becomes past due when payment has not been received within a reasonable period of time (10 days) after the receivable-cycle date for that customer without an authentic, valid reason. An authentic, valid reason includes *only* administrative procedure break-downs by either the subcontractor or the customer.

Collection of receivables (invoices) established as past due can be achieved only by force. Don't forget that the profit made on a job is of *no value* if it cannot be converted to cash. Therefore, a customer that has not paid is of no value. Yet contractors, because of their zeal to not alienate the customer for fear of losing future sales, are notorious in failing to pursue payment of past-due invoices by force. But a contractor who is capable, that is, who can perform and finance the work, will get the next job if he has a low figure, regardless of his past attitude and force used to collect past-due receivables. If a customer owes for a past-due invoice, *why* is the contractor emotionally on the defense? He has done nothing wrong. It is the customer who is creating the adversity. He is the "bad guy," not the contractor.

There are many things available to the contractor to motivate the customer to pay. All, unfortunately, involve proper timing. That is, timing is a major factor, both how soon and at what point. The two major motivators are:

1. Lien

2. Slowdown of work

The lien must be started within a specific number of days after the last day of substantial completion of the work. It is, therefore, important that the unpaid invoice be transferred from receivables due to receivables past due no later than 10 days after the receivable-cycle due date.

Example

Assume the receivable cycle is 6 weeks, or 45 days. After the work is completed it takes 3 to 5 days to invoice. Table 1 shows the various activities and the time they require.

There are two steps to perfecting a lien: notice of lien and perfecting the lien. Liens are usually required to be perfected within 90 days for a

Table 1

Activity	Number of days	Day (consecutive)
Substantial completion of the work	0	0
Invoice forwarded	4	4
Established receivable cycle	45	49
Waiting period	3	52
Investigation and payment request period	10	62
Turnover to receivables past due	0	62
Payment pursued aggressively	15	77
Decision made to start a lien	0	77
Notice of lien perfected	10	87
Lien perfected	33	120

subcontract and within 120 days for a prime contract after substantial completion of the work. The notice of lien is required 10 days prior to effecting the lien. As can be seen by the above time schedule, there isn't any time to lose in any of the activities preceding a lien. The schedule is based on the minimum average receivable cycle. Most receivable cycles exceed 45 days.

A lien during construction stops all payments from the lending institution. The best method available to the contractor during the construction period is to slow the job down. There is absolutely no justification to continue to invest money in a project in the form of labor and materials if the monthly payout payments are not being made. The only way to prevent investing money under these circumstances is to withhold shipments of materials and equipment and to reduce the labor force. It would be unwise to remove the entire labor force because the subcontractor may then be in violation of his contract.

This technique is a very delicate one. If work is stopped on a project in areas that the other trades will cover up, the subcontractor may be required to spend considerable labor later to install his work out of sequence. When this technique is used, the subcontractor must be sure it is in areas and at a time that he is free of the other trades, and in an area and at a time that it will affect construction of the facility to the degree that it will force payment.

The most effective method to obtain payment at any time, before or after the job is completed and before or after the lien rights have expired, is *constant, constant* effort, that is, pursuing the payment with aggressive effort *every day*. There is no substitute for the old saying "The squeaky wheel gets the grease." After the lien rights have expired, there is very little effective legal recourse available. Suing is the only one. Legal costs and the time it takes to pursue payment by suing are in the favor of the customer.

Unless the subcontractor is particularly sure of his customer's payment behavior and payment attitudes, payment *must* be obtained within 90 days. Because time is so important, invoices must be mailed within 48 hours of the work's installation and the payout requests must be forwarded within the cutoff period to the correct place.

Bank Borrowing

The last function of cash in management is control of bank borrowing. Bank borrowing serves two major requirements:

1. It provides working capital for companies not financially independent.

2. It forces the required discipline necessary for efficient cash management. Discipline is so vital to cash management that bank borrowing to force discipline is good for even a financially independent company.

There are two major disciplines involved in cash management:

1. Timely and effective invoicing

2. Collections

Unless both of these functions are efficient, cash flow is immediately adversely affected. Unfortunately, neither of these functions is appealing, especially collecting. Because of this, procrastination is often the rule, the result being a neglected and ineffective cash management function.

Bank borrowing brings into the company a nonowner partner. This nonowner partner immediately and continuously influences timely and effective invoicing and a continuous collection effort. The type of bank borrowing recommended here further forces these two activities to be satisfied. Bank borrowing is a vital part of cash management and cash flow. This is true both for companies requiring bank borrowing for additional cash requirements *and* for the company that is financially independent. For the financially idependent company, funds can be borrowed from the bank for week-to-week cash flow requirements (short-term needs) with surplus funds being invested on a long-term basis. This allows full utilization of funds *and* cash flow control. The use of bank borrowing for cash flow control for the financially independent company is the same as for the company that needs bank borrowing for additional cash requirements.

Bank borrowing is divided into two functions:

1. Establishing a line of credit
2. Determining the amount to be borrowed each week

Establishing a line of credit involves determining the method of borrowing and the amount needed. Borrowing is divided into two types; short-term and long-term. Short-term borrowing is borrowing and paying back in less than 1 year; long-term borrowing is borrowing and paying back in more than 1 year.

Bank borrowing is based on several different methods. The more common methods include:

1. *30-, 60-, and 90-day notes with interest deducted in advance from the amount loaned.* This is called "discounting the note." Collateral for this type of borrowing could be anything the bank would accept, including the total personal assets of the borrower. Payment is by lump sum on the due date.

2. *Notes for longer than 90 days, 6 months, or 1 year.* Interest on this type of note is usually discounted. Payment is usually an equal amount each month for the life of the note. Collateral is anything the bank will accept, usually the total personal assets of the borrower.

3. *Notes for periods exceeding 1 year.* Interest can either be discounted or paid monthly. Collateral is usually the same as for short-term notes. Payment can be either by the month, beginning with the first month, with a moratorium for a period of time other than by the month, or by other agreed-to incre-

ments. Notes for periods of more than 1 year are considered long-term. Long-term lending is looked upon by the banks as investing equity into the business. They will very rarely loan money for periods exceeding 1 year on this basis.

4. *Revolving receivable borrowing.* This type of borrowing involves individual weekly notes. Collateral is current receivables (less than 90 days). Payment is daily, based on the total receipts for each day. All deposits are made to a collateral account. The funds are transferred immediately from the collateral account as payment toward reducing the loan. In reality, the loan is never paid off because all the invoices pledged as collateral are not collected at one time.

A new note is established each week, based on the unpaid amount of the previous week's note, plus the amount to be borrowed. This type of borrowing is considered to be short-term because a new note is established each week which automatically pays off the previous week's note.

The banks historically require this type of borrowing to be suspended for a short period once each year. This requirement, however, is rarely enforced. Short-term borrowing usually continues for 2 to 5 years. In a successful operation, borrowing is necessitated by a rate of expansion requiring more operating funds than retained profits from the preceding year will satisfy. A rate of expansion requiring more than the retained profits from the preceding year should not exceed 5 years. The reason is that after 5 years of accelerated expansion the amount of interest being paid on the money required to be borrowed will cause the expansion to pass the point of diminishing returns. A cooling-off period should be allowed in order to let the retained profits catch up with the need for money. Interest on bank borrowing for operating capital should never exceed 10 percent of the total overhead.

The procedures involved in receivable-type borrowing are very conducive to good cash management. It is, therefore, the recommended type of borrowing.

The next and last step in bank borrowing is determining the amount to be borrowed. Since receivable-type borrowing is the recommended type and involves weekly borrowing, the amount to be borrowed is determined weekly. The amount required for the following week's payables (cash out) automatically determines the amount to be borrowed.

Cash management of *cash out* is the control of all activities involved in cash leaving the company. The cash in activities involve the receivable cycle, which is also the customer's payable cycle. Cash out activities involve the payable cycle, which is the vendor's receivable cycle. These activities include:

1. Establishing specific types and lengths of payable cycles

2. Separating vendors into types of payable cycles

3. Assigning each vendor a payable cycle

4. Preparing of a weekly payable schedule, including payroll transfer

5. Allocating funds to cover payables to be released

6. Releasing payments of payables

Types of Payables

There are several types of payables, including repetitive, immediates, notes, payroll, and major.

Repetitive Payables. Repetitive payables are of a repetitive nature; that is, they come due on a specific day each month and are approximately the same amount each month. They include insurance payments, water bills, electric bills, mortgage payments, rent, gasoline bills, lease payments, telephone bills, and taxes. The payable cycle for repetitive payables is monthly, on the day they become due.

Immediate Payables. Immediate payables are not repetitive and not for materials installed on jobs. They are usually of small amounts and are nonrecurring to the degree that they do not justify establishing a payable cycle. Immediates are scheduled for payment for the week following approval for payment. This allows payment to be made usually within 2 weeks of receipt of the invoice. They include office supplies, invoices for services by small companies not financially able to carry the amount due, and any payable committed to be paid immediately upon receipt of invoice.

Notes. Notes as referred to here are other than the bank notes used to support cash flow. An example may be a 90-day note where the money was used to pay cash for a piece of equipment such as a truck. If a payable cycle of 60 or 90 days is desired with a particular supplier, he may require the amount owed be paid by the tenth of the month by a note. The note then becomes due in 60 or 90 days. The payable cycle of a note is the due day of the note.

Payroll. Payroll is obviously payment for labor, both field and office. It is a payable that covers the total for each week. The payroll payable is paid by transferring the total amount, including burden (insurance, taxes, etc.), from the general bank account to the payroll account. The payroll payable cycle is usually 10 to 14 days.

Major Payables. Major payables are for purchase of materials and equipment installed on the job, tools, and other payables whose payable cycle can be established by the contractor. The payable cycle for the major payables is established to the longest period possible. The longest period possible is the longest length of time that the vendor will permit while continuing to do business with the contractor. For suppliers this is usually 60 days, and some, by special agreement, allow 90 days. With others, such as payables due for professional services such as legal, auditing, etc., longer periods are accepted. The cash discount offered by suppliers and manufacturers is forfeited if necessary to allow extension of the payable cycle beyond 30 days. However, the payable cycle should not extend past the day when the supplier or manufacturer levies a service charge. The common belief that it is prudent and profitable to pay by the tenth of the month and earn the cash discount is erroneous. The following explains why.

VENDOR PAYMENT ANALYSIS

Assumptions

1. The pay period is for materials received from the first of the month through the thirtieth of the month which will become due as a total on the first of the month.

2. The amount due for the total 30-day period can be discounted at an average of 1 percent if paid by the tenth.

3. Bank borrowing is at the rate of 8½ percent.

4. The vendor has extended terms to payment within 60 days with forfeiture of an average of 1 percent cash discount and without additional penalty.

5. Payment must be made on the fifty-fifth day so that the vendor may receive and credit the amount by the sixtieth day.

Analysis

If money is borrowed to make payment by the tenth of the month (10 days) in lieu of paying by the twenty-fifth of the following month (55 days), the money would have been paid out 45 days earlier. The cost of borrowing the money to pay on the tenth day versus the fifty-fifth day (45 days difference) would be 1.047 percent of the amount involved. The difference in the amount of discount earned by paying it on the tenth and the cost of the money involved is 0.047 percent. Based on this, the cost of paying the bills current and taking the discount in lieu of paying on the fifty-fifth day is 0.047 percent. If the interest rate to borrow money is 8½ percent or more, it costs the contractor money to pay suppliers by the tenth and take the cash discount. In addition to this slight cost, bank credit is consumed and, therefore, not available to support additional sales. The higher the interest rate over 8½ percent, the more it costs to discount the vendors' invoices. Assignment of major payables to the longest period possible reduces the number of days between the contractor's payable cycle and the receivable cycle.

There are some myths regarding cash discounts. First, the cash discount for most contractors is not 2 percent. There are some items that carry a 2 percent cash discount. There also are items that carry *no* cash discount. Further, there are items that carry cash discounts that range from 0 to 2 percent. Each subcontractor's average cash discount depends on the mix of the discounts he receives for the various materials and equipment he purchases. This rarely exceeds 1.25 percent. The belief that the discount is multiplied by 12 (for the 12 months in a year) also is a myth. It is a common saying that the cash discount earns the subcontractors 24 percent a year. As explained above, the discount is not 2 percent a month. If the discount is forfeited and the invoice is subsequently paid 45 days later, a month and a half has been obtained for the forfeiture. There are eight 1½-month periods in a year. The saying would be more factual if it would indicate 1 percent a month times 8, or 8 percent a year instead of 24 percent a year.

From the established payable cycle of each invoice, a weekly payable schedule can be developed. This schedule will automatically determine the amount of cash that will be required for cash out the following week. The payable schedule lists the total amount to be paid to each person or firm owed for repetitive, immediate, major, and notes payables. The totals of each, plus the total payroll (including labor burden), equals the total cash required for the following week.

The next activity is to provide and allocate the funds to satisfy the above. This is accomplished by:

1. Using existing funds in the general bank account

2. Transferring money from reserves

3. Borrowing

4. Additional investment by the owner

5. Combination of the above

The most common source of cash is from the balance remaining in the general bank account from the previous week's cash out, plus bank borrowing. Table 2 is a typical cash out summary.

Analysis of Receivable Cycle Versus Payable Cycle

The cash required to support sales depends on the number of days between the time money is paid out for the various costs and the time money is received from the invoices generated by the operation of the company.

Example

If the payable cycle is greater (in days) than the receivable cycle (in days), the amount of cash required to support the payables would be zero. Conversely, if the receivable cycle (in days) is greater than the payable cycle (in days), the amount of money required to support the payables would be the amount represented in the outstanding receivables for the difference of the number of days between the payable cycle and the receivable cycle. Theoretically, if the cash required to support the cost of labor equalled the materials costs, the receivable cycle were less than 7 days, and the payable cycle were 10 days, no cash would be required to support work in process. The average payable cycle for the company is based on the payable cycles of each of the four types of payables, as explained below.

Payroll

Assume the pay period runs from Monday morning to Sunday night and payday is the following Thursday afternoon. The payable cycle starts when the commitment has been made. For payroll this is at the end of each pay period. In the case of a Monday-through-Sunday pay period the payable cycle would start on the following Monday. With payday on Thursday afternoon, the funds to cover the payroll would not have to be

Table 2
CASH OUT SUMMARY

1. Repetitive payables   _____
2. Immediate payables   _____
3. Notes due   _____
4. Payroll (including labor burden)   _____
5. Purchase payables   _____
6. Total payables   _____
7. Variances from previous week*   _____
8. Total cash required   _____
9. Previous bank account balance   _____
10. Cash deficit or surplus   _____
11. Amount required to be borrowed   _____
12. Remaining bank account balance   _____

The above is the cash out for the following week.

Line 6 is the total of lines 1 through 5.

Line 6 plus line 7 equals line 8.

Line 8 plus or minus line 9 equals line 10.

If line 10 is negative, this is the deficit, which is also the amount required to be borrowed.

* NOTE: No matter how proficient a company projects the allocation of funds for the following week, there are frequent needs requiring immediate payment that were not included in the previous week's payable schedule and cannot wait to be included in the following week's schedule. The funds to cover these payables must be included in the following week's cash flow.

transferred to the payroll account until the Monday after the Thursday payday. This would be a 7-day payable cycle. If payday were on Tuesday, funds would have to be transferred by the following Thursday. This payable cycle would be 4 days.

Immediate Payables

Immediate payables are paid immediately; therefore, they have a 0-day payable cycle. It usually takes 3 or 4 days, however, to satisfy the administration requirements to pay, in which case the payable cycle would be 3 or 4 days.

Repetitive Payables

Repetitive payables are usually payables that are for commitments that were concluded at the end of each month and became due within 10 days after receipt of the invoice. These payables are usually paid within the established due period, averaging about 12 days after receipt of the invoice.

Major Purchases

As previously discussed, the payable cycle for major purchases is 55 days, with few exceptions.

To establish the average payable cycle we must average the four types of payable cycles in terms of the number of days of each and the amount of dollars each represents to the total of all. Assume the payroll and major purchases to be about equal, and the repetitive payables about 10 percent of payroll or the major purchases. The payroll is 7 days, immediate payables 4 days, repetitive payables 15 days, and the major payables 55 days. The average payable cycle can be computed by dividing the accounts payable (shown on the balance sheet) by the total costs (shown on the profit and loss statement) of the reporting period times the number of days of the reporting period.

Example

Accounts payable are shown on the balance sheet as $100,000. Total costs for all expenditures as shown on the profit and loss statement for the preceeding year are $950,000. This includes all labor, labor burden, materials, direct job costs, and all overhead costs. The computation is as follows:

$$\frac{100,000 \text{ (accounts payable)}}{950,000 \text{ (year's total costs)}} \times 365 \text{ (days)} = 38 \text{ days}$$

If the accounts payable were $75,000, the payable cycle would drop to 28 days.

The payable cycle is controlled by the frequency with which the bills are paid. It is increased by taking longer to pay bills. It is decreased by paying the bills sooner. The average payable cycle for a company with the above individual payable cycle would be approximately 34 days. Based on an average cycle of 55 days for major payables, this is a realistic average for most subcontracting firms.

The receivable cycle is the average number of days between the invoice date and the day the money is actually received. A subcontractor with poor invoicing procedures and an ineffective collecting effort will have a receivable cycle near 100 days. A subcontractor with timely invoicing procedures and an effective collection effort will have a receivable cycle of perhaps 60 days or less. The type and mix of work will also affect the receivable cycle. Most administrative cycles for construction payouts exceed 50 days, with many taking 75 days. This unfavorably affects the receivable cycle of the average subcontractor.

The average receivable cycle is the average accounts receivable divided by the sales of the reporting period times the number of days of the period.

Example

From the balance sheet the accounts receivable are shown as $200,000. From the profit and loss statement the sales for the preceeding year are shown as $1 million. The receiving cycle would be computed as follows:

$$\frac{200,000 \text{ (accounts receivable)}}{1,000,000 \text{ (year's sales volume)}} \times 365 \text{ (days)} = 73 \text{ days}$$

If the accounts receivable were $175,000, the average receivable cycle would drop to 63 days.

The average receivable cycle is increased by allowing the invoices to be unpaid for longer periods. The average receivable cycle is decreased by collecting sooner.

The difference between the average payable cycle and the average receivable cycle is the cash flow cycle. Cash flow cycle for the above example would be 31 days. The shorter the cash flow cycle, the more the sales that can be supported with the same amount of money. The longer the cash flow cycle, the fewer the sales that can be supported with the same amount of dollars.

The cash flow cycle can be shortened by either increasing the payable cycle or decreasing the receivable cycle. The payable cycle can be increased by holding back payment of all bills as long as permitted by each creditor. The receivable cycle can be decreased by collecting as many invoices as soon as humanly possible. Effective cash management is causing the cash flow cycle to be as few days as possible.

There are two major functions that the contractor historically neglects:

1. Preparing and forwarding invoices

2. Pursuing collection of receivables

He neglects both, even though he knows the stability of the company depends on them. Receivable borrowing requires that both of these functions be pursued aggressively.

Receivable borrowing always has a limit to the amount that can be borrowed. The collateral for the loan is invoices (sales). Reduction of the current outstanding loan is necessary to permit additional borrowing; this requires collection. New invoices are required to generate additional collateral. The line of credit is always limited. To make room in the line for future (next week's) borrowing, collections must be obtained to pay off the current outstanding loan. To provide collateral for future borrowing, additional invoices (sales) must be started. This requires the contractor to pursue these vital functions aggressively.

Collecting and invoicing are so vital, and yet so neglected, that it is wise to use receivable borrowing, *if for no other reason than to force self-discipline by the contractor to pursue these functions effectively.*

For the contractor who does not need bank borrowing to support cash flow, receivable borrowing will more than pay for itself by:

1. Forcing timely billing

2. Forcing aggressive collection procedures and attitudes

These actions will shorten the average receivable cycle. A shorter receivable cycle, plus a longer average payable cycle, will decrease the amount of cash needed to support the company's cash flow. This will free cash for long-term investments.

For the contractor who does not have enough cash to support the cash flow, receivable borrowing will:

1. Force timely billing

2. Force aggressive collection procedures and attitudes

These actions will shorten the average receivable cycle. A shorter receivable cycle, plus a longer average payable cycle, will increase the amount of sales that can be made with the limited amount of cash available.

The contractor not only has to be effective in the field by working effectively to produce a profit, but he also must convert the profit to cash by an effective and timely cash flow.

Filling the Pipeline

For every dollar of sales, an amount of money must be invested to do the work that the sale represents. This is commonly called "pipeline money" or "money in the pipeline." The amount of pipeline money that is available determines the amount of sales (work) that can be in process at any one time. Pipeline money, many times, is called "working capital." Working capital, however, is technically defined as the "difference between current assets and current liabilities" as shown on the balance sheet. If this definition is used, and the amount of sales volume that can be financed is determined by working capital, most subcontractors would have to heavily reduce their sales volume immediately. Fortunately, working capital is not the determining factor regarding the amount of sales volume a subcontractor can finance. The amount of sales volume he can finance is the amount of pipeline money available to him. Pipeline money is

1. Working capital

2. Money that can be borrowed

Extending payable cycles of the vendors is a form of borrowing. By not paying a vendor until 50 days later than the tenth of the month, the subcontractor is borrowing that amount for 50 days. If the subcontractor can shorten the time between his average payable cycle and his average receivable cycle, he can decrease the amount of pipeline money needed to finance his sales.

Timely billing and high-pressured collection activities are about all the subcontractor can do to control his average receivable cycle. He can, however, control the average payable cycle by merely controlling the time when he pays his bills (other than payroll). This is the same way that his customers control his receivable cycle. Pipeline money can best be defined or explained by the following analogy.

Consider an oil storage depot with a 1-in. pipeline extending 100 miles to a distribution tank. Before oil can be pumped from the depot to the tank, the pipeline must be filled. Assume it takes 30,000 gallons of oil to fill the 100 miles of pipe. As long as the oil is being pumped from the storage depot to the distribution tank, the 30,000 gallons in the pipeline are tied up. All they do is push the oil through the pipe. When all the oil in the storage depot is pumped to the distribution tank, then the oil in the pipeline is drained out and sold.

The same thing happens with money on a construction job. The pipeline is filled with costs of labor, materials, and services. The labor, material, and services push out a partial payout; however, at that time more labor, material, and services have continued to be put in, which pushes out another partial payout, and so on, and so on, until the finish of the job when the final payout is made without having to continue to put in more labor, materials, and services. This last payout is represented in the oil analogy as oil draining out of the pipeline. As the oil in the pipeline was tied up as long as it was necessary to pump it from the storage depot to the distribution tank, the money for labor, materials, and services is tied up until the end of the job.

Hopefully, a construction firm is perpetual. Therefore, its pipeline money will never completely drain out because there will always be jobs in progress. The pipeline money is the money tied up between the cash in and the cash out of the cash flow cycle.

If the subcontractor can't get enough pipeline money to finance the job he is trying to get, he had better not take the job. The bonding companies help him to know when he can't get enough. The subcontractor's normal feeling about having enough pipeline money is that he can always handle one more job. Because of greed he overestimates his ability to keep the pipelines full. The bonding companies evaluate the subcontractor's true ability to provide pipeline money for the next job. If he does not have this ability, the bonding company will refuse to provide him with a bond. This will prevent his being awarded the job. In this case, the bonding company has saved the subcontractor from himself. This happens many times.

Required pipeline money is a subject that the subcontractor usually ignores by sticking his head in the sand. The construction industry requires from 15 to 20 cents of pipeline money to support each sales dollar (dependent on the average cash flow cycle for the particular trade and company). This requirement is an undeniable fact. This amount should be determined by each subcontractor for his company and taken into serious consideration each time the sales volume is increased.

As important as it is to produce a profit, it is equally important to control the cash flow of the company effectively.

14 PAYROLL AND LABOR BURDEN

Payroll is a required function of any business involving people. Many years ago, payroll was the simple activity of multiplying the hours worked by the rate per hour for each employee. After this was computed, cash was put in an envelope and given to the employee. Unfortunately, that simplicity does not prevail today. With the advent of income tax withholding, Social Security, union funds, and union contracts requiring reports of earnings came complexity in every sense of the word.

PAYROLL

Payroll is divided into five major activities: earnings, deductions, additions, administration and reporting, and bank account.

I. Earnings

This is the activity where the complexity begins. From the amount earned by each employee, a multitude of deductions are possible. These include:

A. Income tax withholding

B. FICA (Social Security) contributions

C. Union contributions or deductions, which could include:

1. Dues deduction

2. Contribution to paid holiday fund

3. Contribution to vacation fund

4. Contribution to health and accident fund

5. Any other deduction required by the union contract

D. Savings bond purchases

E. Company-sponsored health and accident insurance funds

F. Deductions for wage garnishments

III. Additions

There are two basic types of additions:

A. Allowances for travel, including auto and parking

B. Reimbursement for cash expenditures

IV. Administration and reporting

This payroll function involves five activities. They are accounting, governmental reports and payments, union reports administering and payments, insurance reports and payments, and trade association reports and payments. The following is a description of each.

A. Accounting

Payroll accounting consists of recording the earnings, deductions, and additions in the payroll journal and the individual employee earnings record. It also includes distribution of the payroll. The distribution of payroll to jobs consists of computing the hours and resulting dollars for each job on which labor was expended and then recording the hours and costs to the individual job records. This requires the time for each man to be reported by job. Time cards that permit hours worked to be recorded on the jobs worked on are required. This requires the cost of the labor to be computed for each job that each man worked on, plus the total that each man worked. The total that each man worked is used to establish his pay for the week, and the cost computed for each job for each man is used to distribute the payroll costs to the jobs.

The act of computing earnings, preparing checks, and distributing checks is not part of the managing process. It is strictly an administrative function. The act of distributing labor hours and costs to the individual job records, however, is part of the managing process. This activity contributes vital information for job cost control and billing.

The payroll function must include efficient and timely labor distribution.

B. Governmental reports and payments

This payroll activity requires federal, state, and/or city withholding income tax, FICA (Social Security) withholding, recording, reporting, and disbursing (paying) to the applicable government bodies, including year-end preparation and forwarding of employee earnings and withholding statements (W-4 form). It also includes city and/or state labor tax reporting and paying.

C. Administering union reports and payments

   1. Withholding, recording, reporting, and paying funds withheld from the employee's check, as per the union agreement

   2. Reporting and paying contributions required by union agreement to be paid by the contractor

D. Insurance

   1. Paying all insurance premiums included in the labor burden (see "Labor Burden" section of this chapter)

E. Trade association

   1. Reporting and disbursing (paying) dues and assessments to trade associations (see Labor Burden section of this chapter.)

V. Bank account

The amount of the payroll for most trades in relation to other costs is appreciable. The payable cycle of the payroll is usually shorter than most of the others. The shorter payable cycle and the amount involved cause the payroll to have an appreciable effect on the cash flow of the company. For this reason, and in order not to mix payroll checks with regular checks, a separate bank account is kept for the payroll only.

The payroll bank account can be one of two types: impress payroll account or standard balance payroll account. An impress (zero-balance) payroll account is one that has the exact amount of the net payroll* transferred into the payroll bank account for each payroll period. When all the checks have been cashed and have cleared the bank, the account will have a zero balance. The only checks drawn against an impress payroll account are the payroll checks

---

*Net payroll is meant to be the total amount of checks issued for earnings after withholdings, deductions, etc.

issued to the employees. A standard balance payroll account is one that has the gross payroll* plus the total amount of the labor burden transferred into the payroll bank account. (See "Labor Burden" section in this chapter.)

The use of a standard balance payroll account includes payment of withholding taxes, Social Security, union, and other withholding, and all items included in the labor burden from the standard balance payroll account. This generates a continuing balance in the account. The reason is that monies to cover payment of withholdings, insurance, union fringes, etc., are transferred into the account each week; however, payment of these funds is made biweekly, monthly, and quarterly.

Most industries, accountants, and finance personnel use and advocate the use of an impress bank account for payroll. The withholdings, labor burden costs, etc., are paid from the general account. Because of the cash flow characteristics of construction contracting, it is advisable to use the standard balance payroll account concept. This provides three important functions:

1. It ensures that the money required to satisfy payment of withholdings and labor burden costs will be available when due.

2. It provides the compensating balances necessary to satisfy bank agreements.

3. It allows the contractor to readily evaluate his ability to pay material vendors, since the *entire* balance of the general account is free from the labor burden and withholding tax commitments.

When the standard balance payroll account concept is used, the general account can be treated as an impress account, with no effort to maintain any balances otherwise required.

Table 3 represents a sample of a standard balance payroll account transfer schedule. In the example in Table 3 the total amount of money that will be required to be transferred

---

*Gross payroll is meant to be the total amount earned by all employees prior to deductions, etc.

Table 3
STANDARD BALANCE PAYROLL TRANSFER SCHEDULE

Payroll period week ending Sunday _____10/21/69_____ .

Transfer from general bank account __#3211__ to Payroll bank account __#3271__

on ___10/26/69___ .

		% of gross payroll
$ 3,455.00	Net payroll	
$ 520.00	For FICA (Social Security)	5.2
$ 900.00	For federal withholding tax	
$ 125.00	For state withholding tax	
$ 50.00	National benefit fund (union)	1.0
$ 50.00	Trade association	1.0
$ 137.50	Other insurances at 2¾%*	2.75
$ 275.00	Other insurances at 5½%†	5.5
$ 100.00	Vacation withholding, Local #1782 (20 cents per hour)	2.0
$ 75.00	Working dues withholding, Local #1782	1.5
$ _____	Other	_____
$ _____	Other	_____
$ 5,687.50	Total	

*W.C., O.D., liability $1.712 per C.
State unemployment   0.5
Federal unemployment 0.5
_____
                        2.712 per C.
                      or 2³/₄%
†½% Apprentice fund
  2% Health and welfare
  3% Pension fund
5½%
Note: It is assumed that payday is Friday following the payroll period.

is $5,687.50. The total of the transfer will be part of the cash out summary that establishes the cash requirements for the period involved. (See "Chapter 13, Cash Flow.") Issuance of checks is based on union requirements and mechanical means of delivery. When the total ($5,687.50 in our example) is transferred from the general bank account to the payroll account, all the expenditures and commitments generated by labor have been funded. No future funds will have to be allocated to pay for labor and labor burden.

Preparation of the payroll, distribution of the labor costs, and maintenance of records for income tax withholding, unions, and trade associations is an activity that is appreciable and must be performed weekly, monthly, and quarterly, without fail. In many small companies the payroll activity is performed by the same person who keeps the books, prepares billing job costs, etc. Because the payroll and subsequent reports *must* be done on particular days, the other vital activities take a back seat and many times are neglected. This must not be allowed to occur. Payroll is not necessarily a vital function, but it is a function that requires appreciable time each and every week. The subcontractor should determine the number of hours required to perform the payroll and allied activities and allocate sufficient people-hours to prevent vital functions from being affected.

SEVERANCE OF FIELD EMPLOYEES

The characteristics of construction requires the subcontractor to increase and decrease his field work force frequently. The subcontractor must, therefore, be prepared to sever employees in a systematic, routine manner. Severance of employees is based on one of three actions by either the employee or the employer: quitting by employee, layoff by employer, or discharge by employer. In most union contracts and situations, when an employee quits it is not required that he be paid at the time of severance; hence, his final paycheck can be mailed to him. On the other hand, a layoff or discharge severance requires the man to be given his final paycheck at the moment of severance. On most construction jobs, the employee who is being severed is remote from where payroll checks are prepared. This creates an awkward situation. And most contractors require the job supervisor to call the time into the office. The check is then prepared and physically delivered to the job. The severance is then effected. Most layoffs result from lack of work. The need for a layoff is known in advance. This permits convenient preparation of the final paychecks and delivery to the job in advance of the layoff. Discharges, however, are the result of an undesirable situation, involving one or more employees, that can no longer be permitted to continue. This requires immediate action by the job supervisor. His ability to maintain job discipline is much reduced if he has to call the office, request a check, and have it delivered in several hours, or perhaps even the next day.

There are two procedures that will permit the job supervisor to discharge undesirable employees immediately:

1. The job supervisor has the authority to sign payroll checks at his discretion.

2. A field severance draft system has been established.

To give the job supervisor authority to sign payroll checks at his discretion creates the following undesirable situations:

1. It gives the job supervisor access to the company funds.

2. It requires signature cards to be initiated for the payroll account each time a job supervisor is added or taken off.

3. It lends itself to lack of control of the payroll.

The use of field severance drafts eliminates all the undesirable situations while permitting the freedom and timeliness required for discharge severances.

The difference between a check and a draft is as follows. A check is honored and paid automatically when presented to the bank on which it is written, based on a previously authorized signature; that is, the authorized signature is the authority for the bank to honor and pay the check. A draft is different in that the bank *will not* honor and pay the draft based on the signature. When a draft is presented to the bank on which it is drawn for payment, the bank, at that time and for that specific draft only, obtains *direct* authority to honor and pay. The signature has no authority. Direct authority to pay a draft is obtained by the bank. It calls and receives verbal authority from a person (in the office) previously authorized to authorize draft payment. This eliminates signature cards and gives management full control. The procedure is simple.

When a job supervisor requires a final paycheck for severance, he calls the office and informs the person handling the payroll that John Doe is being severed and will have 26 hours coming at the time of severance. The person handling the payroll immediately computes the gross amount, withholdings, deductions, and net pay. The net pay, deductions, and withholdings, are given to the job supervisor. The job supervisor advises the person handling the payroll the number of the draft he is going to use. The drafts are numbered the same as checks. The drafts have stubs which provide spaces to itemize hours, gross pay, and deductions. The job supervisor then makes out the draft in the net amount and fills in the spaces showing gross pay, withholdings, etc., signs his name, and severs the employee. The person handling the payroll enters the amounts on the employee's earnings record and in the payroll journal and distributes the labor in the same manner as if a regular payroll check were issued by the office.

The number of the draft is also noted. The person receiving the draft then cashes it, the same as a check. A draft looks exactly the same as a check except it has the word "draft" printed on it. When the check arrives at the bank for transfer of the money from the contractor's account, the bank will call and inform the person handling the payroll that draft # _____, in the amount of $ _____ , signed by John Doe, has been received, and the bank then asks for authority to pay the draft. The person handling the payroll refers to the records made at the time the draft was initiated and authorizes the bank to honor the draft.

Assume a draft is written by a job supervisor in an attempt to embezzle funds. When the draft is presented to the bank for payment, the person handling the payroll obviously does not have any record of the draft and, therefore, denies the bank authority to honor the draft. The draft is then returned to the person who cashed the draft. The person who cashed the draft then must recover the funds from the embezzler.

It is, therefore, recommended that the final pay for severances be handled as follows:

1. Quitting: paid on regular payroll check and mailed to the person severed on the following payday

2. Layoff: paid on regular payroll checks and delivered to the job site prior to the scheduled layoff

3. Discharge: paid with the use of field severance draft issued by the job supervisor

LABOR BURDEN

Labor burden is the total of several costs which are generated when labor is expended. These costs would not exist if no labor were expended. They fall into these categories: insurance, payroll taxes, union fringe benefits, and trade association dues and/or assessments.

I. Insurance

  A. Workmen's compensation, occupational disease, and liability insurance premiums

  B. Comprehensive general liability and property damage insurance premiums

  C. State unemployment insurance premiums

  D. Federal unemployment insurance premiums

    E. Umbrella insurance coverage premiums

    F. Costs of other insurances whereby the insurance premiums are based on a percentage of payroll

    The premium costs for workmen's compensation insurance are based on a separate percentage of payroll for each classification of worker. This percentage is based on the experience factor for a particular contractor for a particular classification of worker. For example:

    1. The percentage of payroll used to establish the premium cost for the production employee is greater than for office personnel.

    2. The percentage of payroll used to establish the premium cost for, say, electricians working on transmission lines is much greater than for electricians working inside a building.

    The contractor must know the specific percentage used to establish premium costs for each classification of his employees. This is necessary to establish the exact labor burden for each classification of worker employed by the contractor. (See Chapter 18.)

  II. Payroll Taxes

    A. FICA (Social Security)

    B. Local and/or state labor tax

 III. Union Fringe Benefits

    A. National union benefit fund

    B. Union vacation fund

    C. Union holiday fund

    D. International union pension fund

    E. Local union pension fund

    F. Apprenticeship fund

    G. Health and welfare fund

    H. Other union benefits

 IV. Trade Association Dues and/or Assessments

    A. Local trade association chapter

    B. National trade association

    These costs are usually in the form of dues based on a fixed percentage of the union employees' payroll.

Trade association costs are recognized by the business world as being a legitimate cost of doing business and are accepted as being part of the labor burden, the same as Social Security.

Labor burden is usually calculated in percentage; it can, however, be calculated in dollars. If calculated in dollars, the amount would be per $100 of gross payroll. It is suggested that percentages be used to prevent misunderstandings and errors in computation. Frequently, part of the labor burden may be established in cents. When this occurs, it must be converted to a percentage.

Example

The costs that the contractor must contribute to the union for paid holidays may be established in the union contract as 20 cents per hour. The 20 cents per hour should be converted to a percentage by dividing the 20 cents by the hourly rate. Assume the hourly rate is $10. Then

$$\frac{\$.20}{\$10} = 2\%$$

The labor burden for paid holidays is 2 percent.

A typical list of items and related percentages that make up the labor burden is shown in Table 4. The percentages shown have no validity. They are shown as an example only, not a sample.

Although the percentages shown in Table 4 are representative only, they are relative. Labor burdens of almost 18 percent as shown in the example are not uncommon. Seldom is the labor burden less than the gross markup that can be realized. This fact points out the importance of knowing the exact labor burden for each classification of worker. The production worker's labor is the major product that the contractor sells.

To determine the total cost of labor, the exact labor burden is added to the direct labor costs. It must be kept in mind that the labor burden is constantly changing. It changes annually when the insurance costs change. It changes periodically when the federal, state, and/or local governments change their required insurance costs or labor taxes. It is subject to change with each new labor contract. Rarely does a labor burden percentage remain stable for more than a year. Changes in the

Table 4

Item	Labor Burden, %
Workmen's compensation and occupational disease	1.40
General liability and property damage	0.312
Umbrella liability	0.01
State unemployment insurance	0.05
Federal unemployment insurance	0.5
FICA (Social Security)	5.2
National union benefit fund	1.0
Trade association	1.0
Union vacation fund	2.0
Union holiday fund	1.5
Local union pension fund	3.0
Apprenticeship fund	0.005
Health and welfare fund	2.0
Total labor burden	17.977

labor burden must constantly be anticipated and revised in advance. This ensures that estimates for labor are based on the labor burden that will be applicable at the time the labor is expended.

It is difficult to motivate accounting personnel to include labor burden when reporting labor costs. The accounting profession looks upon the costs listed in labor burden (excluding income tax and FICA deductions) as general administration expenses. When the contractor requests the labor costs for a particular job, he usually will receive the gross labor costs only. The contractor is trained to think of labor cost as including the labor burden. The accountant is trained to think of labor costs as consisting of gross labor cost only. This causes the communication between accounting and the contractor to be in error to the amount of the labor burden, which will run from 10 to 30 percent. To prevent this, the contractor must always be sure the labor cost reports he is receiving include labor burden.

Labor burden is an appreciable part of the total labor costs and always must be recognized as part of the cost of labor and not as an additional cost of doing business.

15 ACCOUNTING, BOOKKEEPING, AND COST CONTROL

Accounting is looked upon by most people, including subcontractors, as a secretive, complicated, holier-than-thou world known only to accountants. It is viewed this way because few (outside the accounting profession) have found it necessary to remove the cloak and make an effort to understand what accounting really is. It appears that business people do not want to remove the cloak of the unknown from accounting because they subconsciously want to lean on the accounting profession as the light that will guide them through the perilous journey of conducting a business. Fortunately, the accounting profession and many individual accountants for small firms have accepted this responsibility and responded with dedication. Unfortunately, in the construction industry—and particularly in subcontracting—the accounting profession, or the individual accountant, *cannot* be the guiding light. The subcontractor *must not* lean on his outside accountant for direction on how to run his business. The accountant must be guided by the subcontractor. The books, ledgers, profit and loss statement formats, and accounting and administrative systems and forms must be in accordance with the actual needs and characteristics of the particular subcontractor, not with what the accountant views the needs to be from his expertise as an accountant.

The average subcontractor is an intelligent, aggressive person who can and does understand most everything that confronts him. But for some unknown human reason, the average subcontractor does not understand the principles, sequence, and functions of accounting. This probably is true for several reasons:

1. The average subcontractor is mechanically oriented.

2. He does not realize the need to understand accounting.

3. He would prefer, out of desire, to "let someone else do that part of the business."

4. Because of the above three reasons, he has learned that his accountant will satisfy what he thinks are his needs.

5. And/or he subconsciously is afraid he cannot understand the accounting functions.

It is the last reason that *must* be overcome.

This attitude of fear regarding accounting is probably enforced by the absolute formality employed. The hard, fancy binders (book covers) with metal spindles probably do much to contribute to the subcontractor's aversion. But a company's accounting books are nothing more than pieces of paper with certain numerical information recorded on them. The paper could consist of paper towels, toilet paper, or any other material on which information could be recorded. For efficiency, the accounting profession has found that by putting both horizontal and vertical lines on the paper, the recording of the numbers involved can be controlled with fewer human errors. So that the sheets of paper may be protected from mechanical injury, they are filed in handsome, expensive binders. Take these binders away and put the forms in manila envelopes, and much of the cloak of the unknown felt by most persons outside the accounting profession probably would be destroyed.

It is not necessary or advisable that the subcontractor become an accountant. It is a must, however, that he understand the accounting principles and the use and purpose of all of the forms. Accounting is a vital part of the contracting business. It can contribute heavily to the daily operating requirements if the subcontractor understands its use and takes advantage of what it can offer. The intent of the following sections on Accounting and Financial Statements is to provide the basic understanding that the subcontractor should have.

ACCOUNTING

Accounting is the process of receiving, accumulating, recording, and reporting information (primarily numerical). In addition, accounting physically handles the company's cash. The processes of accounting are simple and logical. Everything that comes into the accounting department is recorded. Everything that goes out of the accounting department is recorded. A simple recording system has been established over the years and is universally accepted. It consists of four steps. Accounting records summarize specific information resulting from the operation of the company. This information is sales, all expenditures, including payroll, receipt of money, and disbursement of money. Each of the four steps involves the process of summarizing the information. That on which the information is recorded for each step is identified with a name: journals, general ledger, statement of income and expenses, and balance sheet. All information is initially recorded in the journals. This is step one. The totals from the journals are recorded in the general ledger. This is step two. The totals from the general ledger are recorded on the profit and loss statement or the balance sheet. This is step three. The totals from the statement are recorded on the balance sheet. This is step four. The information coming into accounting is recorded in the journals and the general ledger. Summarized information coming from accounting is recorded on the income and expense statement and the balance sheet.

Each category of information has its own separate journal. They are known as the sales journal, purchase journal, cash receipts journal, cash disbursements journal, payroll journal, and general journal. There is only one general ledger to record the totals from the journals. The six journals and one general ledger are all that are used by the accountant to prepare statements, balance sheets, and tax returns. Auditing (confirming) the journals and general ledger and preparing the statements, balance sheet, and tax returns are the total responsibility of the accountant.

There is additional information, however, that is produced by accounting that contributes to the day-to-day operation of the company. This information is a by-product of the information recorded in the journals and is recorded on subsidiary ledgers. The subsidiary ledgers provide information regarding what is owed to each vendor, what amount customers owe and for how long, individual employees' earnings for each week and year to date, cost to date on each individual job, and various other reporting information needs. The main subsidiary ledgers are the accounts payable ledger, the accounts receivable ledger, the employee earnings ledger, the overhead expense account ledger, and the job cost ledger.

The journals and ledgers are sheets of paper or cards which have lines forming columns in which to record numbers. The sheets usually are protected by a binder of some type. If the journals and/or ledgers are cards, they usually are kept in a metal container which protects them from mutilation and wear. There is no set form or size of sheets or cards or size and number of columns and lines required. The format for each is custom-designed to the company, the journal or ledger, and the desires of the person responsible for the format used. The requirement of the format is that it must be compatible with the needs of the company and with the system being used. And to destroy the myth that the journals and ledgers are part of a secretive, holier-than-thou function, any piece of paper with the information written or typed on it becomes a journal or ledger. The journal or ledger is merely a piece of paper on which is recorded specific information.

Following is a definition of each of the journals, the general ledger, and the major subsidiary ledgers, with an explanation of that which is recorded in each. The process of writing the information in the journal or ledger is called entering, posting, or vouchering.

Sales Journal

The sales journal is a sheet or card on which is recorded the amounts of each sale (invoice) by the company. Its purpose is to determine the total sales (invoices) of the company for given periods of time.

Purchase Journal

The purchase journal is a sheet or card on which is recorded the amounts of each purchase for which invoices have been received from the suppliers, manufacturers, or firms providing services. Its purpose is to determine the total purchases of the company for given periods of time.

Cash Receipts Journal

The cash receipts journal is a sheet or card on which is recorded the amount of each cash receipt. Its purpose is to determine the cash received from sales and other sources for given periods of time.

Cash Disbursement Journal

The cash disbursement journal is a sheet or card on which is recorded the amount of each cash payment, whether paid by cash or check. Its purpose is to determine total monies paid out for given periods of time.

Payroll Journal

The payroll journal is a sheet or card on which is recorded the name of each employee and each employee's earnings, deductions, and net pay. Its purpose is to provide a combined record of all employees' earnings, etc. It also provides the totals of amount earned, totals of deductions required to be forwarded to the government for Social Security, income taxes, etc. It also provides the totals withheld for union purposes, which must be forwarded. The payroll journal provides the total of labor expended on all jobs.

General Journal

The general journal is a sheet or card used by the accountant to record all adjustments to the other journals and for other accounting requirements (accruals, write-offs, etc.).

General Ledger

The general ledger is a sheet or card on which is recorded the totals of the amounts recorded in the journals and overhead-expense-account ledgers for a given period of time. The totals of all the journals must equal the totals of all the general ledger accounts. The general ledger is used by the accountants only. It is the source of information required to prepare financial statements.

Subsidiary Ledger

Subsidiary ledgers are sheets or cards on which is recorded the same information that is recorded in each of the journals. The difference between a journal and a subsidiary ledger is that the journal has *all* the transactions recorded, regardless of to whom and from what source they were made. In a subsidiary ledger are recorded only the transactions for the specific source or to whom the transaction is directed. The subcontractor uses this information for his day-to-day functions and decisions. Information from the journals contributes little or nothing to the day-to-day operational needs. The following definitions are for the more commonly used subsidiary ledgers.

Payable Ledger. The payable ledger is a by-product of the purchase journal and cash disbursements journal. *All* purchases are recorded on the purchase journal. *Each* purchase is recorded on an individual payable ledger for each vendor. The purpose of the payable ledger is to record the total invoices from each vendor. It also shows total money owed for each individual vendor for particular invoices. Amounts paid to the individual vendor are recorded on the cash disbursements journal and on the payable ledger for that vendor. The difference between the amounts for what is purchased from each vendor and what is paid to each vendor is that which is still owed to each vendor.

Receivable Ledger. The receivable ledger is a by-product of the sales journal and the cash receipts journal. *All* sales are recorded on the sales journal. *Each* sale (invoice) is recorded on the individual receivable ledger for each customer. The purpose of the receivable ledger is to record the total sales (invoices) to each customer. It also shows the total money due from each individual customer for particular invoices. Amounts received from individual customers are recorded on the cash receipts journal and on the receivable ledger for that customer. The difference between the totals of the amounts of the invoices to each customer and the amounts received from each customer is the amount still due from each customer.

Employee Earnings Ledger. The employee earnings ledger is a by-product of the payroll journal. *All* payroll expenditures are recorded on the payroll journal. The amounts paid to *each* employee for each pay period are recorded on the employee earnings ledger. This information includes gross pay, all deductions, and net pay. The purpose of the employee earnings ledger is to determine total money paid to each employee, total money withheld for federal and state income taxes and social security, and any other money that is withheld for the employee.

General and Administration Expense Ledger. The general and administration expense ledgers are a by-product of the purchase journal and the cash disbursement journal. Their purpose is to separately record the expenses for each overhead expense account shown on the income and expense statement.

Job Cost Ledger. The job cost ledger is a by-product of the purchase journal, cash disbursement journal, and payroll journal. Its purpose is to provide the costs to date generated by each separate job. This information is used by the subcontractor to make the day-to-day cost control decisions.

Of all the journals and ledgers, the job cost ledger is the one that is *most* important to the subcontractor. Other subsidiary ledgers may be established as required. The journals produce totals of items from or to many sources. When the total is required on a repetitive basis for items from or to an individual source, a subsidiary ledger must be initiated for that source. The following diagram shows the flow of information from the journals to the commonly used subsidiary ledgers.

Journals.	Subsidiary Ledgers.
Sales Journal Cash Receipts Journal	→ Accounts Receivable Ledger
Purchase Journal Cash Disbursements Journal	→ Accounts Payable Ledger
Payroll Journal	→ Payroll Ledger (Employees' Earnings Record)
Purchase Journal Payroll Journal	→ Job Cost Ledger

Invoice #	Date	Vendor	Amount
70321	4/1/77	Aetna Plywood Co.	27.33
211	4/1/77	Tremco Mfg. Co.	34.22
176	4/1/77	Structural Glazer, Inc.	174.11
3261	4/2/77	Terrazzo Supply Co.	3,041.00
777	4/2/77	Robt. Stone Co.	426.00
1200	4/2/77	Emyr Fuel Co.	81.30
18421	4/3/77	Consolidated Supply Co.	41.70
8641	4/4/77	Cunningham Wreck, Co.	152.01
6333	4/4/77	Garfield Builders Sup.	176.22
310	4/5/77	Tremco Mfg. Co.	172.01
1295	4/8/77	Emyr Fuel Co.	133.22
358	4/9/77	Tremco Mfg. Co.	947.21
80424	4/9/77	Aetna Plywood Co.	623.18
9876	4/10/77	Standard Supply Co.	18.41
18762	4/11/77	Consolidated Supply Co.	1,043.21
8344	4/11/77	Terrazzo Supply Co.	211.12
6988	4/12/77	Garfield Builders Sup.	.33
987	4/12/77	Robt. Stone Co.	28.40
1380	4/12/77	Emyr Fuel Co.	10,721.18
410	4/15/77	Tremco Mfg. Co.	41.58
85210	4/16/77	Aetna Plywood Co.	723.12
18952	4/17/77	Cons. Supply Co.	824.14
1042	4/17/77	Robt. Stone Co.	918.11
7122	4/17/77	Garfield Builders Sup.	1,811.23
1955	4/18/77	Standard Lumber Co.	1,214.03
1136	4/18/77	Robt. Stone Co.	6,412.13
19211	4/19/77	Consolidated Sup. Co.	28.72
5150	4/19/77	Standard Lumber Co.	.62
19312	4/22/77	Consolidated Sup. Co.	147.18
9994	4/22/77	Standard Supply Co.	342.41
87121	4/23/77	Aetna Plywood Co.	673.12
87533	4/24/77	Aetna Plywood Co.	517.62
19761	4/25/77	Consolidated Sup. Co.	813.12
1301	4/25/77	Robt. Stone Co.	763.71
1450	4/25/77	Emyr Fuel Co.	912.84
7304	4/26/77	Garfield Builders Sup.	1,042.18
94134	4/29/77	Aetna Plywood Co.	1,171.06
19852	4/29/77	Consolidated Sup. Co.	28.72
1466	4/30/77	Robt. Stone Co.	18.13

CONSTRUCTION SERVICES CO.
PURCHASE JOURNAL

CONSTRUCTION SERVICES CO.
ACCOUNTS PAYABLE LEDGER
Name of Account: AETNA PLYWOOD CO.

Inv. #	Date	Amount	Credit
70321	4/1/77	27.33	
80424	4/9/77	623.18	
85210	4/16/77	723.12	
87121	4/23/77	673.12	
87533	4/24/77	517.62	
94134	4/29/77	1,171.06	
	4/30/77		1,373.63

CONSTRUCTION SERVICES CO.
ACCOUNTS PAYABLE LEDGER
Name of Account: TREMCO MFG. CO.

Inv. #	Date	Amount	Credit
211	4/1/77	34.22	
310	4/5/77	172.01	
358	4/9/77	947.21	
410	4/15/77	41.58	
	4/18/77		206.33

CONSTRUCTION SERVICES CO.
ACCOUNTS PAYABLE LEDGER
Name of Account: CONSOLIDATED SUPPLY CO.

Inv. #	Date	Amount	Credit
18421	4/3/77	41.70	
18762	4/11/77	1,043.21	
18952	4/17/77	824.14	
19211	4/19/77	28.72	
19312	4/22/77	147.18	
19761	4/25/77	813.12	
19852	4/29/77	28.72	
	4/30/77		1,909.05

CONSTRUCTION SERVICES CO.
ACCOUNTS PAYABLE LEDGER
Name of Account: ROBT. STONE CO.

Inv. #	Date	Amount	Credit
777	4/2/77	426.00	
987	4/12/77	28.40	
1042	4/17/77	918.11	
1136	4/18/77	6,412.13	
1301	4/25/77	763.71	
1466	4/30/77	18.13	
	4/30/77		1,372.51

Figure 3   Sample journals and ledgers.

Figure 3 is a sample purchase journal with four sample accounts payable ledgers. Note that there can be as many payable ledgers as there are different vendors listed on the purchase journal.

Preparing the profit and loss statement is the third step in summarizing the incoming and outgoing information of the accounting process. The profit and loss statement shows the totals taken from the general ledger for a given period of time.

The balance sheet is the fourth and last step in summarizing information. It is the cumulative totals shown on all the profit and loss statements to date, plus liabilities and assets existing at a particular point and time, plus the initial investment into the company.

To ensure accuracy, a system known as the "double-entry system" involving credits and debits is followed. This system is simple and logical. It requires that every piece of information be recorded in two places. The total of the recordings in each place is required to balance with each other. A more logical explanation of the double-entry system is that anything you put somewhere you must have taken from some place else. If you put down an object you must have moved it from some place else. That is, in the accounting process nothing is created. All information recorded must have been obtained from some place. If the item is a liability, the place you take it from is called a debit, and the place that you put it is called a credit. If the item is an asset, the place you take it from is called a credit, and the place you put it is called a debit.

The entire accounts (bookkeeping) function is the activity of recording information in a specific manner, in a specific place, for specific things, (in journals), then taking the totals from these recordings and recording the totals in another specific manner, in another specific place (in the general ledger), then taking the totals from those recordings and recording those totals in a specific place, in a specific manner (on the statements).

Accounting is the recording of information in a specific series of steps that will provide legal statements required by law for tax and other purposes, and management with information relative to the worth and success or failure of the total business, and day-to-day operational information.

Figures 4(*a*) and (*b*) show the flow of information from its source through the bookkeeping system.

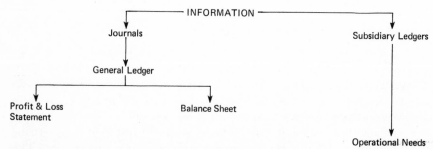

Figure 4a   General accounting information flowchart.

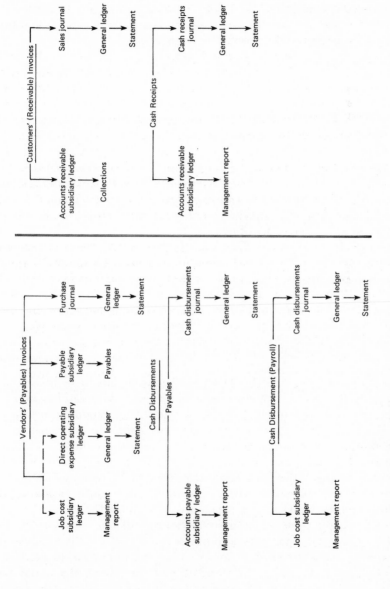

Figure 4b Detailed accounting information flowchart.

BOOKKEEPING FUNCTION

In most companies, the accounting function includes both bookkeeping and the operational functions. The operational function includes these day-to-day activities:

1. Preparation of invoices

2. Preparation of payroll

3. Paying the bills

4. Collecting the money

5. Depositing the money

Just as the human body's vital functions must perform well enough at all times to prevent death from occurring, so too these operational functions must work to keep the company alive. Unfortunately, many companies neglect these vital functions and make them take a second place to many other unrelated activities.

There is no way that the bookkeeping process can function without the operational needs' being performed in an adequate and timely manner. The bookkeeping function provides two basic requirements:

1. A legal statement required by law for tax and other purposes

2. Information to management relative to the worth and the success or failure of the total business

Aside from the legal bookkeeping requirements, a company could theoretically operate without bookkeeping. There is no way, however, that a company could continue to exist without the operational function.

The operational functions in large companies are not a part of the accounting or bookkeeping system. They are often treated as completely self-run functions, and they are often even separate departments. The average manager often has the wrong idea that the operational functions (day-to-day activities) are part of accounting or bookkeeping and looks upon them as bookkeeping functions. This immediately causes him to emotionally put these functions into a category that he feels is unknown to him. He depends upon the accountant completely for the effective performance of the accounting (bookkeeping) function. But the accountant does not apply his effort, etc., toward these operational day-to-day functions. If he does, the system employed in many cases is not applicable and in most cases is not adequate. The average accountant has neither the feel nor the appreciation for the needs necessary to establish and maintain an effective operational function. This leaves the functions in limbo. Because of this it is necessary that management provide accounting personnel with an adequate, applicable system and procedure for the day-to-day operational functions. The system and procedure must meet the practical needs of these activities.

The bookkeeping process can contribute to the operational function if the system is set up to provide more than the two basic requirements. One of the most common and valuable additional functions the bookkeeping system can provide is individual job cost records. In bookkeeping jargon a job cost record is a subsidiary ledger and is usually called the job cost ledger. The job cost ledger will show costs to date for material costs, miscellaneous job costs, and labor. The job cost ledger, or any other accounting function, will *not* show the amount of work installed to date; it can only show the amount of costs incurred to date. Management must determine the amount of work installed to date by other methods.

Remember, all information provided by the accounting (bookkeeping) process is history. However, the system should be as up to date as possible with the historical information. The only way the information provided by the accounting (bookkeeping) process can aid management in decision making is that the information be up to date. Information that is old is of no value toward decision making. The only purposes old information will serve are tax needs and statements for legal needs.

COST CONTROL ACCOUNTING

Included in a company are profit centers. For each profit center there is a cost center. There are no profit centers without cost centers. There are, however, cost centers without profit centers. A job is a profit center. It has costs and a profit or loss. Within each job are additional profit centers. For each profit center within a job there is a cost center. General administration (overhead) is a cost center without a profit center. Estimating is a cost center without a profit center.

One of the greatest contributors to failure in subcontracting is the lack of knowing costs. The accountant presents the subcontractor with a statement of income and expenses each year, and perhaps biannually or even quarterly. The statement shows the total cost of all labor and all material on all the jobs for that period. The statement also shows the cost of all the general administration (overhead). It does *not* show the cost on each individual job, or the cost of estimating, engineering, purchasing, accounting, management, or other appreciable cost centers. The statement is a report of that which has happened, prepared several weeks after it has happened. It is only a report of the final score of the game after the game is over. It gives the score only. It does not give the results of each player's contribution, or lack of contribution.

Unfortunately, the subcontractor cannot coach his team from information on the last game only. He must also have information about the team he is now playing, while the game is in progress. The subcontractor must know the up-to-the-minute costs of each job. For large jobs he must know the up-to-the-minute costs of each cost center in the job. He must also know the cost of each cost center within the general administration (overhead).

The method used to develop total costs for a job differs from that used for general administration (overhead). Total job cost consists of four individual costs: materials, labor, labor burden, and miscellaneous direct job costs. The definition of each is as follows:

> Material costs include costs for all materials and equipment installed into the job.

> Labor cost is the gross cost of all labor expended on the job. This includes productive and nonproductive labor, that is, apprentices, journeymen, and supervision. Supervision includes foremen (working and nonworking), general foremen, and superintendents or project managers who expend their full time on a job. Labor cost for jobs does *not* include a superintendent or area general foreman who has several jobs to oversee. The costs for this type of job management should be included in general administration (overhead) cost. Labor burden costs are generated as a result of labor being expended on a job. They would not exist if labor was not expended. Labor burden costs include payroll insurance costs, payroll taxes, union fringe-benefit costs, and trade association dues and assessments.

> Miscellaneous direct job costs are generated by a particular job. They would not exist if that particular job had not been. They include permit, job performance and payment bond, inspection fees, sub-subcontracts, expendable tools, and other items.

Remember, each job is a profit or loss center and also a cost center. The purpose of developing cost centers is to enable the subcontractor to *control* the cost of each. To control the cost center he must measure and record the costs. He must analyze the results and take a course of action to correct the deficiencies or perpetuate that which is desirable. The job costs are recorded by accounting on the job cost ledger. The accounting system should keep a job cost ledger for each separate job. The information for each of the four separate costs is obtained as follows:

Material and Equipment Costs

All materials and equipment are either purchased directly for a job or are supplied to the job from the subcontractor's warehouse. When materials and equipment are purchased directly for a job, the purchase generates an invoice from their supplier. When the invoice is received by the subcontractor, the amount is recorded in the purchase journal and the job cost ledger. When the material is shipped from the subcontractor's warehouse, a material requisition is initiated, priced, extended, and totaled. This total is entered into the purchase journal (to relieve the warehouse inventory) and the job cost ledger.

Labor Costs

Labor expended on each job is listed on time cards. The time listed is computed to dollars for each job. The dollars for the total labor expended on each job for each week are recorded on the job cost ledger. This is part of the payroll function and is commonly called distribution of labor. It is done immediately after the payroll checks are prepared.

Labor Burden Costs

Labor burden costs are often difficult to include in job costs. The accounting profession looks upon labor burden costs as part of the general administrative costs. Unless the subcontractor insists on these costs being identified as job cost they won't be recorded on the job cost ledger. *It is imperative that they be included as a job cost* and recorded as such on the job cost ledger and the income and expense statement. These are costs that are caused by labor being expended and would not exist if the labor was not expended. Labor burden costs are, therefore, a job cost and *not* general administration costs.

Material and equipment costs, labor costs, and miscellaneous direct job costs are costs that are recorded as a result of money having been paid out or from an invoice for money to be paid out. At the time that labor burden costs should be recorded on the job cost ledger, no money has been paid out for labor burden and/or no invoice has been received for money to be paid out. An accounting system will not voluntarily or automatically act on something that has not yet happened. To wait to record the labor burden costs on the job cost ledger until they were invoiced and/or paid would serve no purpose whatever toward cost control.

Labor burden costs range from 10 to 40 percent of gross labor costs, depending on the classification of the workman and the union jurisdiction the job is in. This amount frequently equals or exceeds the total gross profit of a job. Because of this, a job could show a gross profit when the labor burden was not included but would show a loss when it was included. Job costs that do not include labor burden do not include all the cost and are, therefore, erroneous and deceptive.

To include labor burden costs on the job cost ledger, a percentage of gross labor (payroll) cost must be established. All labor burden costs are either already a percent of gross labor costs or are an amount for each hour of labor. A total fixed percentage can readily be established for labor costs for each classification of workman, union jurisdiction, and period of time in which the work is being performed. This fixed percentage is then computed with the labor dollars recorded for each job for each week to determine the cost of labor burden for that job for that week. This amount is then recorded on the job cost ledger.

It is rare when an accountant will voluntarily develop a bookkeeping system that includes the above. With few exceptions, the subcontractor must *require* the accountant to do it.

Miscellaneous Direct Job Costs

These costs are a result of a purchase of services or expendable tools and other items, performance and payment bonds, etc. From the purchases, invoices are rendered by the firm or person providing the service or money is paid out directly for permits, etc. When the money is paid out, the amount is recorded in the cash disbursements journal and the job cost ledger. When an invoice is received, the amount is recorded on the purchase journal and the job cost ledger. We now have all the costs being recorded on the job cost ledger, and they should be recorded there as soon as possible after the information becomes available.

The subcontractor should insist that all his suppliers and those who perform services on the job invoice him within 3 days after shipment or conclusion of the service. For services rendered on jobs that extend over long periods of time, interim (partial) invoices should be sent. The accounting system should record invoice costs on the job cost ledger no later than 3 days after they are received. Labor costs and labor burden costs should be recorded there no later than 3 days after the payroll is prepared. With this disciplined timing, the information recorded on the job cost ledger is not older than 1 week after the costs have been committed. This allows the subcontractor for small jobs to take action on the next job and the one that is now in progress. For large jobs he can take action before the job is completed.

Knowing the costs for small jobs as soon as possible after the job is completed allows the subcontractor to take corrective measures or to perpetuate methods employed for estimating, layout of the work, field productivity, purchasing, establishing extras, etc., for the next small job, including the ones presently in progress.

On large jobs, knowing the cost expended to date for the entire job is valuable and a must, but it is not enough for effective cost control. Control of large job costs as a whole cannot be effective for most trades. Masonry (bricklaying and concrete pouring) is about the only trade that allows knowledge of total job cost to date to be effective toward cost control, for here it is possible to accurately determine the amount of work that has been installed to date. It is fairly easy to accurately determine the number of bricks that have been laid or the number of yards of concrete that have been poured. The number of bricks laid to date will fairly accurately establish the percentage of work completed to date and, conversely, the percentage of work to be completed. With the cost of work completed to date, plus the projected cost of work to be completed, the total cost can be established at any point in time during the progress of the job. To be able to determine whether the cost of the work installed to date was installed within the estimated cost, two things must be known: the cost to date and that which has been installed to date. To accomplish this, the job must be broken down into cost centers.

The construction industry has researched for years various methods to record and determine that which has been installed to date. The research has been concentrated on using materials as cost centers and quantities installed as the basis for measurement of that which was installed. The methods resulting from this research have not proven to be accurate enough for effective cost control. The problem causing the inaccuracies is the inability to determine and record accurately the quantities of items of materials installed. This is especially true with mechanical subcontractors. An item of material becomes part of a whole when installed. It is no longer an item of material. Because of this, it is almost impossible to accurately determine quantities of materials installed to date directly *after* they are installed and before the whole is completed. Another factor contributing to this inability is that while the count is being made the quantities are continuing to increase.

Cost centers based on materials include only one activity, that of installing that particular material. For the electrical subcontractor, installing 2-

inch conduit is a cost center. Pulling the wire into the conduit is a different cost center. For the plumbing subcontractor, installing ¾-in. water pipe to a sink is a cost center. Installing the sink is a different cost center.

The installation of most materials has no beginning or end, other than the beginning and end of the entire job. For this reason, materials make poor cost centers. A cost center that can easily and accurately be measured should have an easily identifiable beginning and end. It must be readily measurable in its entirety. That is, the extent, size, and length of time of the cost center should be small and short. Because of all these reasons, and the problems and difficulties encountered in basing cost centers on materials, it is recommended that cost centers be based on increments of work.

The reason that a small job can be readily measured accurately is that it has a definite beginning and end. It is small in magnitude, and the length of time between the beginning and end is short. A large job should, therefore, be broken down into as many small jobs as possible. A small job that is part of a large job can be a system or a section of the facility. In a building, each floor can be a cost center. Each floor should, however, be further broken down into smaller cost centers. Remember, each cost center should be as short in duration of time as possible. An entire floor of a building could take several months from beginning to end. Accurate results of a cost center cannot be obtained until the cost center has been completed.

The work involved in *each* section of the rough floor would make an ideal cost center. A section of a rough floor for each subcontractor involved includes several activities, for each of which there is an estimated cost. The total cost of installing the work involved in each section can easily be identified in the estimate. All the materials used and labor expended in each section can easily be measured, reported. and recorded. The duration of time for each section is short. Because it is measured as a whole, the measurement is simple and accurate. Because of the short duration of time, the final results of that cost center are known immediately. From the results of each section, action can be taken toward improving the succeeding sections. When cost centers for large jobs are being established, it is important to remember the simplicity and accuracy of measuring, reporting, and recording a small job in its entirety.

Methods for developing general administration (overhead) costs are also based on the customs and practices of the accounting profession and not necessarily on the needs of the subcontractor. The accounting profession breaks the general administration costs into accounts, which they call a "chart of accounts." The costs for these accounts are reported on the income and expense statements. The breakdown of the chart of accounts is based on the cost of "things" as opposed to "happenings."

For example, a standard chart of accounts will tell the subcontractor how much he has spent for postage, rent, legal and accounting, charitable contributions, dues and subscriptions, heat, light, and water, and other items. It is doubtful that by knowing the cost of each of these the subcontractor will limit the use of postage stamps, stop paying his rent, stop utilizing the services of his lawyer or accountant, stop using water, or turn off the heat and lights. It is also doubtful that the subcontractor will do anything about how much he is spending for "other" or "miscellaneous." The point here is that while the above information may be useful for some purpose, it is of no value to the subcontractor in controlling costs.

Other expenditures in a standard chart of accounts are auto and truck expense, salaries, office supplies and expenses, and telephone. The amount spent for each of these items is very important information to the subcontractor, but unfortunately not in a lump sum as reported on the standard income and expense statement. Autos and trucks are used in various cost centers. Trucks are used for delivery, to perform work with, and for project use. Auto and truck expenses include gas, oil, and repair. The information the subcontractor needs to control auto and truck expenses is how much was spent for repairs. He must ask himself if it is wise to buy new trucks or to continue repairing existing trucks, and if the cost of owning and repairing the delivery trucks justifies the advantages of delivering the material over having the supply house deliver it. This decision-making information cannot be obtained from a lump-sum report on auto and truck expense.

The lump sum for salaries as listed on the standard chart of accounts is the total salaries of general administration (overhead) personnel. Office supplies and expenses and telephone are shown as a lump sum for the entire company. The subcontractor must know, besides this, what his total cost of estimating is. This total includes salaries, office supplies, expenses, and telephone costs for the estimating personnel. The subcontractor must have the general and administration costs (overhead) broken down into functional cost centers if he is to control the costs of each. Basic functional overhead cost centers are management, sales and estimating, purchasing and engineering, accounting, and field control. These may be combined in many companies, while in others they are broken down further. These are the areas of costs that can be controlled by adjusting the personnel and related expenses of each.

Knowing that his company spent $15,000 last year for auto and truck expenses has little meaning to the subcontractor. Knowledge that $3,000 was spent for repairs to delivery trucks last year is very meaningful. This same analogy holds true for all the overhead expenses. The subcontractor has to develop these costs himself. His accountant or accounting personnel will not do this voluntarily.

For effective cost-control information the subcontractor must establish each small job as a cost center and break down large jobs into small job cost centers by system or section. He must break down all overhead costs into basic functions and cause the costs generated by each to be recorded to each.

Day-to-day decision-making information is the most important tool the subcontractor has to be successful—or to prevent failure.

16 FISCAL BUDGETS

To be successful in any business endeavor one must have an overall plan. The results of the plan are called "objectives." To accomplish the overall plan there must be many subplans. The overall plan is called "long-term objectives." The subplans are called "short-term objectives." Because all long-term objectives of all companies include sales and profits, the short-term objectives must also include sales and profits.

As in any human endeavor to go somewhere, one must know where he is going and what route he is going to take to get there. It has been said that the man who does not know where he is going is already there. The same holds true in running a business.

Plans to accomplish the business objectives require budgets. Budgets are usually projections (targets, goals) for the coming year. A business year is called a "fiscal year." Hence, a budget for the coming business year is called a "fiscal budget." Every subcontracting firm *must* prepare a budget for the following year to prevent the events of the following year from just happening as the wind blows. The following is a suggested simple method to prepare the budget.

FISCAL BUDGETS

To accomplish long-term objectives, every company must have yearly profit objectives. To survive, a company must make enough profit to pay for the overhead. Sales must be obtained to provide the vehicle *to produce* profit. After the sales are obtained, the work must be executed *to realize* the profit. There is a maximum amount of profit that can be produced from each sale. The profit from each sale is determined by:

1. Quality of the sale*

2. Efficiency of the execution of the work

3. Price paid for materials required

4. Payment of all work performed

The profit produced by performing the work, that is, satisfying the sale, is called "gross profit." Gross profit is computed by subtracting the costs to perform the work from the amount of the sale. The cost to perform the work is:

*On all new sales projected, assume that gross profit will be as anticipated at time sale is made.

1. Cost of labor

2. Cost of labor burden

3. Cost of material

4. Cost of miscellaneous direct job costs

This is shown on the profit and loss statement, as in the following example:

Sales	$1,000
Less: cost of sales	800
Gross profit	$ 200

Gross profit is measured in terms of percentages. There are two kinds:

1. Percentage of gross profit to costs

2. Percentage of gross profit of sales

When computing and/or evaluating gross profit percentages, it is very important that one understand and realize which kind is being used. There are several percentage points difference between the two, as in the following example:

Sales	$1,000
Cost of sale	800
Gross profit	$ 200

Percentage of gross profit to sale = sale ($1,000) divided by gross profit ($200) = 20 percent.

Percentage of gross profit to cost = cost ($800) divided by gross profit ($200) = 25 percent.

Gross profit to sales = 20 percent.

Gross profit to costs = 25 percent.

In this example there is a 5 percent difference. Gross profit to sales is used in most situations except when developing the selling price. The cost of overhead* determines the minimum gross profit required to prevent a

*Overhead is costs not charged directly to a job or group of jobs.

loss. The minimum gross profit determines the minimum sales required to be performed in the period of time being projected.

Fiscal budgets are divided into two sections:

1. Overhead

2. Sales and gross profit

These are the items that must be projected in order to establish a fiscal budget.

Overhead is projected by establishing the anticipated plus-and-minus variances from each of the previous year's overhead expense accounts. These are shown on the income (profit and loss) statement under "operating expenses." (See sample in this section.) The variances are added to or subtracted from the following year for each expense account. The total of all the expense accounts is the projected overhead and is also the overhead budget for the following year. This process has a very valuable by-product: making management aware of each overhead expense. During this budgeting process, management should readjust overhead expenditures to be compatible with the following year's needs.

The method of projecting sales and gross profit includes identifying the types. There are:

1. Carryover sales and gross profit (sales not performed in previous period)

2. Repetitive sales and gross profit (sales that perpetuate themselves from year to year; example: time and material accounts)

3. Projected new sales and gross profit

Each sale has an anticipated gross profit. Each sale when completed has an actual gross profit. The anticipated gross profit must be tempered with reality by the person preparing the budget.

Carryover sales are contracts that were obtained in the previous year, but have not been completely billed. That is, there is billing still to be invoiced. *The carryover gross profit* is the gross profit that has not been included in billings of the previous year. It should be determined on a more actual basis what part of the job has been completed, thereby providing a means for accurate evaluation of costs to complete. Carryover sales and gross profit should be fairly accurate.

Repetitive sales and gross profit are sales performed for customers year after year which can be anticipated (based on previous years) accurately. The percentage of gross profit also can be anticipated accurately from previous years' experience. Research with each customer must be made to determine the volume of sales that can be expected from him in the following year. Repetitive sales and gross profit should be fairly accurate.

Projected new sales and gross profit form the part of the budget that is the most difficult and requires the most skill. The ability of the company to obtain new sales is determined by:

1. Estimating capacity

2. Sales ability

3. Overall economic conditions

4. Ability and condition of competitors

5. Volume of work available in specific markets

The next step in preparing the budget is to add the gross profit from carryover sales to the gross profit of the repetitive sales and then subtract this sum from the projected overhead. If the overhead exceeds the sum of carryover and repetitive gross profit, more gross profit is obviously required. This additional gross profit can come only from new sales. For example:

Overhead		$40,000
Carryover gross profit	$20,000	
Repetitive gross profit	10,000	
Less total gross profit		30,000
Minimum additional gross profit required		($10,000)

Minimum gross profit required from new sales is $10,000. After the type of new sales that are available and can be obtained is determined, the percentage of gross profit that can be realized from those sales should be calculated. The object is to determine what volume of sales will be required to produce the minimum gross profit to overcome the overhead.

$$\text{Sales} = \frac{\text{gross profit}}{\% \text{ of gross profit}}$$

Assume it is determined that the new sales which can be obtained will produce a gross profit of 10 percent. The minimum gross profit required to overcome the overhead is $10,000.

$$\text{Sales} = \frac{\$10,000}{0.10}$$

$$\text{Sales} = \$100,000$$

Therefore, $100,000 of new sales are required to be obtained and performed in the following year to overcome the overhead.

Net profit is the amount left over from the gross profit after the overhead has been deducted. The same procedure that was used to determine volume of new sales required to overcome the overhead deficit is also used to determine sales required to realize the desired net profit for the projected year.

Carryover sales	$66,000 @ 12% gross profit	$ 8,000
Repetitive sales	80,000 @ 15% gross profit	12,000
New sales for overhead	200,000 @ 10% gross profit	20,000
New sales for net profit	200,000 @ 10% gross profit	20,000
Total projected sales	$546,000	gross profit	60,000
Less overhead			40,000
Net profit before taxes			$20,000

In projecting new sales that are required to overcome overhead and for net profit, reality must be faced in both projecting new sales that *can* be obtained and the percentage of gross profit that *can* be realized from these sales. This is the area where many managers allow the emotions of desire and greed to guide their analysis and evaluations. It is the area that requires the manager to be pessimistic and not optimistic. It is the area where the manager is faced with the realities of his responsibility. If he does not project the new sales and new gross profit with a high degree of accuracy, he will be leading his company toward a loss.

If the realistically projected gross profit from new sales does not make up the deficit created after the overhead is deducted, the manager has a choice of two alternatives:

1. Reduce overhead to equal obtainable gross profit.

2. Prepare for a loss.

After the budget is completed, it should be the manager's bible throughout the year. With it he should control overhead costs and gross profit from each job and pursue new sales. The following are suggested forms for preparing a fiscal budget.

Figure 5 is suggested form for use to project the following year's overhead. The items listed under "Operating Expenses" should be the same items as listed on the particular subcontractor's statement of income and expenses (profit and loss statement) as prepared by the accountant.

Figure 5 is a suggested form for use to project the following year's

OVERHEAD BUDGET SCHEDULE

Operating Expenses	Previous Year	+ — Variance	= Projected
Accounting and Legal			
Advertising			
Bad Debts			
Collection Costs			
Depreciation			
Dues and Subscriptions			
Entertainment			
Employee Welfare			
Gas and Oil			
Heat, Light, Water			
Insurance — Miscellaneous			
Insurance — Overhead Personnel*			
Interest			
Janitor Service			
Licenses and Miscellaneous Taxes			
Miscellaneous			
Office Supplies			
Office Services			
Rent — Building			
Rent — Equipment			
Repairs — Trucks			
Salaries — Office			
Salaries — Officers			
Salaries — Supervisor			
Sales Promotion Activities			
Small Tools			
Telephone			
Training			
TOTAL OPERATING EXPENSES			

*Labor Burden for overhead personnel only.

Figure 5 Overhead budget schedule.

The previous year's statement will show the actual expense incurred by each account. The amount of each should be written in the column headed "Previous Year." For each item, the amount of increase or decrease anticipated for the following year is filled in in the column headed "+ − Variance." In the column headed "= Projected" is added or subtracted the amount of increase or decrease for each item listed in the column headed "+ − Variance." The total of the "= Projected" column is the projected overhead for the following year.

Figure 6 is a suggested form for use to project sales and gross profit. The form is divided into two sections. One section is for groups of jobs of the same type, and the second is for individual large jobs. The type or groups of jobs are listed in the first column, headed "Type of Jobs." In the adjacent columns are listed for each group of jobs and/or large individual jobs the carryover sales that will be performed the following year, the forecasted repetitive sales and anticipated new sales that will be performed the following year, and the carryover sales that will *not* be performed the following year.* The next column is the arithmetical results of adding the sales carried over from the previous year to the forecasted repetitive sales and the anticipated new sales and subtracting the carryover sales that will be performed the following year. In the column headed "Times *%," is written the percentage of gross profit to sales anticipated for each group of jobs and/or individual large job. The next column, headed "Equals Gross Profit," is the arithmetical result of multiplying the projected sales by the percentage of gross profit to sales for each group of jobs and/or individual large job. This amount is the anticipated gross profit in dollars anticipated for each group and/or individual job. The total of the column headed "Equals 1992 Sales" is the total sales budget for the following year. The total of the column headed "Equals Gross Profit" is the total gross profit anticipated and projected to be earned the following year. This also is the gross profit budget for the following year.

Figure 7 is the suggested form to be used to summarize the sales and gross profit projections. The year for which the projection is being made is entered in the space marked "Year." In the space listed as "Maximum Overhead" is written the amount of total overhead anticipated. This total is taken from the overhead budget schedule. The maximum average percentage of gross profit to sales that is realistically obtainable is written in the space listed as "Maximum Percentage of Gross Profit to Sales." This should be based on the market and performance ability of the individual

---

*On some large jobs there will be a portion of the contract that will not be completed the following year. This will become the carryover sales for the year following the next year.

PROJECTED SALES AND GROSS PROFIT SCHEDULE

YEAR ___1992___

Type of Jobs	1991 Carryover Sales	Plus 1992 Repetitive Sales	Plus New Sales	Less Carryover Sales to 1993	Equals 1992 Sales	Times *%	Equals Gross Profit
New Residential							
Residential Remodeling							
Commerical Remodeling							
New Small Construction							
Service Work							
Time and Material							

Individual Jobs in Progress	Total Contract	Less 1991 Sales		Less Carryover Sales to 1993	Equals 1992 Sales	Times *%	Equals Gross Profit

*Percent of gross profit to sales.

Figure 6 Projected sales and gross profit schedule.

PROJECTED OVERHEAD AND SALES SUMMARY
YEAR _____

Maximum Overhead $ _____

Maximum Percentage of Gross Profit to Sales   % _____

Maximum Overhead Divided by Percentage of Gross Profit to Sales = Minimum Sales

$\frac{MO}{\%Gr.} = MS$

_____ = _____

_____ = _____

Types of Jobs	Sales	*%	Gross Profit
New Residential	_____	_____	_____
Residential Remodeling	_____	_____	_____
Commercial Remodeling	_____	_____	_____
New Small Construction	_____	_____	_____
Service (Time and Material)	_____	_____	_____
_____	_____	_____	_____
_____	_____	_____	_____
_____	_____	_____	_____
Individual Jobs	_____	_____	_____
Total Objectives	_____	_____	_____
Less Overhead			_____
Net Profit before Taxes			_____

*Percent of gross profit to sales.

Figure 7 Projected overhead and sales summary.

subcontractor. The remaining spaces are for mathematically working the formula shown to determine minimum sales required. Information for the columns headed "Sales," "*%," and "Gross Profit" are the totals from the projected sales and gross profit schedule. The totals of these columns are the projected sales and gross profit for the following year. The maximum overhead is subtracted from the total gross profit (top of form). The result is the projected net profit for the following year. This also is the net profit budget for the following year. If a loss is shown after the overhead is subtracted from the gross profit, management must take one or more of four courses of action:

1. Reduce overhead.

2. Increase new sales.

3. Increase percentage of gross profit.

4. Prepare for a factual loss.

At this point in the preparation of the budget, when a loss is shown the human thing to do is to say, "Self, the budget is wrong so I'll increase the anticipated sales and gross profit beyond reality, which will cause the summary sheet to show a net profit and all will be well." The results of this type of action need not be discussed. The results are self-evident. On the other hand, the subcontractor who prepares a realistic budget can accurately determine in advance the deficiencies which lie ahead. Proper use of the budget will enable the subcontractor to develop and implement courses of action that many times can reverse adversities.

17 FINANCIAL STATEMENTS AND PERFORMANCE REPORTS

Financial statements are produced by the auditors at the end of each fiscal year. Income tax laws require information that is part of the financial statement. These and other legal requirements cause all businesses to have a financial statement completed. The initial purpose of financial statements is, therefore, to satisfy requirements of others, not the subcontractor. Remember the case of Frank Cletsowitz. The need that required him to obtain a financial statement was a requirement of the supply house to establish credit, not Frank's need for decision-making management information.

Because most subcontractors do not have a formal system for reporting cost and gross profit, they use the financial statement as their source for decision-making information. Financial statements were neither designed nor intended to provide management with the day-to-day operating information that is so vital to the decision-making process. Financial statements report that which has happened as a result of the day-to-day decisions made by the subcontractor.

It is important that the subcontractor be able to understand a financial statement. It is his scoreboard. The subcontractor should be able to read the scoreboard and determine if he is winning or losing. He cannot, however, determine from the scoreboard what play he should call next. This information comes from the result of the previous play. The quarterback calls the next play based on the number of downs, his position on the field, amount of time left, his opponent's ability and defense strategy, plus many other factors, most of which are not shown on the scoreboard.

The subcontractor must watch the day-to-day costs of each job from the job cost ledger. He also must watch the overall results of all the jobs combined, week to week and month to month. For the job cost information on the job cost ledger to be meaningful it must be compared with the estimate and the work installed to date. For the overall results of all the jobs on a week-to-week and month-to-month basis to be meaningful, the results must be compared to something. That something is a budget. When a sales, gross profit, overhead, and net profit budget is established, then it can be determined by comparison if the week-to-week and month-to-month overall results are meeting the requirements and the objective. These week-to-week or month-to-month reports are in reality performance reports of the combined results of everyone in the company.

The yearly sales, gross profit, overhead, and net profit budget can be divided by 12 to show the monthly budget or even by 52 to show a weekly budget. The job mix of most subcontractors is such that weekly performance reports are not realistic. This is because it is difficult to cause the reporting of sales and job costs to track each other on a weekly basis. This is because of the lag of time between the invoices (sales) being established and the time the costs are accumulated, or vice versa. Tracking sales with the related cost is more easily achieved monthly than weekly. Monthly performance reports resemble a profit and loss statement. The following is a typical format of a performance report:

Sales

Job costs

Gross profit

Overhead

Net profit

The three vital signs to monitor are sales, gross profit, and overhead. There must be enough sales to produce enough gross profit to overcome the overhead with some left over for net profit. Gross profit is the key to net profit. The percentage of gross profit is a measurement of materials management and field performance. Of course, gross profit is directly affected by the quality of the sales. Overhead can be forecast very accurately. The forecast is also a budget. Keeping the overhead costs within the budget automatically causes the forecast to come true. The overhead forecast for the coming year divided by 12 gives the overhead budget for each month. Overhead for most subcontractors is fairly stable. The uneven cycle of sales performed has very little effect in causing overhead to go up and down.

The cycle (for most areas) of sales being performed increases during the summer months and decreases during the winter months. The cycle in some Southern states may be slightly different. A typical sales performance cycle is shown below.

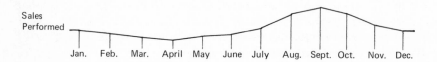

Gross profit is directly proportional to sales performed, quality of the sales, and productivity of the performance. Productivity will go down during the winter months as a result of inclement and cold weather. The decline of sales performed and productivity during December, January, February, March, and April causes the gross profit to drop. The gross profit for these months for many firms drops below the overhead for these months. This causes net profit losses for these months. Hopefully, the gross profit in excess of the overhead for the months of May, June, July, August, September, October, and November will overcome the losses for the other months and produce a net profit for the year.

A typical year will show a loss accumulating for January, February, and March. April may show a near break-even for the month, with May and June showing a net profit, but not enough to overcome the losses incurred in January, February, and March. Many times it will take the net profit produced in May, June, and July to overcome the earlier losses. The net profit from August, then, becomes net profit for the year to date, as does that of September, October, and November. December usually is a break-even month. If the fiscal year is from January 1 through December 31, the first 7 months of the year will be a break-even period with the net profit of the year being earned in the following 4 months, with the last month breaking even.

The following graph shows the sales, gross profit, overhead, and resultant net profit cycles.

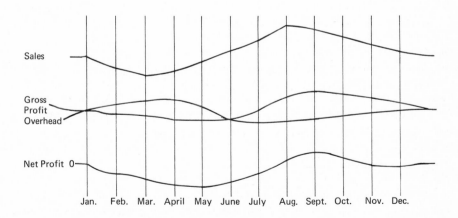

The subcontractor should know well in advance when his gross profit is going to decline. When he takes a job with a poor gross profit, his overall gross profit will be affected. The degree depends on the size of the job involved.

There is a lag of from 15 days to 6 months between the time a sale is made and the time it is performed. When sales decline, the overall gross profit will be affected 1 to 6 months later (dependent on the average lag of the particular subcontractor). This lag allows the subcontractor to know how, when, and how much his gross profit is going to be affected. For monthly performance reports to be meaningful they must be compiled no later than the fifteenth of the following month. This requires that all sales and costs for the month be recorded by the tenth. For sales to be recorded they must be invoiced. Invoicing must, therefore, follow costs by no more than 10 days.

The subcontractor must know where he is at all times. A profit and loss statement will tell him where he's been. A timely performance report will tell him where's he's been, plus where he is going. Profit and loss statements and performance reports show trends which become standards that are very valuable in determining causes of particular results. Productivity trends can be measured by the percentage of labor cost to sales. This percentage should remain approximately the same regardless of the amount of sales or labor costs. Variations in this percentage indicate a drop in productivity, poor estimates of labor costs, or a change in job mix where the ratio of material and labor cost to sales has changed. The subcontractor should know offhand the average percentages of material costs, labor costs, gross profit, and overhead to sales for his company. When these percentages vary, he immediately knows a change has occurred in his company. Knowing this, he can take immediate action to correct an adverse change or to perpetuate a desirable change.

Monthly performance reports are vital to running a subcontracting firm. Financial statements are the final performance reports for a period of time and tell the results of the performance for that period. The financial statements also tell the subcontractor the condition of his company. Information from performance reports and financial statements is necessary to guide the firm profitably through the years.

FINANCIAL STATEMENTS

Financial statements consist primarily of an income statement (also known as a profit and loss or operating statement) and a balance sheet. The purpose of financial statements is to:

1. Satisfy legal requirements for tax purposes

2. Provide information required to be made public (for publicly owned companies only)

3. Provide necessary information for credit purposes (bank, bonding companies, etc.)

4. Provide management and/or owners with information relative to the success or failure of the total business for a specific period of time (profit and loss or operating statement)

5. Provide management with the financial condition (total worth, etc.) at a specific point of time (balance sheet)

Both the balance sheet and the income statement contain specific information which is combined and listed under specific terms. The definition and explanation of these terms are as follows:

1. The first group is relative to the income statement.

2. The second group is relative to the balance sheet.

Income Statement

(Profit and Loss or Operating Statement)
  The income statement is broken up into these parts:

1. Sales

2. Cost of sales

3. Gross profit or loss

4. General operating expenses (overhead)

5. Net profit or loss

6. Income taxes

7. Retained earnings

The sequence used on an income statement (profit and loss) is the same sequence followed in the actual operation; that is, one must have sales before all else. To execute sales there are costs which are called "costs of sales." The results of the sales versus the costs of sales is gross profit. To cause the sales to be executed requires general (operating) expenses (overhead). The end result of deducting the general (operating) expenses (overhead) from the gross profit results in the net profit. From this, income taxes must be paid, which further reduces the amount to retained earnings.

Definitions of Terms

Sales. The total of all invoices rendered for which it is reasonably assumed that payment will be made in cash from a source other than the company itself, in exchange for the services and/or product supplied by the company.

Cost of Sales. (Direct costs of contract performance). The total of all costs expended to provide the service, or procure the product, including the following:

1. All materials used directly to perform the services or procure the product, including waste

2. All labor expended to provide the service and/or install the material, including:*

    a. Workmen's compensation, occupational disease, liability

    b. State unemployment insurance

    c. Federal unemployment insurance

    d. FICA (Social Security)

    e. National benefit fund (union)

    f. Trade association

    g. Vacation (union) (or prorated)

    h. Local pension (union)

    i. Apprenticeship fund (union)

    j. Health and welfare fund (union)

3. Job costs (other than materials)

4. Other miscellaneous direct job costs:

    a. All costs, other than the cost of the materials, and labor which are required to provide the service, or install the materials, or to permit the installation of the materials

*See detailed analysis of labor burden in Chapter 14.

Examples: Tool depreciation, subcontracts, permits, bonds, tool rental, gas, oil, and maintenance and repairs for on-site vehicles and equipment.

Gross Profit. The difference between the total sales and the total of the costs of sales. This is the profit before the general (operating) expenses (overhead) are deducted. The gross profit indicates the effectiveness or efficiency of the profit-producing activities of the company.

General (Operating) Expenses (Overhead). All expenses other than those costs required to provide the services or procure the products that are sold. These costs are also referred to as the costs for the support activities, including the facilities and the wages paid to the support (overhead) personnel. These are the costs that are not related to, or identified with, the service itself.

Net Profit. The difference between the gross profit and the general (operating) expenses (overhead). Where the gross profit was an indicator of the effectiveness and efficiency of the profit-producing activities, the net profit is an indicator of the effectiveness and efficiency of both the profit-producing activities and the support (overhead) activities combined.

The relation of the ratio of general (operating) expenses (overhead) to sales and the ratio of gross profit to sales is an indicator of the feasibility of the cost of the support (overhead) activities. In other words, the overhead costs must not exceed the gross profit generated. As a result of the support activities one could build an overhead machine that would provide 100 percent efficiency and support the profit-producing activities most effectively and still cause a net loss because the cost of these support activities would exceed the resultant gross profit.

Income Taxes. The amount of taxes that will be required to be paid on the net profit.

Retained Earnings. The amount of net profit, less the amount of taxes that will be required to be paid, retained in the business. This amount is carried forward to the balance sheet. This is the end result of all the costs of the entire operation and the effort expended by all concerned.

Balance Sheet. The balance sheet consists of:

1. Current assets
2. Fixed assets

3. Other assets

4. Current liabilities

5. Other liabilities

6. Net worth

The total of all assets is balanced with the total of all liabilities and net worth. This is why it is called a balance sheet. The balance sheet is a measurement of assets, liabilities, and subsequent net worth at a particular point in time. A particular point in time means, say, midnight on a particular day.

BALANCE SHEET DEFINITIONS

Assets. Everything owned by the company that has real value established in dollars and cents. The assets are divided into three categories:

1. *Current assets.* These are all cash owned by the company, plus all things of value that will automatically become cash within a short period of time (usually within 90 days). These are assets which are continually moving into or out of the business or converted from one form to another.

   Example: Cash is converted to inventory; inventory is converted to accounts receivable; accounts receivable are converted to cash; cash is converted to work in progress; work in progress is converted into invoices; invoices are converted into accounts receivable; and accounts receivable are converted into cash.

2. *Fixed assets.* Assets that are of a relatively permanent nature and are necessary to carry on the business, such as a building, furniture, desks, typewriters, trucks, etc. These assets do not change from one form to another as do current assets. Fixed assets depreciate in value as they are being used and subsequently worn out. The value of fixed assets is the original cost of the item less the depreciation amount to that particular date.

3. *Other assets.* Tangibles such as prepaid insurance, cash value of life insurance policies owned by the company, investments, advances, long-term notes (money owed to the company that will be paid back over a longer period of time usually over 90 days), etc.

Liabilities. Everything owed (indebtedness) by the company. Liabilities are divided into two categories:

1. *Current liabilities.* These are those debts owed which must be paid within a short period of time (1 year or less).

2. *Other liabilities.* These are liabilities that are not required to be paid within 1 year.

   Example: If you purchase a truck on a 3-year installment plan, the first year's installment will become a current liability. The last 2 years' installments will be other liabilities.

Net Worth. This consists of the initial value of the stock of the company, plus the retained earnings accumulated to date. The total of net worth plus the total of liabilities will always equal the total of all assets. When this is accomplished numerically, the books are then considered to be in balance.

The most significant information available to management from the balance sheet is the difference between current liabilities and current assets, which is called "working capital." Working capital is the criteria for the company's ability to financially support the execution of the sales. There are, however, many other items of information valuable to the subcontractor on the balance sheet. Most items of information are expressed in ratios. The subcontractor should become familiar with the more important applicable ratios.

Tables 5 and 6 show a typical statement of income and a typical balance sheet, respectively.

FINANCIAL STATEMENTS FORMAT

Balance Sheet

The format for the balance sheet has been established by the accounting profession and is adequate to the needs of management. A typical balance sheet is shown in Table 6.

Income Statement

(Profit and loss or operating statement)

The format for the income statement can be established almost in its entirety by management. In determining the format, management can get the breakdown of information for tax purposes from the income tax return relative to a corporation, sole ownership, or partnership. The

Table 5
CONSTRUCTION SERVICES CO.
STATEMENT OF INCOME
January 1, 1977, through December 31, 1977

Sales		Period	% to Sales
		$90,458.20	100.0
Less: Direct costs			
Materials	$25,418.35		28.1
Direct labor	33,909.01		37.5
Labor burden	8,475.06		9.4
Other direct costs	1,720.60		1.9
Total direct costs		$69,523.02	76.9
Gross profit on sales		$20,935.18	23.1
Less: Operating expenses			
Accounting and legal	$ 433.00		0.5
Advertising	0		
Bad debts	0		
Collection costs	0		
Depreciation	2,142.18		2.4
Dues and subscriptions	108.30		0.1
Entertainment	48.93		0.1
Employee welfare	261.52		0.3
Gas and oil	1,475.54		1.6
Heat, light, and water	0		
Insurance—miscellaneous	1,451.69		1.6
Insurance—overhead personnel (labor burden)	0		
Interest	878.28		1.0
Janitor service	0		
Licenses and miscellaneous taxes	378.50		0.4
Miscellaneous	118.45		0.1
Office supplies	591.35		0.6
Office services	380.00		0.4
Rent—building	46.00		0.1
Rent—equipment	7.28		
Repairs—trucks	788.12		0.9
Salaries—office	3,026.00		3.3
Salaries—officers	535.00		0.6

Table 5 *(Continued)*

Sales	Period	% to Sales
Salaries—supervisor	5,723.87	6.3
Sales promotion activities	898.70	1.0
Small tools	702.68	0.8
Telephone	831.42	0.9
Training	0	
Travel expense	373.17	0.4
Total operating expenses	$21,199.98	23.4
Net operating profit (or loss)	(264.80)	(0.3)
Add: Purchase discounts (other income)	539.16	0.6
Net profit (or loss)	$ 274.36	0.3

breakdown and format used other than required on the income tax return is strictly up to the desires and needs of management. A typical income statement is shown in Table 5. The format generally consists of:

Sales

Cost of sales

Overhead (operating expense)

Profit or loss

The format of the breakdown of the cost of sales should be compatible with the breakdown used to estimate cost of sales. For example, if the estimate of costs format includes labor, material, direct job costs, and all fringes to labor, the format breakdown for cost of sales on the income statement should include all these items. Every item that is used in the estimate as a job cost should also be included as a cost of sale on the income statement. All items of costs not included as a job cost should be included under overhead (operating expense) on the income statement.

Too often, items listed on the estimate of costs are included in the overhead (operating expense) on the income statement. For example, most subcontractors consider workmen's compensation, liability, and occupational disease insurance costs for productive personnel a direct job cost. These insurance costs for overhead personnel should be listed under overhead (operating expense). Unless the accountant is specifically

Table 6
CONSTRUCTION SERVICES CO.
BALANCE SHEET
December 31, 1977

ASSETS

Current assets

Cash in bank—general account (overdraft)	(7.95)	
Cash in bank—payroll account	2,902.92	
Accounts receivable	20,392.17	
Advance to employees	165.00	
Inventory—warehouse materials	7,777.14	

Work in progress:

Inventory—labor (expended, unbilled)	$5,101.60	
Inventory—labor burden (expended, unbilled)	1,329,95	
Inventory—other direct costs (expended, unbilled)	766.01	
Total work in progress	$ 7,197.56	
TOTAL CURRENT ASSETS		$38,426.84

Fixed assets	Cost	Depreciation	Net
Trucks	$11,127.22	$2,317.65	$8,809.57
Automobiles	6,349.00	1,210.14	5,138.86
Tools and equipment	1,816.98	377.63	1,439.35
Office equipment	1,082.80	106.88	975.92
	$20,376.00	$4,012.30	$16,363.70

NET FIXED ASSETS	$16,363.70

Other assets

Prepaid insurance	$ 272.57	
Deposits	40.00	
TOTAL OTHER ASSETS		312.57
TOTAL ASSETS		$55,103.11

Table 6 *(Continued)*
LIABILITIES AND NET WORTH

Current liabilities

Accounts payable	$ 5,951.77	
Notes payable—Bank of Utopia (current portion, vehicle loans—4)	3,304.80	
Notes payable—State Bank & Trust Co. (current portion)	5,000.00	
Notes payable—State Bank & Trust Co. (A/R loan)	9,059.87	
Accrued payroll taxes (labor burden)	1,073.94	
TOTAL CURRENT LIABILITIES		$24,390.38

Other liabilities

Loans from officers	$14,954.95	
Notes payable—Bank of Utopia (noncurrent portion, vehicle loans—4)	3,345.02	
Note payable—State Bank & Trust Co. (noncurrent portion)	1,249.97	
TOTAL OTHER LIABILITIES		$19,549.96

Net worth

Capital stock		$10,000.00	
Retained earnings, December 31, 1976	$ 888.41		
Net profit for the period	274.36		
Retained earnings, December 31, 1977		1,162.77	
TOTAL NET WORTH			$11,162.77
TOTAL LIABILITIES AND NET WORTH			$55,103.11

directed to separate these costs, the entire costs will inevitably be included as overhead expense (operating expense). The result of this is that the cost of sales would not include all the costs; therefore, the gross profit would be erroneously increased and the cost of overhead (operating expense) would be greater than it actually is. It is, therefore, very important that management direct the accountant on the specific format desired.

Assume that the summary of the estimate is as follows:

Material and equipment costs

Miscellaneous direct job costs

Labor

Labor burden

Gross profit

Selling price

The format of the income statement (profit and loss statement) should then be as follows:

Sales

Cost of sales

Materials and equipment

Miscellaneous direct job costs

Labor

Labor burden

Total cost of sales

Gross profit

The other remaining item on the income (profit and loss) statement is overhead (operating expense). The only tax requirement for a breakdown of this item is that within a corporation the officers' salaries must be kept separate and depreciation must be separate. All other expenses not listed as a cost of sales can be broken down in any fashion desired by management. This breakdown should be such that it helps to measure the costs involved for cost control purposes. Remember that prudence should be employed in order to avoid superfluous detail in the breakdown. Breakdowns should not include items that are not going to be measured by management for cost control and analysis purposes. Major items of overhead (operating expense) include:

Officers' salaries (corporations)

Other overhead salaries

Estimating and engineering fees

Taxes

Travel

Automobile and truck expenses

Sales promotions

Insurances

Professional services

Utilities

Telephone

Office supplies and expenses

Advertising

Depreciation

Bad debt expenses

Cost of facilities (rent, maintenance, etc.)

These items can be broken down into as many increments as desired for cost analysis and control purposes. For example, insurances could be broken down into:

Building (fire, etc.)

Inventory

Building contents

Difference in conditions

Fidelity and forgery

Auto and truck

Group hospitalization

Life insurance

Workmen's compensation

General liability, etc.

Unless there is a specific need for a breakdown other than insurance, no breakdown on the income statement (profit and loss statement) should be included in the format. The breakdown of operating (overhead) expenses is called the "chart of accounts," with each breakdown an expense account.

Management, however, must understand that if the breakdown is not included in the format, it is a laborious and costly task for the accounting personnel to provide the breakdown at the request of management. The breakdown is achieved in accordance with the format of the income statement (profit and loss statement) by establishing an expense account for each item of the breakdown. When the costs are incurred, they are recorded to expense accounts in accordance with the breakdown. Obviously, the more items in the breakdown, the more expense accounts are required. If management wants information broken down that is not previously included in the format, the accounting department must then separate on existing expense account records all the items recorded. Obviously, the greater the breakdown, the more expense accounts that are required and the more accounting activities that must be performed. Too often, management fails to direct the accountant as to the desired format. Then, after receiving the statement of income (profit and loss) they ask, "What does this item include?" It is much easier for management to direct the accountant on the breakdown desired *prior* to the reporting period. In this way the accountant can set up the accounts so that they will automatically produce the breakdown of costs desired.

TYPES OF REPORTING

There are two methods of recording all job costs on the profit and loss statement and balance sheets:

1. On a completed job basis

2. On a percentage of completion basis

The completed-job basis involves holding all partial payout invoices (sales) in an accrual account (inventory) until the job is completed. The costs of labor and material for these sales are considered unbilled costs and are shown on the balance sheet as such under "current assets." This means the profit or loss from all jobs would not be accepted as such into the books until the job is completed. There are few advantages to this method of accounting. It is considered to be a method that can be maneuvered to put profits or losses into the most advantageous tax year. There are disadvantages, too. It is more difficult to measure the true results of the company's efforts for a specific period of time. It is very important to measure the results of the company's total efforts by the month, quarter, and year.

If the company's job mix includes any appreciable percentage of jobs that have more than one billing, that is, larger jobs requiring partial billings and payouts, the percentage of completion method of reporting job costs into the accounting system is more advantageous.

The subcontractor must understand both methods thoroughly and then direct the accountant to use the method most applicable to his needs. This is a decision the subcontractor must make, not his accountant. Remember: the accounting function must provide a service to management.

ANALYSIS RATIOS

There are hundreds of sources of ratios that can be used to evaluate financial statements. These ratios include the ratios of current assets to current liabilities, net profit to assets, and all the combinations one can develop by comparing one numerical value to another numerical value on the profit and loss statement and balance sheet.

The more common ratios which appear in any accounting or finance handbook are of value. The most useful ratios, however, are the common ratios of percentage of overhead to sales, gross profit to sales, net profit to sales, etc. These ratios are of no value without a standard of measurement to compare them to. Fortunately, most trade associations have compiled information from financial statements in a standard format from companies throughout the country for each particular construction trade: electrical, plumbing, heating and ventilating, general contracting, painting, etc. This information has been averaged for different size firms in related geographic locations. The ratios shown for the average company of a particular size must be the minimum standard used for comparison. This information is most valuable. Every subcontractor should take advantage of it and use it as the guide for his minimum performance.

Reading financial statements is primarily an art of detecting variations in the average amounts and ratio percentages established by previous statements. For instance: The balance sheet shows the amount of receivables due. An increase in receivables due would indicate a problem that should be investigated and corrected. A drop in the ratio of current assets to current liabilities indicates a decrease in the ability to finance the jobs. The cause of this drop should be determined and corrected. An increase in payables indicates that a cash flow problem exists. The subcontractor must be familiar with the financial statements and through the statements must develop a feel for his company's condition and financial ability.

18 INSURANCE AND BONDS

Insurance represents the largest expenditure of all costs other than direct labor, materials, and overhead salaries. Even though it is one of the major costs of operating a contracting firm, it is the least understood and also the least controlled. With few exceptions, control of insurance coverages and costs is left to the seller of insurance.

PURPOSE OF INSURANCE

Insurance required by law and contract is to provide monetary recovery of employees, the public, and the customer for loss caused by the negligence of the contractor or other causes. Insurance not required by law or contract is to protect the contractor against losses and/or claims that would affect the company financially.

Insurance rates are based on the individual company's loss experience. That is, a company that has few or no paid claims over a period of years will have a lower rate than a company that has had several incurred claims over the same period of time. The premiums paid are directly related to the incurred claim experience of the individual company. Laws allow the insurance company to adjust the premium rates, based on previous incurred-claim experience of the individual company. This, in effect, assures the insurance company a profit. The laws hopefully cause the insurance company to remain financially capable of satisfying all claims of the insured to the limits of the coverage.

Theoretical Analysis of Insurance

The minimum loss ratio (paid premiums to incurred losses) by which the insurance companies operate is approximately 55 percent. This means that for every dollar paid to the insured to satisfy a claim, the insured will eventually pay back to the insurance company a minimum of $1.55. In effect, it is the same as if the contractor were to borrow the money to pay for a particular loss and pay back to the lender over a period of time on an installment basis the amount borrowed plus 55 percent.

Example

Assume the contractor has tools insured against theft with $100 deductible. A theft occurs with the loss of $1,000. The contractor immediately pays $100. The insurance company immediately pays $900. The tools are immediately replaced. All is well. However, the incurred loss causes the loss ratio to exceed 55 percent. The contractor's premium rates are increased.* The insurance company receives the $900 back, plus an additional $495. The $1,000 tool theft eventually cost the contractor $1,495. For a cost of $100 immediately, plus $1,395 over a period of time, the contractor was allowed to have $1,000 worth of tools replaced immediately, with an outlay of only $100 of cash and paying the additional $1,395 over a period of time.

Insurance, in reality, is a form of financing losses. An important advantage of financing losses through insurance is that the liability of paying for the loss is not shown on the balance sheet as a liability. Knowing this, the subcontractor can establish a definite company insuring policy based on the following criteria:

1. Insurance in minimum amounts required by law must be carried.

2. Insurances in the specified amounts required by individual contracts must be carried.

3. Analysis of all other exposures:

   a. For each exposure, the amount of loss that the company can sustain without appreciably affecting its cash flow and financial stability must be determined.

   b. The exposures should be separated into two categories:

      (1) Exposures that can potentially produce losses greater than the company can financially sustain.

      (2) Exposures in which the potential losses produced will not appreciably affect the cash flow or financial stability of the company.

Based on these criteria, the company policy should be:

1. Insure all exposures which can potentially produce losses that will affect the cash flow and financial stability of the company. To minimize the cost, the insurance covering these exposures should each have a deductible amount that the company can comfortably sustain.

*Note: The higher the losses, the higher the premium.

2. The exposures that potentially produce losses that can be comfortably sustained should not be insured (as in the previous example regarding tool theft).

The company that can replace a $1,000 tool theft immediately without appreciably affecting the cash flow or financial stability should not insure against a $1,000 tool loss. The possibility of experiencing ten $1,000 losses in a short period of time should, however, be considered.

The construction subcontractor should consider his liability for the following exposures:

1. Liability under the workmen's compensation act of the state in which the work is being performed.

2. Claims by persons other than employees for bodily injury and for property damage. This includes on-the-job exposure during construction, off-the-job exposure at any time, anywhere, and on-the-job exposure after completion.

3. Claims by employees and nonemployees for libel, slander, defamation of character, false arrest, invasion of privacy, etc.

4. Explosion, collapse, and underground damage to utilities, building foundations, etc. This is commonly called "XCU."

5. Claims for damage to equipment furnished by others but handled and/or installed by the contractor. This exposure is called "care, custody, and control."

6. Construction equipment and tool losses resulting from acts of God, theft, fire, accidents, etc.

7. Losses of material and equipment furnished by the contractor that have not been installed resulting from acts of God, fire, accidents, theft, etc.

8. Losses of material and equipment installed on the job resulting from acts of God, fire, accidents, theft, etc.

9. Dishonest acts by employees resulting in loss of money, securities, personal property, etc.

10. Burglary.

11. Forgery.

12. Motor vehicles:

    a. Claims resulting from bodily injury

    b. Claims resulting from property damage

    c. Physical damage to the vehicle

13. Damage losses to real and personal property owned by the contractor, including buildings and contents, furniture, fixtures, equipment, and inventory:

    a. Fire

    b. Vandalism

    c. Malicious mischief

The contractor could normally be liable for all of the above exposures.

There are additional exposures that the contractor may be liable for by contract. These are called contractual, or assumed, liabilities. There are basic contractual (assumed) liabilities that should be insured on a blanket basis. These are the result of "hold harmless" agreements in a contract. Hold harmless agreements indemnify other parties from exposures for which they are, or could be, liable.

Contractual liability is usually one of three forms:

1. Limited—contractor's negligence

2. Intermediate—joint negligence

3. Broad form—sole negligence of the other parties

    a. For the general contractor the other party would be:

        (1) Owner

        (2) Developer

        (3) Architect

        (4) All others

    b. For the subcontractor the other party would be all the above, plus the general contractor.

It is common practice for owners, architects, developers, engineers, and general contractors to attempt to pass the liabilities of all their exposure down to others contractually. They succeed in this by including indemnification (hold harmless) clauses in the specifications and contracts. This leaves the general contractor and/or subcontractor no choice but to sign the contract and insure the liability he has assumed.

Blanket contractual coverage is based on the three forms: limited, intermediate, and broad. Most blanket contractual policies include all forms of indemnification (hold harmless) exposures. This, however, depends on the specific insurance carrier (company). The policy may be called a blanket contractual policy, and the agent may infer that it covers all hold harmless exposures. It would be wise, however, for the contractor to make sure and fully understand what *exclusions* his blanket contractual policy contains.

NOTE: Most blanket contractual policies exclude coverage for liability of exposures resulting from faulty design, maps, plans, or specifications. Liability for this exposure can be covered under a professional liability policy. The terms of the indemnification (hold harmless) clause in the contract could or could not (depending on interpretation) pass this liability down to the contractor.

It is important for the contractor to know what coverages are included in each of his insurance policies. It is, however, more important for him to know what *exclusions* are in his policies. The contractor can better evaluate his insurance coverages if he knows what exposures he is liable for that are not covered and/or what exclusions are in his insurance policies. The insurance policy that contains no exclusions, conditions, and/or deductible is nonexistent.

Other insurances required as a provision of a specific contract may include:

1. Performance bonds
2. Builders' risk

An effective, monetarily justifiable, and adequate insurance program must include:

1. Minimum coverages required by law.
2. Coverages which would protect the company against the catastrophic type of loss.
3. Coverages that will prevent voids. This very frequently occurs.

4. Continuity of coverages that will prevent overlaps. That is, the same exposure covered in more than one policy. (This also very frequently occurs.)

5. Deductibles which are the maximum that can be sustained without affecting the financial stability and/or cash flow of the company.

6. No insurance coverage for the potential loss which will not affect the financial stability or cash flow of the company. Remember, insurance is a costly form of financing losses. It represents installment payment for losses before *and* after the loss.

Money paid out for insurance is *money out of use.* The contractor should establish his own policy and criteria for his insurance program. He should not allow them to be established by the insurance agency. Because of the complexities of insurances, the contractor should not, however, attempt to determine alone the specific types and amounts of coverages of insurance he should have to satisfy the policy and criteria of his insurance program. He must select a *trusted* and *capable* insurance agent, tell the agent of his policy and the criteria of his insurance program, and then collectively select the types, amounts, and specific carriers that will satisfy and conform to his insurance program.

A detailed review and subsequent modification of the insurances must be made yearly to conform to the growth and changes of the company. Again, this must be done *jointly* by the contractor and his agent.

NOT BY EITHER ALONE!

To assure that the contractor is covered for all the exposures requiring indemnification (hold harmless), each specific contract and specification should be reviewed by the insurance agent *before* the contractor signs it.

Insurance falls into two categories:

1. Job-related

2. Overhead-related

Types and amounts of job-related insurance are, with few exceptions, required by law and/or as a provision of the construction contract. Types and amounts of overhead-related insurance are, with few exceptions, at the discretion of management. Job-related insurances are job costs and must be charged to the individual job. Overhead-related insurances are overhead expenses and must be charged to overhead. Job-related insurances are either part of the labor burden or are specific insurances required for specific jobs. The costs of insurances that are part of labor burden are automatically charged to individual jobs through the distribution of labor (including labor burden) to the jobs upon which the labor was expended. The costs of specific insurances required for specific jobs are charged to the particular jobs directly.

The premiums for job-related insurances that are part of labor burden are based on a percentage of expended labor or contract amount. The premiums for specific insurances required by specific jobs are based on the specific exposure and coverage and usually are a fixed amount. The premiums of overhead-related insurances are based on the specific exposure and coverage and usually are fixed amounts.

Job-related insurances that are part of labor burden are:

1. Workmen's compensation and occupational disease liability

2. Comprehensive general liability and property damage

3. Umbrella liability insurance

Specific job-related insurances are:

1. Performance bonds

2. Builders' risk

3. Care, custody, and control

4. Explosion, collapse, and underground (XCU)

5. Completed operations

6. Tool and equipment floater

7. Watercraft

8. Aircraft

Exposures 3 through 8 can be covered on only those jobs where the exposure exists or on a blanket basis, depending on the job mix of the contractor. If they are covered only on specific jobs, they are job-related and the costs are charged to the specific job. If they are covered on a blanket basis, the costs are charged to overhead. These exposures can also be included in the umbrella liability, in which case the cost automatically becomes part of the labor burden.

Overhead-related insurances include:

1. Fidelity bonds

2. Property—fire, etc.

3. Vehicle and auto

4. Crime—dishonesty

5. Forgery

6. Personal injury (not bodily injury)—false arrest, etc.

7. Host liquor

PRINCIPAL COVERAGES

Following is a summary of the principal coverages which must and/or should be carried.

Workmen's Compensation Insurance

This covers the employer's liability under the workmen's compensation act of the state or states involved. The act is statutory, and the benefits are determined by the legislature of the appropriate state. In Illinois, for example, the act provides for payment of all medical expenses without limit, for weekly disability payments of varying amounts if the injured employee is off work beyond 6 working days, and for payments for permanent or partial disability (loss of a finger, eye, etc.). Under the Illinois Workmen's Compensation Act, the employee, with one or two rare exceptions, must take the benefits provided by the law and cannot sue the employer. He can, of course, sue a third party whose negligence caused his injuries. There have been one or two rare exceptions where the employee has the right to sue the employer, and so the policy provides employers liability coverage with a basic limit of $100,000.

Comprehensive General Liability Insurance

This coverage protects the contractor against claims arising out of bodily injury or property damage made against him by persons other than employees. The policy has several sections of coverage as follows:

1. *Operations.* This covers injuries occurring directly as a result of the operations of the employer. An example would be an

employee of another contractor who was hit in the head on the job site by a tool dropped by an employee of the insured.

2. *Contractors' protective.* This applies to any claims made against the contractor as a result of injuries or damage caused by a subcontractor.

3. *Contractual.* This coverage applies to liability assumed by the insured under contract. It can be written two ways: (1) each contract is submitted to the insurance company and a premium is developed for the "hold harmless" clause in the contract; (2) a so-called blanket contractual liability basis automatically provides coverage for all written contracts. This is the case with most larger contractors.

4. *Completed operations.* This applies to claims made against the contractor for either bodily injury or property damage which may occur after the job has been completed.

Various extensions of coverage can be provided under the comprehensive general liability policy. The principal ones are:

1. Personal injury coverage, which extends the policy to provide coverage against such things as libel, slander, defamation of character, false arrest, invasion of privacy, etc.

2. Explosion, collapse, and underground damage. Certain types of work as classified in the general liability rate manual *exclude* coverage for these hazards unless specifically provided for by payment of an additional premium. For example, operations involving machine trenching for underground conduit would normally *exclude* underground damage to cables, etc. Coverage can be provided on a job-by-job basis where the exposure exists, or on a blanket basis so that specific jobs do not have to be reported to the insurance company.

3. Care, custody, and control. The general liability policy *excludes* damage to property in the care, custody, or control of the insured. Normally it is very difficult to remove this exclusion, but in some cases it can be done if a modest limit (for example, $10,000) is placed on the coverage. The umbrella policy, which will be discussed later, would cover this hazard, but subject to the self-retention or deductible usually of $10,-000, or $25,000, as the case may be.

Comprehensive Automobile Insurance

Automobile insurance coverage is divided into two sections—liability, and physical damage. The liability coverage protects the insured against claims arising out of bodily injury or property damage arising out of the ownership, maintenance, or use of motor vehicles. The physical damage coverage provides comprehensive (practically any loss or damage to the vehicles except that caused by collision) and, optionally, collision insurance with varying deductibles from $50 and up. An optional coverage is medical payments which will pay the limit of insurance for all medical expenses for each person injured. The limits for medical payments run from $500 to $5,000 per person, and such benefits are payable without regard to negligence.

A mandatory coverage in Illinois, and in certain other states, is "uninsured motorist." In this coverage, if injuries to persons in the insured vehicle were caused by an uninsured driver who is at fault, the insured's own insurance company would negotiate a settlement with these persons, just the way the other party's insurance company would, had insurance been provided. This coverage applies only to injuries and not to property damage.

Umbrella Liability

This is a liability insurance coverage which is written to be excess over primary general liability, automobile liability, and employers' liability insurance. The minimum limit of coverage is $1 million per occurrence and this can, of course, be increased for an additional premium. In addition to providing excess insurance over the primary coverages, it also provides coverage against a number of types of liability claims that may not be covered under the primary policies. On these types of claims, there is a self-insured retention or deductible which is a minimum of $10,000, and in some cases $25,000. Therefore, umbrella coverage (1) provides high limits of liability to guard against the catastrophic claim and (2) covers certain exposures that are not covered at all under the primary policy with a reasonable and realistic deductible to be assumed by the insured. Legal defense coverage under the umbrella policy is optional, but it always should be provided, since any claims that exceed the primary insurance, or that are not covered by the primary insurance, will undoubtedly involve heavy legal expense.

Property Insurance

These coverages apply to real and personal property. The more common ones are:

1. Fire insurance on building or buildings if the contractor owns the building which he occupies for office, warehouse, etc. This coverage should be provided to protect the building against the common hazards of fire (extended coverage), vandalism, and malicious mischief.

2. The same type of fire insurance that is provided on the building also should be written to cover the contents, which would consist of furniture, fixtures, equipment, and inventory.

3. Builders' risk coverage on new construction or remodeling is carried either by the owner or contractor, based on the terms outlined in the specifications. If provided by the owner, the general contractor and subcontractor should be named as insured as well as the owner so that the interest of all parties on the job will be protected. The insurance is customarily written for the completed value of the work involved and the premium paid annually or for the duration of the job.

4. Difference in conditions coverage. This is basically an all-risk coverage which is written to supplement the fire insurance on buildings and/or contents. It is not a standard form of policy but can be tailor-made to cover the particular situation. The policy always excludes the perils of fire (extended coverage), vandalism, and malicious mischief, since these are picked up under the fire insurance policies. The difference in conditions policy can be written with varying limits of liability and usually carries a deductible of at least $250, although higher deductibles are common.

5. Contractors' equipment floater. This policy also is a nonstandard one and is designed to cover the contractor's exposures to loss of his equipment, either on the job site, in transit, or at other locations. A policy can be written on either a named-perils or all-risk basis and usually has deductibles applying to either all hazards covered or some of the hazards.

   Certain specific pieces of equipment can be listed on the policy, in which case only those shown are covered, or the insurance can be written on a blanket basis to cover all equipment owned or leased by the contractor. In the latter case, a coinsurance clause is used (as is the case with fire insurance policies) to require the insured to carry insurance equal to a stipulated percentage (usually 80 or 90 percent) of the total values at risk.

6. Installation floater. This coverage can be written on a named-peril or all-risk basis to cover machinery and equipment as well as materials during transit and installation at the owner's premises. Coverage normally applies until the installation is accepted by the owner.

Crime Insurance

For the ordinary contractor, the most important coverage in this area is dishonesty insurance, which protects the insured against dishonest acts committed by employees, either alone or in collusion with other employees. Loss of money, securities, and personal property is covered. Various limits are available starting at $10,000, and such limits apply to any dishonest act committed by one or more employees acting together. If any exposure exists with respect to money or securities, coverage can be provided against their disappearance or destruction. This coverage can be provided either on the insured's premises or away from premises, as needed.

Burglary insurance can be carried to cover loss of personal property. Burglary is defined as breaking into the premises. There must be visible evidence of such a break-in. If a difference in conditions policy were carried as described above, the burglary insurance would not be needed, since it is included under that coverage.

Forgery coverage is frequently written with the fidelity bond mentioned above. This protects the contractor against loss resulting from forgery of his bank deposits or checks, drafts, or other written promises or orders to pay issued by him. If the contractor has corporate credit cards that are in the hands of employees, coverage can be extended under the bond to cover this exposure.

THE INSURANCE AGENCY

The insurance function consists of three entities:

1. Insurance company (carrier)

2. Insurance agency

3. Subcontractor

The three form a team to furnish protection to the subcontractor against exposures to liabilities required by law, contractual commitments, and other exposures. The team is similar to the team of:

1. Manufacturer

2. Distributor (supplier)

3. Subcontractor

The insurance company (carrier) sells the insurance coverage to the insurance agency, which in turn sells it to the subcontractor. As in the manufacturer-distributor-subcontractor relationship, where the distributor plays a vital role, the insurance agency plays a similar vital role in its relationship with the insurance company and the subcontractor.

The insurance agency should be an expert in the types of insurances required by a subcontractor. The subcontractor must select first an insurance agency that specializes in construction insurance, and second, an insurance agency that has an agent who is an expert in construction insurance. The key is the agent, not the agency. The agent must be compatible to the subcontractor as a person. The subcontractor must have confidence and trust in him. The agent must be totally and continually informed about the subcontractor's business. He must have an intimate knowledge of the subcontractor's financial condition, his objectives, etc. To achieve this the subcontractor must take the agent into his total confidence. If he feels he cannot, or does not want to, he has the wrong insurance agent and perhaps the wrong insurance agency.

The subcontractor, however, must always be aware that the prime motivator for the insurance agency is to sell insurance. Many insurance agencies do a fine job of advising the subcontractor regarding what insurances and limits he should carry, but because these agencies are sales-motivated, the subcontractor could be overprotected with expensive and needless insurance. Insurance is like any other commodity. It always can be purchased somewhere else cheaper. But also, like every other commodity, "you get what you pay for." The objective is to obtain the best *needed only* coverage and service at the most reasonable cost (not the cheapest cost). To make sure he is not being sold insurance coverages that are not needed and/or at limits in excess of need, the subcontractor *must* know his insurance needs and understand the exposures and coverages. This advice he can get from his insurance agent. He must, however, decide what coverages, limits, and deductibles he needs. For example, auto collision insurance at a cost of $150 per year on a truck with a market value of $300 would be coverage that is not needed. It is important that the subcontractor find from his insurance agent that he is not carrying unneeded insurance, that he does not have duplicate or overlapping coverages, and most important, that there are no voids of coverages against critical exposures between where the coverage of one policy stops and another begins.

BONDS

There are many types of bonds; however, only five types are basic to the subcontractor. These basic bonds are guarantee bonds and include bid, performance, payment, wage, and license bonds.

The bid bond guarantees the owner that the subcontractor will enter into a contract in accordance with his bid. The penalty for refusing to sign the contract is forfeiture of the amount of the bid guarantee. Many bids require a cash bid deposit, usually 5 or 10 percent of the total bid. After the bids are opened, and the amounts of all the bids are exposed, a natural reevaluation takes place by the bidders. If a bidder finds he is appreciably lower than his competition and/or has left out an appreciable cost, he would be inclined to rescind his bid. To prevent this, a bid deposit or bid guarantee frequently is required by the owner. In lieu of actually depositing cash in the form of a certified or cashier's check, a subcontractor is, in many cases, permitted to provide a bid bond. There is a nominal annual charge for bid bonds. It is a common belief that if the bonding company will provide a bid bond, they will automatically provide performance and payment bonds. This is not true. A bid bond guarantees to the owner that the bidder will enter into a contract in accordance with his bid and nothing else. A bid bond in no way obligates the bonding company to provide performance and payment bonds.

The performance bond guarantees the owners of a project that the subcontractor will perform the work in accordance with the plans, specifications, and contract. This guarantee is terminated upon acceptance of the building, facility, bridge, etc., by the owner. If the subcontractor's performance on the job is judged to be incompetent by the owner, the owner has the right, in accordance with the contract, to require the bonding company to assume the responsibility of completing the job. Incompetent judgment comes when the subcontractor does not have personnel who have the know-how and experience necessary to perform the work, and the subcontractor himself does not have the experience and/or the support organization that is necessary to support the field operation. When incompetence is judged, the bonding company is required to subcontract the remainder of the job to a capable subcontractor of the bonding company's choice. The bonding company would be entitled to all payments due to the subcontractor who failed to perform. The bonding company would then expect payment from the subcontractor who failed for the remainder of the costs incurred to finish the job. If the subcontractor who failed refused to reimburse the bonding company, the bonding company would attach the assets of the subcontractor through legal action. (See section on Contracts, Owner's Recourse, in Chapter 8.)

The payment bond guarantees the owners that all materials, services, and labor used and expended on the project will be paid for. If for any reason the subcontractor cannot pay suppliers for materials and sub-subcontractors for services and cannot meet his payroll, the owner has the right, in accordance with the contract, to require the bonding company to assume the responsibility of job completion. When this occurs, the bonding company can immediately attach all the assets of the subcontractor. These assets include:

All work installed, not paid for

All payments not received to date

All material and equipment on site not installed

Any other assets of the subcontractor

The bonding company would have the prerogative of dismissing the subcontractor who failed to perform and sub-subcontracting the remainder of the work to another subcontractor of the bonding company's selection. Costs incurred in excess of payments received at the conclusion of the job would be recovered from the subcontractor who failed to perform the contract. The bonding company could also allow the subcontractor who failed financially to finish the job, with the bonding company providing the required financing.

The wage bond guarantees the union that all wages will be paid to union employees and all fringe benefits will be paid to the union in accordance with the union contract. If the subcontractor became financially incapable of meeting his payroll, and/or of paying union fringe benefits, the bonding company would be required to make the payments for the subcontractor.

The license bond guarantees the village, city, county, and/or state that all work will be installed in accord with the codes and requirements of that village, city, county, and/or state.

By providing a bond for any of the above, the bonding company accepts all the responsibility of satisfying the guarantee if the subcontractor fails to do so. In effect, the bonding company is gambling that the subcontractor will satisfy the guarantee and that they (the bonding company) will not have to. To decrease the odds of the gamble, the bonding company *must* know the capabilities of the subcontractor. More often than not the true capabilities of the contractor are not indicated on a balance sheet or profit and loss statement. If bonds were provided based on outward appearance of the subcontractor, the majority of subcontractors would never receive bonds!

Appraisal of the true capability of a subcontractor becomes a personal endeavor. This is why the relation between the bond agent and the subcontractor must be of a confidential and personal nature. As it is important for the bond agent to be personally compatible with the subcontractor, the subcontractor must also be compatible with the bond agent. The bond agent must be enthused with the objectives and believe in the capabilities of the subcontractor and must be motivated to "go to bat" for the subcontractor when obtaining bonds.

At any period of growth of a subcontracting firm, the need for performance bonds always exceeds the outward apparent justification required to provide the bond. The bonding company only sees the subcontractor through the balance sheet, profit and loss statements, and the eyes of the bond agent. If the bond agent knows of the financial details, the objectives, behavior, etc., of the subcontractor and his organization, he can (and in many cases is required to) sell the bonding company on providing the required bond. Remember, when the bond agent does this he puts his reputation and personal security on the line. Performance and payment bonds are a necessary requirement of a subcontractor. A knowledgeable, personable, and compatible bond agent is a must to establish and maintain a desirable bonding capability.

To grow, a subcontractor needs a good, understanding banker; a good, *practical* auditor; a lawyer who has a personal interest (not part ownership) in the subcontractor; and a capable, personally interested, construction-oriented bond agent (*and* a similar insurance agent).

The subcontractor can fool his banker and make out well; he can mislead his auditor and prolong taxes. The subcontractor should listen to his lawyer with discretion; and he *must* be truthful with, tell all to, and take complete advice relative to bonds from his bond agent. (See Chapter 13, "Filling the Pipeline," reference to bonding.)

It must be thoroughly understood by the reader that the information and material presented in this chapter is to be used only to acquaint the subcontractor with the depth, complexity, and importance of insurance and bonds. No one should use the information and material presented herein as a basis or as a guide in general or otherwise to establish or maintain insurance coverages. The subcontractor *must* consult a knowledgeable, capable, construction-oriented insurance agent and establish the required and/or desired insurance coverages himself.

The purpose of the above statements is to release the author from any potential liability whatever regarding the actions of any reader of this manual as a result of having read the information contained herein.

SEE YOUR INSURANCE AGENT FOR ADVICE ON INSURANCE!

19 SUBCONTRACTING BY THE SUBCONTRACTOR

Subcontractors are required from time to time to subcontract work. Many do not recognize that the hiring of a firm or person to perform a service on the job site is a subcontract. A subcontract many times is confused with a purchase. There is an important technical difference between the two. The following definitions will help explain the difference:

> To purchase—To buy a product whose labor to produce was done away from the purchaser's responsibility and/or control.

> To contract—To buy a service. Service means providing a product and/or expenditure of labor.

> To subcontract—To contract part of a contract to others. To subcontract also is to join with another person or firm to perform a service. The document of agreement is called a subcontract.

> A purchase order—A vehicle of communication for the mechanical data of a product being bought. It also serves an internal administrative function.

> A contract—A legal document which is a vehicle of communication for the mechanical data of a service plus the liabilities that go with the service.

Many purchase orders include descriptions of liabilities to be assumed by the person or firm furnishing the product or service. Many purchase orders also require written acceptance of the order with all its provisions and qualifications. This type of purchase order is also a contract. A purchase order which includes the provisions of an incomplete contract is an extension to that contract.

Thus, there is a fine line between a purchase order and a contract. Important to the subcontractor is his exposure to the liabilities that go along with each. When he buys a product or service whose labor to produce is out of his area of control or responsibility, he is not exposed to certain liabilities. He *would* have to face them if the labor were done *in* his area of control or responsibility.

The subcontractor is responsible for the acts of all persons employed by him, either directly or indirectly, who work where he has responsibility or control. But while he must insure against the exposures to liabilities for all persons employed directly, the insurance does not have to cover persons employed indirectly. These persons are those who work for another person or firm employed by the subcontractor. Protection against exposures to liabilities by these indirectly employed persons must be by the person or firm they work for directly. Protection against such exposures is insurance coverage. To assure that exposure to liabilities of personnel being employed indirectly (through another firm or person) to perform a service is protected, the subcontractor must *contract* the service, *not purchase* the service.

Liabilities that must be considered by the subcontractor are:

1. Liability under the workmen's compensation act of the state in which the work is being done.

2. Claims by persons other than direct employees for bodily injury and property damage, including on-the-job exposure during construction, off-the-job exposure at any time anywhere, and on-the-job exposure after completion.

3. Claims by employees and nonemployees for libel, slander, defamation of character, false arrest, invasion of privacy, etc.

4. Underground explosion, collapse, and damage to utilities, building foundations, etc., resulting from acts of the person or firm performing the service.

5. Claims for damage to equipment furnished by others but handled and/or installed by the person or firm performing the service. This exposure is called care, custody, and control.

6. On-the-job losses of construction equipment and tools owned by the person or firm performing the service resulting from acts of God, abuse, theft, fire, accidents, etc.

7. Losses of materials and equipment not yet installed, but furnished by the person or firm performing the service, resulting from acts of God, fire, accidents, theft, etc.

8. Losses of materials and equipment already installed on the job by the person or firm performing the service, resulting from acts of God, fire, accidents, theft, etc.

9. Motor vehicles used in the performance of the service, owned by the person or firm performing the service.

   a. Claims resulting from bodily injury

    b. Claims resulting from property damage

    c. Physical damage to a vehicle

These liabilities always exist. Protection against them must be the responsibility of the firm or person performing the service. If this person or firm does not have enough protection (insurance) against them, the liabilities become the subcontractor's responsibility.

There are two kinds of work that a subcontractor may have to contract to others:

1. For services not related to a contract (job)

2. For services related to a contract (job) to which the subcontractor has committed himself

For services not related to a contract (job) where work will be done where the subcontractor has responsibility or control, the listed liabilities must contractually become the responsibility of the person or firm performing the service.

For services related to a contract (job) which the subcontractor has committed to, where work will be done at the job site, or any other site where the subcontractor has responsibility or control, the listed liabilities of the contract that apply must become the responsibility of the person or firm performing the service.

On every job the subcontractor is committed by contract to specific responsibilities and exposures to specific liabilities. (For more details on contractual liabilities and indemnification, see Chapter 8.) Contractual liabilities are those that are included in and specific to the subcontractor's contract. Protection against these liabilities must also be the responsibility of the person or firm performing the service. (See Chapter 18.)

THE ONLY WAY TO ENFORCE THE PROTECTION AGAINST ALL LISTED LIABILITIES IS TO CONTRACT FOR THE SERVICE, NOT PURCHASE THE SERVICE.

The subcontractor must require the person or firm furnishing the service to submit certificates of insurance as proof of adequate protection against the listed liabilities.

In addition to protecting himself against liabilities from the person or firm performing the service, the subcontractor must hold this person or firm responsible for the applicable contractual responsibilities of the subcontractor's contract. These responsibilities may include:

1. Time limitations

2. Legal recourse by the subcontractor against the sub-subcontractor. (If the contract which the subcontractor is working
   under is a sub-contract, the contract for part of the subcontract is technically a *sub*-subcontract.)

3. Schedule of payment

4. Waivers of lien

5. Changes

6. Guarantees and warranties

7. Governmental requirements

8. Special

The provisions of a contract that a subcontractor is responsible for, or
the recipient of, must be part of the sub-subcontract.

Because of the exposures to liabilities and the importance of legal
ramifications, a brief discussion of specific examples would help to make
matters more clear. In each example, a mechanical subcontractor wants a
service or an item, and a specific way to get that service or item is
recommended. The following examples further illustrate this point:

Example 1

The subcontractor wants a painter to paint his office. The painter's
services must be contracted to make him responsible for all the liabilities
that may occur while he is on the subcontractor's premises.

Example 2

The subcontractor wants a painter to paint pipes on a job. The pipe
painter's services (where pipe painting is a part of the subcontractor's
contract) must be sub-subcontracted to make him responsible for all the
liabilities and applicable contractual responsibilities that are part of the
subcontractor's contract.

Example 3

The subcontractor wants to obtain the services of a data processing firm.
He may procure these by a contract *or* a purchase order, because the labor

required to perform the service will be done away from the subcontractor's area of responsibility or control. Thus, the subcontractor is not exposed to any liabilities. Also, the services performed are not a part of a contract to which the subcontractor has committed himself. All that is necessary is a means for communication of the understanding of what the data processing firm is to furnish, for what amount, and when. A purchase order does this well. The data processing firm may, however, want a contract, instead of a purchase order, to commit the subcontractor to the service for a minimum period of time, and to require advance notice of cancellation of the services. In this case the seller prepares the contract.

In most industries the seller of services prepares the contract for his convenience and protection. In the construction industry the buyer prepares the contract for his convenience and protection. The subcontractor must always be aware that when he is procuring a service he is the buyer. If the service has any connection with the construction industry, he should prepare the contract, not the seller. (See Chapter 8.)

Example 4

The subcontractor wants to obtain a product for a job. This can be done by issuing a purchase order. Because the labor to produce the product is done away from the subcontractor's area of responsibilities or control, he is not exposed to any liabilities or failure of contractual responsibilities that may occur in the manufacture of the product. Qualification relative to quality, approvals, time of delivery, etc., can be a condition of the purchase order and made part of the purchase order.

Example 5

The subcontractor wants to get a desk for his office. The desk can be purchased. The procurement of a desk, or any other product to be used by the subcontractor and not be installed on a job, has the same characteristics as if the product were to be installed on a job. A product is a product, no matter where it is to be used. A service is a service, no matter where it is to be performed.

CONCLUSION

IF IT INVOLVES PEOPLE, CONTRACT IT.

IF IT INVOLVES PEOPLE ON A JOB, SUBCONTRACT IT.

IF IT INVOLVES A PRODUCT, PURCHASE IT.

20 JOINT VENTURES

When two or more parties agree to jointly share the responsibilities, profits, and/or losses of a construction contract, a "joint venture" exists. There are no rules, customs, practices, or laws governing joint ventures. The joint venture can consist of any type of agreement that two or more parties elect to share. Projects are undertaken on a joint venture basis for many reasons and/or purposes. These include:

1. To share the risk

2. To generate required bonding capacity

3. To satisfy minority participation requirements

4. To reduce the number of competitors

5. To satisfy the customer's desires

6. To satisfy local customs and practices and acquire local representation on a project in an unfamiliar area

7. To acquire specialty capability on a job requiring unfamiliar expertise

8. To acquire an additional source for manpower

9. To acquire an additional source for supervision

10. To acquire a source for additional finance

11. To provide more than one estimate on the job for comparison

A subcontractor must make several evaluations before joining a joint venture. These include:

1. Is there a justifiable need for a joint venture?

2. Is the selection of the other partner or partners a prudent one? This evaluation should include:

   a. Is he financially sound?

   b. Is he compatible as a person?

   c. Is his method of operation compatible?

   d. Is he trustworthy?

   e. Will his participation satisfy the need to joint-venture the job?

3. Will the joint venture be beneficial to all the partners?

4. Is joint venturing the only means to satisfy the need?

   Example: a subcontractor may desire to bid a large job requiring a performance bond in excess of his bonding power. He elects to joint-venture the job with another sub-contractor to satisfy the need for a bond. The job carries a potential gross profit of $250,000. The only need to joint-venture in this case is to satisfy the performance bond requirements. He is capable of mechanically performing the work.

   To joint venture on a 50/50 percent basis would cost one-half of the $250,000 potential gross profit. This is the price for the required bonding capacity. But there are other, less costly ways to satisfy this need. The bonding company's restriction is based on its concern about the subcontractor's ability to finance the job. The bonding company would accept $250,-000 placed in escrow for 1 year and $100,000 for 6 months to guarantee financial capability. The bonding company also would allow the $250,000 to be used to finance the job. It does, however, require that the $250,000 come from sources other than the company's working capital. The subcontractor could borrow the $250,000; however, to motivate the lenders he would be forced to pay 20 percent interest. The interest charges would total $60,000. The difference between the interest costs and the costs of joint venturing is $65,000. By borrowing the required capital instead of joint venturing, the subcontractor would realize an additional $65,000 gross profit and provide autonomous working capital for the job.

   Many times there are other desirable methods that will satisfy the needs without having to joint-venture the job.

After it has been established that the particular need can be best satisfied by a joint venture and the partner or partners have been selected, there are two activities required to establish and function the joint venture:

1. Prepare and execute the joint venture agreement.

2. Determine what activities each partner will be responsible for in the execution of the job.

The Agreement. The joint venture agreement is vital to the success of the joint venture. It serves two purposes:

1. It is the vehicle of understanding between the partners.

2. It is the legal document for the protection of each individual partner.

The ideal joint venture is made up of partners who are thoroughly acquainted, compatible, friends, similar in size financially, financially sound, trustworthy, have similar business philosophies and methods of operations, and have a similar need to joint venture. While this combination appears to be hypothetical, the partners of most successful joint ventures ironically *do* possess it. When this happens, the agreement can be confined to being a vehicle of understanding. Establishing a legal document for the protection of each partner is not necessary if this combination exists. It is not necessary for the vehicle of understanding to be prepared by an attorney. A written agreement prepared by the partners is sufficient.

The vehicle of understanding must make these points clear:

1. What will be the percentage of total capital required to finance the project that each partner will be required to provide?

2. What will be the percentage of profit to which each partner is to be entitled?

3. If the contract produces a loss, what percentage of the loss will each partner be responsible for?

4. What will be the accepted definitions of net profit and net loss?

5. Who will maintain the accounting books for job costs and total receipts and what method will be used for doing so?

6. From what source will the tools be procured?

7. If the joint venture is to own accumulated assets, such as tools, what procedure will be followed to dispose of them or divide them between the partners at the conclusion of the job?

8. What will be the method of distribution of profits and when will distribution be made?

The second activity in developing a joint venture is to determine what activities each partner will be responsible for in the execution of the job. Execution of the job includes:

1. Project management

2. Purchasing

3. Procurement of journeymen and apprentices

4. Manpower control

5. Furnishing of supervision

6. Job administration, including billing

7. Accounting

8. Payroll

9. Engineering

10. Liaison

These activities may be divided any way the partners want. Experience has shown that the best way is for the most competent partner to assume all the activities possible. The remaining partner, or partners, will then act in a consulting capacity only. The partner who assumes the total responsibility of executing the job is paid an agreed-to fee for his services. Joint ventures in which partners divide the activities are breeding grounds for ineffective performance and misunderstandings. The partners usually end up blaming each other for the failure. When one partner is responsible for all the activities, he can be held accountable for an effective performance. The agreement must include a detailed description of who is to be responsible for what. If one partner is to be totally responsible, in return for a fee, the details of the fee should also be included in the agreement.

The following is a sample of a simple joint venture agreement that serves as a vehicle of understanding only.

JOINT VENTURE AGREEMENT
(VEHICLE OF UNDERSTANDING ONLY)

THIS AGREEMENT, MADE AND ENTERED INTO AS OF THE 25th day of May, 1998, by and between MOTOROTZ CONSTRUCTION CO., INC., hereinafter referred to as "MOTOROTZ," and CLETSOWITZ CONTRACT-ING CO., INC., hereinafter referred to as "CLETSOWITZ";

WITNESSETH:

WHEREAS, the above companies have entered into a contract with the MICHEL BITSKO CO., General Contractors, to perform certain construction work as set forth in Contract dated April 1, 1998, titled: Subcontract with MOTOROTZ CONSTRUCTION COMPANY and CLETSOWITZ CONTRACTING CO., INC., D/B/A MOTOROTZ—CLETSOWITZ, JOINT VENTURE, covering the Walacuty County College, Penaday, Illinois.

WHEREAS, MOTOROTZ AND CLETSOWITZ have mutually agreed to pursue the project to completion as a JOINT VENTURE in the manner hereinafter set forth.

WHEREAS, the parties hereto wish to reduce their agreement into writing.

NOW, THEREFORE, in consideration of these premises, it is hereby agreed by and between the parties hereto as follows:

1. The parties hereto agree that they shall mutually assist in the performance of the aforesaid contract; however, certain administrative services shall be provided by CLETSOWITZ.

2. MOTOROTZ and CLETSOWITZ agree to advance equally from time to time the necessary funds as required for the purpose of providing adequate working capital.

3. MOTOROTZ and CLETSOWITZ agree that MOTOROTZ will furnish the Project Manager and General Foreman for the project. All wages and other costs directly incurred by the Project Manager and General Foreman shall be paid for by the Joint Venture.

4. MOTOROTZ and CLETSOWITZ agree that procurement of Journeymen and Apprentices necessary to complete the work will be a dual responsibility.

5. MOTOROTZ and CLETSOWITZ agree that CLETSOWITZ will furnish the project Management Personnel which will perform all purchasing, engineering, administration, and liaison with the General Contractor, Engineers, Architect, and Owners.

6. The first TWENTY-FIVE THOUSAND DOLLARS ($25,000) of net profits from the contract heretofore referred shall go to CLETSOWITZ as compensation for their aforementioned Management, Purchasing, Engineering, Administration, and Liaison with the General Contractor, Engineers, Architect, and Owners. CLETSOWITZ agrees that TWENTY-FIVE THOUSAND DOLLARS ($25,000) is the maximum amount that will be charged to the Joint Venture for the aforementioned Management, Purchasing, Engineering, Administration, and Liaison Services.

All net profits after TWENTY-FIVE THOUSAND DOLLARS ($25,000) shall be divided equally between MOTOROTZ and CLETSOWITZ.

CLETSOWITZ may, at their discretion, invoice the Joint Venture each month for a proportionate share of the above fee, not to exceed $1,200. If there is any loss incurred on the performance of the aforesaid contract, such net loss shall be borne equally by MOTOROTZ and CLETSOWITZ. Net profit or net loss as herein used shall mean total receipts from the aforesaid contract, less direct cost of performing the services and furnishing the material to perform said contract.

In the event of a loss, CLETSOWITZ agrees to forfeit the $25,000 fee for aforementioned Managing, Purchasing, Engineering, Administration, and Liaison services.

7. CLETSOWITZ shall maintain a separate set of books for the contract covered by this agreement. The books shall be set up mutually by accounting personnel of MOTOROTZ and CLETSOWITZ. Accounting methods and procedures shall be as mutually agreed to by MOTOROTZ and CLETSOWITZ.

8. MOTOROTZ and CLETSOWITZ agree that CLETSOWITZ may, at their discretion, employ a clerk to perform administrative duties at the job site. Cost of said clerk will be paid for by the Joint Venture.

9. MOTOROTZ and CLETSOWITZ agree that all tools, office facilities, job storage facilities, shall be procured new and will be paid for and owned by the Joint Venture. At the completion of the contract *all* such items will be equally divided in a manner mutually agreed to at the time. In the event that no mutual agreement can be made, all items will be sold at market value and the monies received therefrom shall be equally divided.

MOTOROTZ and CLETSOWITZ agree that no distribution of profit shall be made until thirty (30) days after costs certification, and proof of job completion and receipt of the total monies due from the contract and others whom the joint venture may perform work for have been received. Surplus funds shall be invested in short-term investments, as mutually agreed to.

IN WITNESS WHEREOF, the parties hereto have caused this agreement to be executed by their duly authorized officers this *25th* day of *March,* 1998.

MOTOROTZ CONSTRUCTION CO., INC.

By: _____

ATTEST: _____

CLETSOWITZ CONTRACTING CO., INC.

By: _____

ATTEST: _____

The above sample is relative to a job approximating $2 million, requiring 2½ years to complete.

The agreement, which is the vehicle of understanding, is always in two parts:

1. Prebid agreement

2. Postbid agreement

The prebid agreement is similar to the postbid agreement with three modifications:

1. The prebid agreement states that the partners desire to form a joint venture to bid said job.

2. The prebid agreement includes a provision that requires all partners to join into a postbid agreement.

3. The prebid agreement should include a provision which will prevent all the partners from submitting a bid and/or entering into a contract on the same job individually.

SAMPLE PROVISION:

It is further agreed by MOTOROTZ and CLETSOWITZ that no agreement other than this agreement has been made, or will be made, with any other parties, and that no bid will be submitted by MOTOROTZ or CLETSOWITZ other than the joint venture bid. MOTOROTZ and CLETSOWITZ further agree that neither will pursue or accept the award of the contract individually.

When the partners are somewhat unknown to each other, and/or if an appreciable variance as to size of company, net worth, financial ability, etc., exists, then the joint venture agreement must include the vehicle of understanding plus legal protection for the individual partners.

There are several potentialities that each partner must be legally protected against:

1. If one partner becomes insolvent during the life of the joint venture, the agreement must protect the other partner or partners from the liabilities of the insolvent partner from becoming a liability of the joint venture.

2. The agreement must protect the vested interest of each partner if one partner is unable to provide his share of the required working capital.

3. The agreement must include provisions that will provide forfeiture of participation in the profits by a partner if that partner fails to provide his share of the required working capital or other required contribution.

4. The agreement must legally confine the joint venture, its restrictions, requirements, etc., to the specific job or jobs. The agreement must clearly indicate the termination of the agreement. That is, that the agreement will terminate at the completion of the job. This is to protect the partners from being legally committed to the joint venture on future work.

5. The agreement must provide for whom, where, and how the money is to be banked, accounted for, etc. This is to protect the partners against embezzlement by one of the partners.

The portion of the agreement that provides legal protection to the partners *must* be prepared by an attorney. When it is felt that a legal document prepared by an attorney is required, extreme thought should be employed to make sure the partner or partners selected are honorable and desirable. Joint ventures of partners who have no trust and/or confidence in each other, or one to the other, seldom are successful. The major prerequisite of a joint venture is *know, trust, and have confidence in your partners.*

21 CONCLUSION

A construction subcontractor should not think of his business as that of an electrical contractor, sewer contractor, bridge builder, plumbing contractor, etc. His first and foremost identification of his business must be that of making money. When asked, "What kind of business are you in?" he should immediately think and even respond, "I am in the business of making money." The second logical question would then be, "Well, what does your company produce, or what type of service does it perform to make that money?" The answer would then be, "My company constructs bridges," or "My company is a painting contracting firm," or whatever the title of the particular construction being performed may be.

Construction subcontracting is the process of investing cash into the activities required to control, administer, and construct a facility, and then the conversion of the investment back into cash. The objective of this process is to convert back to cash more than was invested for any given period of time. The result of this conversion process is the money that can be taken from the business by the owner or owners as the return on their investment. Between the investment of cash and the conversion back to cash lies the game of running a business. The end product is not the building of a sewer, bridge, etc. The end product is profit.

As in football, the end product is not touchdowns or field goals. The end product is the total score for 1 hour of play. As the score in a football game indicates a win, loss, or tie, the score resulting from all activities of the business for a particular period of time indicates a profit, loss, or break-even.

The players in the game of construction subcontracting are architects; engineers; general contractors; union business managers and representatives; OSHA inspectors; municipal, federal, and state code inspectors; competitors; trade association managers; material and equipment suppliers; bank representatives; lawyers; accountants; auditors; customers; professional employees; tradesmen employees; and the federal, state, and local governments.

The federal government is playing an ever-increasing role and is assuming more and more authority that appreciably influences the operations and profit of the subcontractor. First of all, the federal government is a full-fledged partner who does not invest any money or constructive effort into the business but makes positively sure that it takes every penny of its share of the profits each year. It does not leave any of its share of the profits in the company to help finance and support the following year's needs and growth. The federal government does, however, share in the losses by returning its share of profits to the extent of the profits taken.

The rules governing this process are the income tax laws. Income taxes are confined to profit and losses. Other federal government involvement includes administrative requirements, direct involvement in the actual field operation, and involvement in whom the subcontractor employs. Federal government involvement presents a very interesting situation. The federal government is a partner and recipient in the profits. At the same time, it imposes requirements, procedures, and restrictions that adversely affect the ability of the subcontractor to produce a profit and/or add administrative burdens which increase overhead costs.

First, let's identify the administrative burdens. The federal government, as well as some state and city governments, requires every company to be the collector of income taxes and social security payments from its employees. This collection process is called withholding taxes. In reality, the employer collects the taxes by withholding them from the employees' pay. The employer is then required to deposit the money collected (withheld) periodically with the particular governing body. The employer is then required to account for the money collected (withheld) and deposited for each employee for each required period of time. In many areas, if the subcontractor resells any materials or equipment, he is required to collect sales taxes from the buyer. Again, this requires accountability and depositing of the funds.

The collecting, being responsible for, accounting for, and forwarding of employee social security payments and income and sales taxes is in addition to the taxes paid for the company's own activities. The company's own tax responsibilities can include such taxes as income, personal property, capital stock, employee head, vehicle use, labor (on man-hours of labor expended), etc. Although these types of taxes involve administrative activities and costs, they are for the company itself and not a function being performed for the government at the company's expense.

Another administrative burden required by the government is the administration of the Occupational Safety and Health Act (OSHA). Records and reports of accidents and other pertinent information relative to employee work safety and environmental compliances must be maintained.

Still another administrative burden is the maintenance of records and reporting of race of employees. This requirement is primarily confined to those subcontractors performing jobs involving federal funds. It is rare when new construction does not involve federal funds in one form or another which qualifies the federal government to influence the hiring practices of the subcontractor.

Certain defense department projects require all contractors, including subcontractors, to submit detailed reports of their costs, reflecting profits. These types of records and reports differ and are in addition to the job cost records the subcontractor must keep for cost control.

These and many more administrative functions required by federal, state, and local governments add administrative (overhead) costs that cannot be considered as insignificant.

Aside from the costs that these requirements represent there is a *real* exposure of the subcontractor to criminal actions. Subcontractors and heads of other businesses have served and are serving prison terms for not adhering accurately and honestly to the collecting and depositing of employee social security payments, employee income taxes, and sales taxes. Many have paid fines that have caused personal bankruptcy for failure to comply with government requirements.

The laws, rules, procedures, record keeping, and reporting forms for all government requirements are detailed infinitely by explanation and illustration and are all readily available.

Government involvement in individual businesses includes, in addition to costly administrative burdens, requirements that affect the operation and the profit-producing ability of the company. No one can quarrel with or challenge the moral aspects of the Occupational Safety and Health Act or the requirements of giving everyone an equal opportunity to pursue an occupation of his choice and to gain a living. There are, however, some practical aspects relative to the construction industry that the subcontractor must recognize and cope with. For example, a guard rail must be constructed around every elevator opening during construction of a building. No law is necessary to make that a practical requirement. Logic makes it a requirement. OSHA, however, (in the early days of field representative interpretation) insisted that all elevator openings be protected with a substantial guard rail *before* any construction worker be allowed to work in the area. If a construction worker was found to be working in an area where an elevator opening was not guarded with a railing, all the contractors on the job were subject to severe fines. The practical problem to this safety requirement was that some construction worker had to construct the guard rail around the opening and while doing so was in fact working in an area where an open elevator shaft existed without a guard rail.

OSHA laws, interpretations, and methods of enforcement are constantly being changed, improved, and made more practical. The subcontractor must, however, be completely familiar with the *latest* OSHA requirements applicable to each and every job undertaken. When and if an impractical situation exists such as described in the foregoing example, the subcontractor *must* obtain from the OSHA enforcement officer an interpretation and ruling *in writing* as to what method to satisfy the problem will be accepted.

The equal opportunity requirements of the federal government, which require the work force of a construction contract involving federal funds to include certain balances of races with no other regard, many times present the subcontractor with some impracticalities. These impracticalities include the necessity of frequently utilizing inexperienced workers who are also unfamiliar with the hazards involved. The need to constantly change the size and type of work force with workmen who are not completely experienced and familiar with the hazards, customs, and practices of construction and to be required to obtain construction tradesmen from sources other than those which have evolved over the years through trial and error, present the subcontractor with some very challenging and costly problems.

The fact is that the government is appreciably involved in subcontracting and that the laws, rules, procedures, forms, reports, and requirements are there and are real and costly. Detailed knowledge and full compliance of *all* government requirements is absolutely necessary and cannot be neglected or avoided. Satisfying government requirements does not produce profit. Compliance requires no management expertise but must be recognized by the subcontractor as an integral part of the business.

With each player and circumstance of the construction subcontracting game of business are activities that the subcontractor can either control, influence, or just cope with. Those activities and players that can be controlled must be controlled. The activities and players that cannot be controlled must either be influenced or coped with. Controlling, influencing, or coping with the players, situations, problems, elements, and money is the managing expertise that the subcontractor must have. The short- and long-term success or failure of construction subcontracting is directly related to the ability of the subcontractor to manage effectively.

INDEX

INDEX